Women in Patriarchal Society

Women in Patriarchal Society

Profulla C. Sarker
(Senior Policy Advisor)
National Food Security and Nutrition
Surveillance Project and Adjunct Professor,
James P. Grant School of Public Health
BRAC University
66 Mohakhali, Dhaka-1212
Bangladesh

SERIALS PUBLICATIONS
NEW DELHI (INDIA)

First Published – 2010

ISBN: 978-81-8387-330-7

Published by

SERIALS PUBLICATIONS
4830/24, 1st Floor, Ansari Road
Darya Ganj, New Delhi-110002 (India)
Phone : 23245225. Fax : 91-11-23272135
E-mail: serials@satyam.net.in

CONTENTS

PREFACE

This volume is a compilation of different papers written by the scholars of various disciplines which cover anthropology, sociology, social work, psychology, public administration, journalism and mass-communication. The main focus of this volume is to examine the problems of women in the different phases of their life cycle and to what extent the women want that patriarchal social system should exist. The main intention of this volume is to address the situation of disabled women and how they are being the victims of gender discrimination in connection with education, health care, rehabilitation and violence. This volume also discusses the impact of credit programs of Grameen Bank on the changing role of women in relation to their life style, awareness, and living standards. This volume highlights the political participation of women in local government and also the impediments in their participation in local government administration. Further, widowhood and the problems of widows in traditional peasant society in India, status of women journalists and how they are being discriminated in different perspectives in male dominated societies. Also discussed in this volume are aspects of human rights, and the situation of women's health, and to what extent the women arsenic victims are being subjected to domestic violence along with their children, these are some of the problems which have been discussed in this volume. Beside these the problems of married working women and their nature of adjustment, women's bid for equality in the USA, and to what extent the complex interplay of socio-economic, political, and cultural forces are associated with marginal position of women in rural China and socio-cultural parameters of gender disparity and old age insecurity of the women in patriarchal society.

The academics, researchers, administrators, policy makers and the students of anthropology, sociology, social work and social policy, women studies, women development, and social development will be benefited from this volume. This volume will enrich their thinking, knowledge, and will encourage them to develop newer ideas through their everyday experiences. This volume also highlights the contemporary situation of women in different dimensions. We hope that this book will address the needs of the students and the instructors alike by speaking to students where they are in relation to feminist issues. Our expectation is that the information included in this book will invite scholars and the students into productive dialogue and encourage them to involve in feminist work. The instructors will be able to utilize the various pedagogical procedures from this volume to develop teaching plans for their class sessions.

Like other women studies, this book covers the variety of issues. Pragmatically, this will facilitate the instructors to decide how they want to organize their own courses. The articles that have been chosen in this volume are based on empirical studies. All the articles are interesting in terms of both topics and writing styles emphasizing the techniques of analyzing the specific problem of the women and their way of life in the patriarchal social system. It is hoped that this volume will help the administrators and policy planners to chalk out appropriate, pragmatic and realistic policies for overall development and well-being of the women in difficult circumstances in patriarchal social system in global perspective.

Profulla C. Sarker

ACKNOWLEDGEMENT

This volume covers a collection of articles contributed by many scholars. I express my gratitude to the scholars for their valuable contributions to this volume and for helping me to organize this volume in its present form for publication.

I would like to record my intellectual and academic debt to Professor Clarence T. Maloney, Professor Peter J. Bertocci, Professor Jean Ellickson, and Professor Joanna Kirkpatrick along with other teachers who taught me in different phases of my life and in different academic institutions. I always acknowledge their scholarly intellectual teaching capacity and advice which gradually helped to develop my intellectual and academic capability and self-confidence and the present volume is the out come of those pursuits.

I am greatly indebted to Professor Ajit K. Danda, Dr.Depali Danda, and Professor P.Dash Sharma for their constant inspiration and suggestions to organize this volume. I would like to express my sincere thanks and gratitude to Professor S.T. Edmund Kwok, Executive Vice President, Beijing Normal University-Hong Kong Baptist University, United International College (UIC), Zhuhai, China, for his support and cooperation to prepare the manuscript of this volume. Thanks are also due to my colleagues of the Department of Social Work, University of Rajshahi, Bangladesh, and to the colleagues of Social Work and Administration, United International College, Zhuhai, China, for their cooperation.

Finally I express my thanks to Jhang Hui, a Ph.D. scholars of UIC and my assistant Miss Serena for their technical support especially for the computing the manuscript of this volume. Special thanks are due to Pangkaj, our son for constant silent support for my academic activities.

Profulla C. Sarker

LIST OF CONTRIBUTORS

Sanzida Z. Habib, Ph.D. Scholar, Center for Women and Gender Studies, University of British Columbia, Vancouver, Canada.

Dr. Tahmina Akhtar, Professor of Social Welfare, Institute of Social Welfare & Research, Dhaka University, Dhaka, Bangladesh.

M. Omar Faruk, Lecturer in Social Welfare, Institute of Social Welfare & Research, Dhaka University, Dhaka, Bangladesh.

Azizur Rahman, Lecturer in Social Welfare, Institute of Social Welfare & Research,Dhaka University, Dhaka, Bangladesh

Pranab Kumar Panday, Associate Professor of Public Administration, University of Rajshahi, Rajshahi, Bangladesh. [Ph.D. scholar of City University, Hong Kong]

Prafulla Chakrabarti, Retired Professor of Sociology, Indian Statistical Institute, Kolkata, India

Pradip Kumar Panday, Assistant Professor of Mass Communication, University of Rajshahi, Rajshahi, Bangladesh [Ph.D. scholar of Sheffield University, U.K.]

Dr. P. Dash Sharma, Retired Professor of Anthropology, Ranchi University, Ranchi, Jharkhand, India

Dr. Bhaswati Roy, Lecture in Sociology, Kalyani University, Kalyani, West Bengal, India

Dr. Soumyajit Patra, Lecturer in Anthropology, Vidya Sagar University, Medinipore, West Bengal, India

Dr. Samita Manna, Professor of Sociology, Kalyani University, Kalyani, West Bengal, India

Dr. Katherine Van Wormer, Professor of Social Work, University of Northern Iowa, Cedar Falls, IA,U.S.A.

Dr. Maria Cheung, Associate Professor of Social Work, Manitoba University, Winnipeg, Canada

Dr. Meng Liu, Associate Professor, National Women's University, Beijing , China

Dr. Toula Heinonen, Manitoba University, Winnipeg, Canada.

Dr. Profulla C. Sarker, Senior Policy Advisor, National Food Security and Nutrition Surveillance Project and Adjunct Professor, James P. Grant School of Public Health, BRAC University, 66 Mohakhali, Dhaka-1212, Bangladesh

1

INTRODUCTION

Profulla C. Sarker

A society that expects males to dominate in all family decision making is termed as patriarchy. It describes a political system ruled by men in which the women have inferior social and political status, including basic human rights (Kottack, 2005:198). In patriarchal society authority is vested upon the man who takes the responsibility for maintenance of the family and plays dominant role to take any decision of the family (Sarker, 1997). In many cultures women are devalued as human beings from the day they are born; from very early childhood girls are made conscious of the fact that unlike their brothers, who are assets to the family, they are liabilities. In the process of socialization, girls are made to understand from childhood that once married, they should learn how to adjust with their husbands and others relatives (Rahman,1984:30). Adjustment means total submission to the will of the husband and other members of the family. In many societies girls are taught the two virtues — patience and sacrifice, the ideal motherhood in patriarchal society. They also learn to accept the inferior status of women in society. For example, as girls grow up they perceive the preferential treatment given to their brothers, fathers and other male members of the family and they are also taught that getting less of every thing and not complaining about it, is the ideal behavior pattern for good women.

In patriarchal society, the wives are expected to be modest, submissive and dutiful to their husbands and other members of the family. Culture of many societies does not permit equality between men and women. Because in many cultures gender dichotomization has its genesis in religion (Sarker,1999:205). Almost every religion has either directly or indirectly propagated the concept of inequality between man and woman. Patriarchy values male dominance as a natural, inalienable right, thereby enforcing the inferiority and subordination of women. Normative behaviors derived from this value include institutional discrimination against women in education, health, and in the labor force, resulting in restricted opportunities, lower wages for vwork, and relative economic, social, and political deprivation (Neubeck and Glasberg,1996:111). Consequently, women have to depend upon men in different phases of their life cycle. Even the employed women are not independent in real sense though they have the liberty of movement and have scope of social interaction with the cross-section of people. In many societies, women have no individual identity; rather they are addressed by their kinship positions vis-à-vis others, such as daughter, wife or mother of some one. In patriarchal society, only the relatives of the father are significant under the kinship system (Scheafer, 2006:324).

Barbara Miller (1997), in a study of Systematic Neglect of Females, describes women in rural northern India as "the endangered sex". Societies that feature a full-fledged patrilineal-patrilocal complex, replete with warfare and inter village raiding, also typify patriarchy. Such practices as dowry murder, and female infanticide exemplify patriarchy, which extends from tribal societies. Baden et al, (1994) pointed out that in rural Bangladesh husband is the guardian of his wife; and thus women's labor, income, sexuality, and access to education, jobs, markets, etc. are strictly controlled by their husbands. Slaves are purchased with money, but in patriarchal society, directly or indirectly, women become slaves by paying their husbands money in the form of dowry. Even developed countries, despite their advancement in higher education, women still face major barriers when they attempt to use their educational achievements to advance in the work place. For example, women rarely hold more than 1 to 2 percent of top executive positions (Schaefer, 2006:280). Moreover, women almost always work in occupations with lower status and lower pay scale than men. In both developing and developed countries, many women work as unpaid family laborers. Despite social norms and values regarding support and protection, many widows around the world receive little concrete support from their extended family net works system. Laura Nader (1986:383) has observed, even in the relatively more egalitarian society of the West, women's subordination is "institutionally structured and culturally rationalized, exposing them to conditions of deference, dependency, powerlessness, and poverty."

About 50 percent population of the world is of women especially in Asia .The male domination on women is one of the socio-economic and psychological problems in patriarchal society, not only at the household level but also in every other spheres where women have to face these problems. Consequently, dependency on man by woman has already been imprinted in the mind of the women which is one of the constraints to make them self-reliant and self-dependent. Under the circumstances, if the existing situation of patriarchy is allowed to continue, the 50 percent human resource i.e., women, will be unutilized and de-touched from the main stream of development and as a result, all the development efforts will be ended like smoke. On the other hand, the reduction of patriarchy and social, economic and psychological development of women are not possible without active cooperation of the counter part men. This volume addresses to understand the social, economical, political and cultural situation of women where the patriarchal social system exists and male domination is prominent. If the future patriarchy is to day's reality, then the millions of people especially the women and children will be the main victim of oppression and depression and the human rights will be declined throughout the world.

Sanzida Z. Habib in her paper "Disability, Poverty and Patriarchy: A Feminist Analysis of the Situation of Disabled Women in Bangladesh" has analyzed the socio-economic conditions of the disabled women in Bangladesh, both in mainstream society and in the disabled community. Exploring the relationship between poverty, patriarchy and disability in Bangladesh, she uncover that women's lack of entitlement to nutrition, health care and medical treatment makes them more vulnerable than man to disabling conditions and systematically creates disabilities for a large number of women. She high lighted in her paper that the situations and experiences of disabled women are shaped not only by their gender, but also by the wealth and social status of their families, and by where they live. Sanzida pointed out that the patriarchy or gender discrimination, disabled women are usually at a greater disadvantage than their male counterparts in terms of getting a diagnosis, accessing health care, education, rehabilitation and employment, and being more likely to encounter violence but less likely to get married. In her conclusion, she has suggested the limits of viewing patriarchy as a closed and monolithic system, and the importance of using gender as a ' contested image' in future research in the area.

Tahmina Akhtar, M. Omar Faruk and M. Azizur Rahman in their paper "The Impact OF Grameen Bank Credit Programs on the Role of Rural Women in Bangladesh: An Empirical Assessment" has examine the change in roles of the rural women. The changes in relation to their income, savings, life style, living standard, occupation, decision-making capability etc. were analyzed in this study, which had indirect impact on the socioeconomic status in their families, society, and political affiliation. This study was conducted only on the borrowers of Grameen Bank of Lamakazi Branch, Sylhet. One hundred and ten borrowers were interviewed out of 1275 borrowers of that branch. Social survey method was used to collect data and statistical tools such as, measure of central tendency, measures of dispersion, measurement of inequality were used to analyze the data. The results show that a significant change was made in the roles of rural women by the credit program of Grameen Bank. It changed the life styles, awareness and living standards of the rural women.

Pranab Kumar Panday in his study " Women's Political Participation in Bangladesh and India: Symbolic or Real? has presented the state of women's political participation at the local government level in Bangladesh and India. What factors led both governments to initiate several affirmative actions for the enhancement of women's participation? What factors impede their participation in the political arena? And what happens to women of both the countries once they participate in the local government bodies? The present study seeks to answer all these questions. The study is based mainly on the analysis of the secondary data. The available findings substantiate that despite having initiated several affirmative actions by both governments, women are still victimized by structural, religious and cultural impediments. The finding also suggests that once they make their way to the political process they are not cordially accepted by their counterpart. Although few NGOs and women organizations have been vocal in favor of women's equal rights and carrying out several programs but their initiatives remain quite inadequate. Another important finding is that women members can not exert any influence in the local level decision making. Once they go for asking their rights, they are very often victimized, assaulted and harassed.

Prafulla Chakrabarti has given a brief description in his paper " Widowhood in Rural Purulia" about the situation of widows in Purulia district of West Bengal, India. He high lighted in his study that the widowhood as a general problem has not gained much importance ion India. The author examined the pattern of widowhood in an economically backward community of rural Purulia through comparative analysis of the trend of widowhood between the rural and urban locations. He also examined the nature and extent of variations, if any, in the ratio of widowhood by religion, caste, class and education along with the socio-economic characteristics of the widowhood at the household level.

Pradip Kumar Panday has given an account in his research work "Women Journalist in the Print Media of Bangladesh and their Professional Challenges" about the existing status and position of women journalists in the print media especially newspapers in a patriarchal social system of Bangladesh. The trends of participation of women journalists in newspapers have also been discussed. Both primary and secondary sources of information have been used for this article. Emphasis has been given on secondary sources of information. A few case studies have been conducted to supplement the secondary information. The main focus of this paper is to examine the extent of devaluation of women journalists in newspapers in connection with wage and salary, access to information and employment and gender discrimination. From the analysis, it has been found that although the rate of participation of women journalists in newspaper industry is increasing gradually, but they are still discriminated in this industry of Bangladesh.

P. Dash Sharma in his research paper "Human Rights and Women's Health in India" has analyzed the status of women in the context of Indian mythology. He examined the process of gender discrimination is started right from the birth of a new born baby in patrilineal society where the gender preference of baby is highly prized in kinship network relations. It is set as a notion of right. The findings of his paper are that the Government of India has enacted laws against the gender discrimination in order to establish the equal rights of the women but the position of women in India remains same excepting the women who are educated and employed in urban settings but their number is insignificant.

Profulla C. Sarker in his paper "Arsenicosis and Domestic Violence against Women and Children in Bangladesh" discusses the cultural aspects of domestic violence against women and their children associated with arsenicosis in arsenic prone areas of Bangladesh. About 70 million people out of the total 140 million are at risk of arsenicosis due to arsenic contamination of ground water which is used as drinking and cooking purposes. The findings of this research show that domestic violence directed at the arsenic affected women includes desertion, separation and divorce, along with the physical and psychosocial torture, and sometimes they are victims of trafficking, which also affects the wellbeing of their children and probability of HIV/AIDS.

Bhaswati Roy, Soumyajit Patra and Samita Manna explained the problems of married women in India and their nature of adjustment. Indian society is too much restrictive in the matter of women's economic work participation. Even now the men folk want that the working women must fulfill their domestic duties first and after that they may go to attend their work place. In most cases the male members do not want to extend any cooperation to the working women in household activities, as they regard all the household duties are basically 'feminine'. Working women have to carry out both inside and outside burdens of home and office and bear tensions simultaneously that often exceed the tolerance limit. So working women, especially who are married and have children, are in a dilemma.

Katherine Van Wormer in her article Women's bid for equality in the United States: two steps forward and one step back" discussed that the women in United States of America have made great strides in achieving equality and human rights as a result of activism and political climate of the late1960s. This article recalls that progress but then show that a counter-reaction has set in, a reaction that is being paid by women at the lower economic levels and among the poor members of minority groups and even the professional women are thriving in American society.

Maria Cheung, Meng Liu, and Toula Heinonen depicted in their paper women's status and roles in patriarchal rural China. The authors use a gender lens to analyze inequality between women and men in China and examine institutional barriers, such as the household responsibility, household registration (*hukou*), political systems, and traditional cultural values. After economic reforms in China, have rural women enjoyed benefits similar to other groups in society? Has China improved gender equality in rural areas? The gender analysis illuminates the interplay of economic, political, social, and cultural forces which marginalize women in rural China. Rural women have always been at the bottom of the social strata. In China's the long history, rural women have faced patriarchal and patrilineal social arrangements. After communist rule, patriarchal values remained strong in rural areas. However, the collective system and the communes provided a basic social safety net for women. After economic reforms, gender inequality has intensified, partly due to the reversal of welfare policies and partly because the revival of traditional patriarchal values. Although our focus is on the analysis of gender and patriarchy in rural China, we do not imply that urban women are not affected by patriarchal societal values, but that because urban and rural development in China differs, different analyses need to be employed for the two respective populations. This chapter is divided into four sections: (1) the patriarchal social structure and values - how they affect the role and status of rural women; (2) household responsibility system how a lack of land ownership poses a problem for rural women; (3) household registration (*hukou*) system – how this system limits women's mobility and contributes to feminization of agriculture and poverty in the interior and remote areas; (4) limited participation of women in the political process; and (5) impact of gender inequality on rural women from birth to old age. The concluding section discusses some ways to overcome the institutional barriers imposed on rural women.

Profulla C. Sarker discusses in his paper that the advancement of medical science, public health care services, and technological advancement the longevity of the people is improving through out the world and as a result the number of aged person is increasing. On the other hand, the culture of gender disparity is a deep rooted problem especially in the patriarchal society where the women have to depend upon men in kinship network relations in different phases of their life cycle. The women perceived the preferential treatment in patriarchal social system given to their counter part men at the family, community, and societal levels. The culture of patriarchal society does not permit equality between man and woman in real sense. Gender disparity has its genesis in religion and value system which differentiate men and women in different dimensions. The main focus of this paper is to examine to what extend the socio-cultural parameters of gender disparity of the patriarchal society affects insecurity of the women especially in old age in relation to basic needs in terms of food, clothing, shelter, and health care along with the other civic facilities.

REFERENCES

Baden, S., Green C.,Goetz,AM and Guhathakurta, M.(1994), Background Report on Gender issue in Bangladesh, Report No26, BRIDGE

Kottak, C. Philip (2005), Mirror for Humanity. New York: McGraw-Hill.Miller, B. D.in (ed) Sex and Gender Hierarchies. New York: Cambridge University Press

Rahman, Habibur (1984), Changing Status of Women in Bangladesh. Current Sociological Perspectives. 3(1). pp.30-38

Sarker, Profulla C.(1997), Social Structure and Fertility Behavior. Dhaka: Center for Social Services.

Sarker, Profulla C. (1999), Gender Dichotomization, Use of Contraceptive Devices and their Impact on Social Development in Bangladesh. Indian Social Science Review.1(1), pp203-211

Nader, Laura (1986), "The Subordination of Women in Comparative Perspective." Urban Anthropology 15 pp. 377-397.

Neubeck, Kenneth J. and Glasberg (1996), Sociology: A Critical Review. New York, McGRW-Hill, Inc.

Schaefer, Richard T.(2006), Sociology: A Brief Introduction. New York. McGraw-Hill.

2

DISABILITY, POVERTY AND PATRIARCHY: A FEMINIST ANALYSIS OF THE SITUATIONS OF DISABLED WOMEN IN BANGLADESH

Sanzida Z. Habib

INTRODUCTION

Adrienne Asch and Michele Fine (1988, 1992) are among the leading feminist disability scholars who have explicated the complex interaction between gender and disability, and analyzed the social, psychological and economic consequences for women with disabilities in developed countries like the US and Canada. Some activists and feminist scholars of disability have illustrated the dual or multiple oppressions of women with disabilities due to their gender, disability, race, first nation or immigrant status, sexuality and so on (for example, Abu-Habib 1997; Begum 1992, 1996; Demas 1993; Driedger 1991; Ferri & Gregg 1998; Fine & Asch 1988; Fine 1992; Nancoo 1993). There are also some anthologies by women with disabilities that portray the lived experiences of disabled women and the barriers they face, as well as the way they organize and work together to overcome those barriers in both developed and developing countries (see Driedger & Gray

1992; Driedger, Feika & Batres 1996; Keith 1996; Stewart, Percival & Epperly 1992). The social conditions for rural disabled women in developing countries in general, have been portrayed in Boylan (1991). Wahab (1997) has also outlined the situations of disabled women, particularly in rural areas of underdeveloped countries in Asia and the Pacific region. Ghai (2001, 2002), a disabled woman herself, has written about the marginalized status of disabled women in India and their exclusion from the disabled people's and women's movements in that country.

Little is known about the particular situation of women with disabilities in Bangladesh. There is a dearth of research and of relevant literature, especially literature written from a socialist-feminist point of view that challenges the gender hierarchy within the disabled people's community and explicates how gender, age, class, marital status and level of education interact to shape the lives of disabled women in Bangladesh. Indeed, I have not found any writing by Bangladeshi women who identify themselves as disabled.

The Feminine Dimension of Disability: A Study on Situation of Adolescent Girls and Women with Disabilities in Bangladesh, the report of the first countrywide survey carried out by the Center for Services and Information on Disability (CSID) on the particular situations of disabled girls and women, was published in March 2001. The fact that the CSID study focuses on the "feminine" rather than the "gender" dimensions of disability, however, tends to explain its lack of comparative and critical analysis of the different needs and situations of disabled men and women in a patriarchal society such as Bangladesh. It does provides important information about the overall socio-economic and psychological situations and experiences of disabled girls and women in Bangladesh, but lacks critical analysis of either the gender hierarchies between disabled men and women, or the broader socio-economic and political reasons behind disabled women's exclusion from and marginalization in both the mainstream society and the disabled community. In other words, the study reveals how disabled women in Bangladesh face discriminations, negative attitudes and oppression because they are disabled and they are women, but overlooks how their disability and gender interact to create discriminations between disabled men and women.

In this paper I analyze the conditions for disabled women in the patriarchal society in Bangladesh. I have adopted a socialist feminist approach to analyze the marginalization of Bangladeshi disabled women both in the mainstream society and in the disabled people's community. A socialist feminist point of view towards disability (which seems to be absent in the prevailing writings on disability and disabled people in Bangladesh) not only acknowledges the power relations between disabled and/or non-disabled men and women, but also addresses the differences or unequal relations among disabled women on the basis of such factors as class, ethnicity, educational status, occupation and employment status. I argue that in Bangladesh, poverty and patriarchy systemically create disabilities among some women. I also demonstrate that disabled women are likely to be at a greater disadvantage and in worse-off positions than their male counterparts under the same socio-economic conditions in a patriarchal society like Bangladesh.

I consider disability both as a physiological and/or psychological condition, and as a social construct created by socio-economic factors, including society's negative attitudes and prejudices towards disabled people, as well as the structural arrangements that prevent disabled people's participation in mainstream activities of society. I conceptualize patriarchy or male dominance as a complex ideological, psychological, social, political and economic symtem of power and control that manifests in a number of both overt and covert ways in Bangladesh society - unequal and unfair distribution of labour and resources between men and women, women's unpaid or even unacknowledged housework and underpaid wage work, women's double burden of childcare and wage work, rape and violence against women, objectification and control of women's bodies, and purdah, to name a few.

POVERTY, PATRIARCHY AND DISABILITY

Nobel laureate economist Amartya Sen believes that poverty and deprivation rarely occur due to the scarcity of resources, but rather due to a person's lack of entitlement to the basic necessities of life. Sen's (1982, 1990) entitlement approach to starvation and poverty focuses on the in/ability of people to command food or other commodities through the legal means available in the society, including trade opportunities, the use of labor power and production ability. This approach explains poverty in terms of the individual's lack of ability to claim his/her entitlement to the set of commodities necessary for satisfying the basic needs of life. A person's relative ability or inability to command any commodity depends on "entitlement relations". These relations are determined by two main factors: endowment (what one initially owns including labor power) and exchange entitlements (what exchange possibilities are offered to one through production and trade, what is given free, or what is taken away).

Studying a number of famines that occurred largely during the second half of the last century in South East Asia and Africa, Sen (1981, 1990) showed that the famines and starvation resulted not so much from "food availability decline" as from entitlement failures related to decline in endowment (such as, alienation of land or loss of grazing rights), or to decline in exchange entitlement (for example, loss of employment, failure of wages to match with food prices, failure of incomes earned through sales of animal products, crafts or services to keep up with the costs of basic food), or to both. He also noticed that even when famines were indeed accompanied by a shortfall in food supply, specific occupation groups were demolished while other occupation groups remained unaffected. Therefore, rather than focusing on the question of food supply, Sen's entitlement approach explores the broader socio-economic, political and legal circumstances in order to explain why certain groups of people fail to get a hold of the available food, why they do not have the income or ability to buy food, and what factors determine inequitable distribution of food between different sections of the community.

Sen's (1981) entitlement approach to starvation and poverty, which considered household as the basic unit of analysis and analyzed the household's command over goods and services, was extended in his later work (Sen 1990), to explain the issue of mal/distribution within the household. Sen (1990, p.140) has pointed out that although intra-household distribution is not typically controlled by laws, which govern "who can have the use of what" (as, for example, in the case of property ownership, market transactions, or wage employment), it operates through deep-rooted notions of "legitimacy" within a powerful structural basis, namely the social norms, beliefs and practices centering around the idea of male superiority. As Kabeer (1994) has argued, the fact that women and children are disproportionately represented among the poor cannot be explained by the problem of inadequate (formal or legal) entitlements alone: structurally reproduced distributional inequities must also be considered. Different members in the household may have different entitlements, which stem from the unequal distribution of family resources within the household according to the gender, age, perceived contribution, and prestige of each family member. Thus, women's inadequate extended entitlements to food, health care and other family resources are caused not only by their limited opportunities for outside employment and earnings, but also by patriarchy and socially legitimized gender bias in intra-household distributions.

Sen's (1990) theorizations about entitlement relations and extended entitlements also seem to be useful in analyzing disabled people's experience of deprivation, economic oppression and poverty. A man or woman's entitlement to social goods and services is certainly curtailed by his or her disability, since it tends to constrain mobility and limit the use of one's own labor power, which in turn hinders income earning and/or trade opportunities, in other words, "exchange entitlements". Disabled people are also likely to have inadequate claims over family resources as a result of their dependence and lack of bargaining power. They are not perceived as making any "contribution" to the family, which is likely to weaken their claims over both tangible and intangible resources. Thus, disabled people are likely to face poverty and inadequate entitlement to food and other resources due to their disability.

On the other hand, a person's lack of entitlement to basic necessities of life can cause disabilities. An exploration of the relationship between poverty and disability in the Bangladesh context makes apparent that a woman's lack of entitlement to food, nutrition, education, health care and medical treatment, security and other tangible and intangible resources systemically creates disability for some women. Below, I demonstrate how the intersection of poverty and patriarchal practices creates disability in a large number of women. The discussion, exploring factors contributing directly or indirectly to disabilities among "the poor", also reestablishes that disability is socially created.

MALNUTRITION, FERTILITY AND MATERNAL MORBIDITY

Poverty, malnutrition, chronic disease, and conditions of ill health tend to form a vicious circle for women in Bangladesh. While severe physical deprivation and malnutrition are common among the majority of the population living in poverty, several authors have suggested that women and young children, young girls in particular, are more likely to suffer from malnutrition (Kabeer 1994; Ostergaard 1992). A survey of the nutritional status of rural children in Bangladesh found 14% of girls to be severely malnourished compared to 5% of boys, and 26% of the girls to be severely stunted, compared to 18% of the boys (Royston and Armstrong 1989, as cited in Ostergaard 1992).

Most women in poverty-stricken rural Bangladesh are malnourished due to economic as well as social or gender factors. Women are subject to unequal distribution of food due to certain socio-cultural values and practices that reflect the preference for and prestige of males over females. Usually, adult male members of the family are fed first and served the best food, while women eat last, and often the leftovers. The gender and age bias in food distribution and feeding practices is prevalent across different classes in Bangladesh, but certainly affects women and female children the most who live below the poverty line. Mahmud and Mahmud (1985) noticed that children suffer from substantial deficits in terms of calorie intake vis-a-vis requirements even in the richest households, while female adults suffer from larger deficits than male adults in the poorest, and enjoy a smaller surplus in the richest households (cited in Kabeer 1994). It has been suggested that women's participation in wage-labor, particularly gainful outside employment, improves their bargaining power within the household and thus strengthens their claims on household resources like food and health care (Kabeer 1994; Sen 1990). However, Paul-Majumder (1996), in her study of garment workers in Bangladesh, found a poorer food-intake among female workers than among the male workers due to the traditional discriminatory feeding practices, which they could not overcome even after entering wage employment. This gap in food-intake also partially accounted for the differential health conditions–measured by physical weakness–found between male and female workers.

There is a complex relationship between poverty, high infant mortality, fertility and maternal morbidity, which is potentially disabling for thousands of women in rural Bangladesh. High infant mortality is the result of malnutrition, poor obstetric and maternal care, and lack of education, all of which are associated with poverty (Ostergaard 1992; Zakir and Wunnava 1999). High infant mortality may lead to high fertility by creating increased pressures on poor mothers to have more children, which in turn leads to poor health for the mother. Thus Kabeer (1994) correctly notes that a major cause of female malnutrition in Bangladesh is the superimposition of early, frequent and closely spaced childbearing on already high levels of nutritional deprivation.

Malnutrition and multiple pregnancies in the absence of adequate maternal care can cause maternal morbidity, disability, and increased vulnerability to disabling diseases. Malnourished mothers are also likely to give birth to malnourished, underweight and diseased babies whose chances of survival are very low and who are at greater risk of getting disabilities than healthy babies. The 1998 World Bank data show that 68% of children under age five in Bangladesh suffered from malnutrition during the years 1990-1996, while 34% of babies were of low birth weight for the years 1989-1995 (Srinivasan 2000, p. 270). Both of these rates are the highest among countries in the South Asian region. Siddiquee (2003) has mentioned that a UNICEF study (2000) found only one in three young pregnant women to have met the iron requirements for their bodies. Sufi, Yamashita and Nazneen (1996) note protein and iodine deficiencies, both in a mother's diet during pregnancy and in the baby's diet after birth, as potent causes of lower intelligence or impaired intellectual development among children. Thus, malnourished mothers run the risk of disabilities both for themselves and their children. As Ostergaard (1992) has remarked, WHO (1986b) figures show that each time a woman in rural Bangladesh becomes pregnant she faces a risk of dying which is at least 55 times higher than the risk for women in Portugal and 400 times higher than the risk for women in Scandinavia. The health risks involved in pregnancy and childbirth among poor women in Bangladesh cause high rates of maternal mortality, as well as high rates of severe disability among the large number of women who somehow escape death.

Around 20 years ago, Chen (1986) noted that most village women in Bangladesh work an average of 14 hours a day. Undoubtedly, too much work combined with too little food causes malnutrition and poor health in women. Women in low-income households are also often involved in piecework like sewing, weaving, embroidery and making handicrafts, which not only increase their workload but can also diminish their eyesight. Long working hours, seven days a week throughout the year, often cause various conditions of ill health among malnourished women in poor households. An empirical study by Pratima Paul-Majumder (1996) has shown the adverse impact of the double burden of wage work and household work on the health of poor working class women in garment factories. A number of illnesses, and particularly physical weakness, which may be a symptom of some serious diseases like anemia and tuberculosis, were found to be common among female garment workers in Bangladesh. These were attributed to overwork and sleep deprivation, since it was found that in addition to the average 12 hours of labor in garment factory, female workers spent an average of 2.5 hours on domestic chores, and further, 70 percent of these female workers slept less than 6 hours a day.

ACCESS TO HEALTH CARE

In Bangladesh, a densely populated and poverty stricken country, it is quite understandable that general health conditions are unsatisfactory due to inadequate health care facilities. People living in poverty cannot even access the health care facilities that exist. Elwan (1999) has pointed out that lack of adequate and timely health care can exacerbate disease outcomes and can turn a remediable impairment into a permanent disability.

Most girls and women in Bangladesh also lack entitlement to medical care due to the discrimination they face in utilizing existing health care facilities. There is some empirical evidence of gender bias with respect to accessing health care in developing countries including Bangladesh (Sabir & Ebrahim 1984). Chen, Haque and D'Souza (1981) found that more ill boys were brought to the health clinics and hospitalized than girls (cited in Kabeer 1994, p.147). Sue Tackwell (1991) mentions that a study of a Bangladeshi village found a 6.9% prevalence rate of psychiatric illness among the villagers, and an increased vulnerability of women over men to such illness by a ratio of 2:1. She mentions another study, carried out at the post-graduate hospital in Dhaka, which showed that most of the psychiatric outpatients were male, despite the fact that more women than men suffer from mental illnesses.

The high rate of maternal mortality and morbidity in Bangladesh is also associated with undernourished mothers' inadequate access to basic maternal and obstetric care. Most women in the villages of Bangladesh risk their lives during labor and childbirth because deliveries are facilitated by traditional birth attendants under very poor sanitary conditions. Sufi, Yamashita and Nazneen (1996) report many incidents of difficult and defective births among very young women in the village of their study. They claim that difficult or defective birth processes, infantile illnesses (such as high fever, meningitis and infection), and the indiscriminate use of drugs (including antibiotic, homeopathic and Ayurvedic medicines) during pregnancy are the major causes of disabling conditions in the village they studied. Sorcar and Mondal (1992), in their study of developmentally disabled children at the "Bogra Institute for the Mentally Retarded" in Bangladesh, also found developmental disability to be associated with such factors as harmful conditions experienced by mothers during pregnancy (for example, through taking highly potent medicines, suffering from serious illnesses during pregnancy and experiencing birth hazards), and diseases or trauma during infancy and early childhood (most commonly typhoid, whooping cough, meningitis, kidney infection and asthma). Thus, women's disadvantaged claims to proper health care, especially during pregnancy and childbirth, again greatly increase the potential for disabling conditions, both for themselves and their children.

Hosain and Chatterjee (1998) have noted that certain socio-economic and cultural barriers prevent women and dependent young children from accessing health care, while those individuals who are perceived as economically beneficial to the family usually are able to utilize health services. They have also noted that generally the decision to obtain health care in rural Bangladesh is made through a social process based on prioritization of scarce resources and keeping the earning members healthy. But in the case of women, besides the sheer economic prioritization, deeper socio-cultural and patriarchal practices such as purdah, along with the general negative attitudes towards women in the society, contribute to non-utilization of existing medical services. Khanum (1999, pp. 116-118) mentions a number of factors, other than the directly economic ones, as barriers to women's utilization of prevailing medical facilities in Bangladesh: time constraints, geographical inaccessibility (distant locations of medical centers), poor infrastructural facilities, inadequacy of medicine and medical staff, health professionals' apathy, and popular norms and values including purdah.

Yet another important socio-cultural patriarchal attitude that restricts women's access to medical care is the socialization of women not to complain about illness or pain, and to be strong enough to endure pain and continue working against all odds for the welfare of their families (Hosain & Chartterjee 1998). Kabeer (1994) refers to the UBINIG study (1987) on health-seeking behavior in village households in Bangladesh, which found that male household -heads were most likely to report on their own illnesses, with the reporting of illness among women to be scanty, even in cases where interviewers clearly noticed a woman's sickness, because women's health problems are not recognized either by themselves or by the community. The study suggests that women's illnesses are indeed doubly ignored–they remain frequently unidentified as illnesses requiring treatment, and even when they are identified, women have little clearly recognized entitlement to the necessary health care.

Disabled people in rural Bangladesh face yet further difficulties in using the medical facilities that exist. Inadequate services, coupled with the absence of a disabled-friendly social environment, actually make disabled people's access to health care systems more difficult, even for basic medical needs (Hosain & Chatterjee 1998). Considering the gender bias and the socio-cultural barriers that prevent women's access to medical facilities, it can be assumed that disabled men will get priority over disabled women in utilizing health care facilities. Hosain and Chatterjee (1998) have suggested that in rural Bangladesh a female child who is congenitally disabled or an older female who has become disabled later in life would probably be the least likely to obtain treatment or even to be perceived as having a problem. They maintain that the socio-cultural practice of purdah in rural Bangladesh inhibits disabled women from utilizing health-care services outside of their villages.

Sufi, Yamashita and Nazneen (1996) found that due to restrictions on movement outside the home, women in the village of Bandaikhara received medicine during their illnesses via the male members of their families, who brought it from village physicians after describing the symptoms on behalf of the women. In a different study, Khanum (1999) found that 69% of the women in the village she studied showed hesitance to talk to male doctors about any complaint regarding female diseases. Rahman and Ahmed (1993) have mentioned that, according to Islamic religious beliefs, if a male physician or physio-technician touches a woman's body, it is a sin. So, despite the fact that an increasing number of women in Bangladesh are entering labor markets outside of their courtyards, thus breaking the patriarchal control of purdah, it appears that certain religious codes and social beliefs still play a vital role in preventing numerous disabled and even non-disabled women from getting medical treatment. Sarah White (1992, p.14) has pointed out that although there are continuing debates about the ideal roles for women, or the true interpretation of gender in Islam, "there is no doubt that its political expression in present day Bangladesh acts significantly to curtail women's room for manoeuvre."

Hosain and Chatterjee (1998) report that more than half of the respondents in their study sample had seen an unqualified medical practitioner, one-third of them had seen a practitioner of an alternative medical system, such as homeopathy or Ayurvedic medicine, and a third had consulted a spiritual healer. Hosain and Chatterjee, however, did not examine any gender difference in the utilization of alternative or traditional healing methods. Other studies have also explored the different health care options and the utilization of the existing medical options by men and women in Bangladesh (see, for example, Banik 2003; Desmet et al. 1999a, 1999b; Khanum 1999; Sultana 2003). None, however, have conducted a gender analysis of their findings – for example, whether women utilize alternative health care more often than men do, or what impacts the differential utilization of alternative care may have on women's health. It seems that women (with or without disabilities) in rural areas of Bangladesh would be more likely than men to utilize traditional health services because these are less expensive than modern or specialized medical services, are readily available within the villages, and do not require touching or thorough examination of the body. The spiritual healer, often, is herself a woman who lives in the same village and is known as one of the villagers, so women may feel comfortable talking about their ailment with her. The greater possibility for women to utilize traditional, spiritual, or non-medical treatment, again, can exacerbate their disease conditions, and turn a remediable disease into a permanent disability.

Women in rural Bangladesh are deprived of education and so are more superstitious about the causes of disability and disease. Sarder and Chen (1981) found social perceptions and beliefs about causation of illnesses to influence the selection of a particular healer or utilization of a particular health service. According to the general beliefs among the rural people in Bangladesh, disability is caused by a supernatural factor such as the effect of an evil spirit, an evil eye, or a curse of God. Such beliefs are particularly strong among rural women and lead them towards seeking treatment from traditional healers. Until and unless their illnesses take a serious turn and become life threatening, they are not generally taken to hospitals or health clinics where they can get modern medical services. Sometimes they even die within their households without having had any modern medical treatment.

GENDER, PATRIARCHY AND DISABILITY

Examining the socio-cultural and gender factors that interact with economic ones to create malnutrition among women and female children and limit their utilization of existing medical care makes it clear that many of the disabilities among Bangladeshi women stem from preventable impairments, and that women are more vulnerable than men to disabilities and disabling conditions. Many women in Bangladesh become impoverished and disabled due to the biased, discriminatory socio-cultural practice of preferential treatment of males in distributing household resources, a practice that in effect legitimizes women's lack of entitlement to social goods and services. Indeed, a large number of women in the country encounter the problems of malnutrition, early marriage and early pregnancy, and lack of health care and medical attention, all of which make them more vulnerable than men to disability.

STATISTICS AND THE INVISIBILITY OF DISABLED WOMEN

Statistics, quite ironically, show a higher rate of disability among Bangladeshi men than among women. Although current and reliable data on the nature and extent of disabilities is not available for most of the developing countries in the Asia-Pacific region, including Bangladesh (Wahab 1997), some national level statistical data show the crude disability rate among the female population in Bangladesh in the year 1996 to be 11.0 per 1,000, compared to 12.9 per 1,000 among the male population, with an average of 12.0 per 1000 population (Bangladesh Data Sheet 1999).

As Elwan (1999) cites from Harriss-White and Subramanian's findings (1999), estimates from India and Pakistan indicate male disability rates to be higher than female rates. Overall, disability rates for women seem to be lower than those for men in developing countries, and higher in developed countries (Elwan 1999). Paradoxically, an International Labor Organization survey (1989) carried out in six Asian and Pacific countries, as the ESCAP paper (1995) notes, showed a relatively higher incidence of disability among women between the ages of 15 and 44 compared to men of the same age range, despite the overall lower number of disabled women. The ESCAP paper explains this situation by noting that women in this age group suffer more from ill-health caused by too many pregnancies, inadequate medical and health care, and poor nutrition, all of which put them at greater risk of disability. The paper also holds that the lower number of disabled women than men in general in developing countries, despite the fact that women generally live longer than men, could indicate that girls and women with disabilities receive less care and support than men, which ultimately leads them to die at younger ages. Moreover, it is likely that in most developing countries with patriarchal social structures like Bangladesh, men will be diagnosed as disabled and will get rehabilitation services, while women's disabilities may remain unrecognized. Elwan (1999) contends that another reason for the lower number of disabled women in developing countries is that the gender division of labor is such that disabled women contributing to household activity are not identified as disabled, whereas the visibility of disabled men is greater.

Sen (1990, pp. 123-124) has argued that the overall socio-economic inequalities between men and women are crudely reflected by a simple statistic, namely the sex ratios, or female to male in some developing countries, including Bangladesh and India. Sen believes that the lower number of females per male in the less developed countries as a whole (.97), regardless of the proven fact that women have some general biological advantages for survival and longevity over men, points to the importance of treating gender as a vital parameter in studies of poverty and development. Drawing upon Sen's argument, I would make a similar claim: the lower number of disabled women than disabled men in developing countries such as Bangladesh, on its own, signifies the necessity for acknowledging the gender perspectives and politics of disability, or, in other words, the relative deprivation of disabled women vis-à-vis disabled men, which is quite often ignored by researchers and policy makers working in the field of disabilities.

GENDER AND OVERALL SITUATIONS OF DISABLED WOMEN

In developing countries, as Driedger notes, "women with disabilities face triple jeopardy: discrimination due to disability, gender and developing world status" (1996, p.10). Rahman and Ahmed further illustrate the developing world status and the gender conditions for disabled women in Bangladesh: "In a country where it can be a curse to be born a woman, the problems of a woman with a disability are fourfold: she is a woman; she has a disability; she lives in poverty; she is a victim of illiteracy and superstition" (1993, 47). In developing countries like Bangladesh, women in general are worse-off than men in terms of socio-economic and educational status. In the context of overall patriarchal or gender discriminatory conditions, disabled women are at a greater disadvantage than their male counterparts. Disabled women are discriminated against in terms of being diagnosed, and in getting access to health care, education, rehabilitation and employment, and are more likely to encounter violence and less likely to get married, and thus are in worse off positions than their male counterparts under the same socio-economic circumstances in Bangladesh.

Bangladeshi Disabled women, however, are by no means a homogeneous group. In addition to gender, the status and experiences of women with disabilities in the country likely to depend on socio-economic class, level of education, area of residence, age, employment and marital status, and types and severity of disabilities among other factors.

The extent to which a girl child or woman with a disability is accepted and the extent to which she gets medical, educational and other attention, seem largely to depend on the socio-economic status of her family. In a patriarchal society, where the birth of a girl is not always welcome, it seems that a girl born with a visible deformity or with physiological or mental impairment will rarely be accepted. But, according to Rahman and Ahmed (1993), a disabled child in an upper-class family in Bangladesh is relatively fortunate, because even though viewed as an extra responsibility, s/he will have access to modern amenities and treatment, as well as to social facilities, and will enjoy the protection of economic security. In stating the conditions for developmentally disabled children in upper-class Bangladeshi families, Sufi, Yamashita and Nazneen (1996) suggest that the higher socio-economic groups can afford to, and usually do, appoint nurses or attendants to care for their developmentally disabled children, although there is a general tendency among these groups to hide their disabled children from others.

The life of a disabled woman in a middle class family is likely to be full of uncertainties, dilemmas and conflicts. Middle class people are usually the most conservative, but due to the pressure to conform to the norms of modern industrialized life, they juggle the old and new beliefs, values and ideologies, and they almost always have to compromise between their desires and capabilities. Hence, as Rahman and Ahmed have correctly commented, "a person with a disability in a middle class family, is always a burden" (1993, p. 47). The life of an adult female with a developmental disability in an urban area, according to Sufi, Yamashita and Nazneen, (although they do not explain why) is far more miserable than that of an adult male with a similar disability. I suppose these women remain completely confined within the walls of their homes, with the least opportunities for social interaction, since there is almost no institution in Bangladesh for taking care of adult persons with developmental disabilities. There is also a risk of road accidents and a fear of harassment and abuse outside the home bringing shame to their families. Disabled women in middle-class families thus face more discrimination, isolation, negative attitudes and skepticism about their potential than disabled men in the same class. The overprotection and neglect of middle-class disabled women hinders their development of social skills, which in turn weakens the possibilities for their social and community participation, as well as their chances of marriage.

Conditions for disabled women in rural Bangladesh vary significantly from those for women living in urban areas. In general, the plight of disabled women living in rural Bangladesh is even more severe, since they encounter more problems in their daily living and fewer opportunities for education, employment and rehabilitation. But developmentally disabled persons in lower socio-economic conditions, according to Sufi, Yamashita and Nazneen (1996), enjoy more freedom of movement than middle-class urban women in both urban slums and in rural areas. Developmentally disabled children of both sexes in rural areas get opportunities to go out to the agricultural fields and village markets, due to less risk of road accidents. In rural Bangladesh, women with developmental disabilities usually get involved in household activities, take care of their nephews or nieces or other children in their families, and have relatively better scope for socialization: overall, they enjoy more social acceptance compared to their urban counterparts (Sufi, Yamashita & Nazneen 1996). I think there is good reason to believe this also to be the case for persons with other kinds of disabilities in rural Bangladesh as rural life is less competitive and simpler than it is in urban areas. People, particularly women in rural areas, spend a lot of time socializing with each other, since it is the most affordable recreation in their lives, and most of the time disabled women can also take part. As well, men with moderate physical or mental disabilities can do some simple manual work in fields or village markets.

Disabled men and women in less individualistic agrarian society of rural Bangladesh therefore seem to experience less exclusion or isolation from the mainstream social, and, to some extent, economic, activities. It should be noted that Oliver (1996) has argued that disabled people only began to suffer economic and social exclusion and to be considered as "individual and medical problems" as the capitalist mode of production and individualized wage labor in factories were introduced. In addition, disability theorist Finkelstein (1980) has argued, reviewing the history of disability in Western culture, that disability is an outcome of the development of Western industrial society (cited in Barnes 1996). According to Finkelstein, people with impairments were first excluded from employment and economic activities with the advent of industrialization because they were perceived to be unable to cope with the new factory-based work system and as a result became socially isolated or marginalized. These theories imply that people with disabilities are more likely to enjoy greater social and economic integration in less competitive and less individualistic agrarian societies than in industrialized urban societies, which seems to be true for disabled people in rural Bangladesh.

Disabled women are not only de-humanized; they are also de-womanized. Throughout the world they are denied and restricted from performing the roles considered traditional for woman as "nurturers." A disabled woman is not considered "marriageable," due to the perception of her disabilities as "defects," the fear that she could pass the disability onto her children, and the doubt that she would be able to look after her family and home (ESCAP 1995). Shah (1992) states that in the South Asian regions marriage is the most important and sometimes only "career" for a woman. But due to the society's negative attitudes towards disability, disabled women are denied their rights to marriage and family. The CSID study (2001) found that despite the 48% prevalence of early marriage among women in Bangladesh, only 2% of 150 adolescent girls with disabilities were married, and 50.63% of the 160 adult disabled women in the study reported never being married. The study also reports an 8.13% rate of divorce and 2% of separation among the group of disabled women. It should be mentioned that 28.6% of the rural and 36.6% of the urban women of age 10 and above in Bangladesh in the year 1996 were never married, while 0.7% of the rural women and 1.1% of the urban women of the same age were either divorced or separated in the same year (Bangladesh Data Sheet 1999).

The marriage of a disabled woman in Bangladesh appears to depend on her economic status and class position, as well as on her level of impairment or type of disability.

Sufi, Yamashita and Nazneen (1996) state that marriage of develop mentally disabled persons is less common among the educated class, apparently high among the illiterate class, and more frequent among rural people than among the urban middle-class. The CSID study (2001) points out that well-off families often encourage their disabled girls to get an education rather than to get married. Rahman and Ahmed (1993) assume that a woman with a disability can still marry in exchange for a handsome dowry. But the CSID study (2001) found that even though some disabled women got married after offering generous dowries, their marriages did not last long.

According to the ESCAP report (1995), universally the incidence of marriage for disabled women is lower than that for disabled men. While a man's eligibility or potential to be a husband is primarily judged by his ability to earn money or financially run the family, a woman's chances of getting married depend heavily on her beauty and attractiveness, her physical and sexual abilities, and her housekeeping and child-bearing abilities. Friesen (1992) found that if a Bangladeshi woman acquires a disability after marriage, her husband would likely divorce her, a fact which also seems to be true worldwide. On the other hand, if a man becomes disabled after marriage, it is usually his wife who is supposed to take care of him.

Zaman has argued that in Bangladesh, women are everyday targets of discrimination, exploitation and violence because

The existing social, economic, and political structures, such as property rights, state laws, policies, and discriminatory treatment along gender lines are exploitative in nature and ultimately deny women their socioeconomic autonomy at every stage of their lives. Subtle yet overt forms of violence are used on various occasions and at different stages of women's lives (1999, p. 37).

Considering the pervasive and systemic nature of violence against women in Bangladesh society, it can be assumed that a considerable number of women among those who do not die become disabled as a result of violence, either domestic or public, although there are no data or reports available regarding this issue. In Bangladesh, as the CSID study (2001) points out, a good number of studies have focused on the issue of domestic violence and sexual assault against women without incorporating the issue of violence against disabled women. However, in the overall scenario of violence against women in Bangladesh, it is not surprising that the CSID study (2001) found 92% of the disabled girls and women with disabilities to be victims of emotional, physical or sexual abuse both inside and outside the family.

One example of the discrimination and negative attitudes faced by Bangladeshi women with disabilities, both as disabled people and as women, is documented in the work of Francine Arsenault, a representative of the Council of Canadians with Disabilities (CCD) and a board member of International Center for the Advancement of Community Based Rehabilitation (ICACBR):

The disabled women I met in Bangladesh at the ICACBR National Forum in 1992 were very resourceful, and yet very reticent about speaking out or coming forward with their suggestions. When I was asked to be a role model and give a keynote address at the forum, I overheard an argument between the conference coordinator and other guest speakers (mostly Muslim men) who refused to sit at the table with a disabled woman. I reminded them that I represented one of the co-sponsors of the event (ICACBR) and so had paid for their participation! No wonder women with disabilities lack confidence if they must battle such negative attitudes about their right to represent themselves (1996, pp. 132-133).

Disabled women do share some common experiences of oppression with non-disabled women, as well as some experiences of discrimination and exclusion, with disabled men. Yet the compound effect of gender and disability puts disabled women in a situation that is unique and different from that of both disabled men and non-disabled women. Lina Abu-Habib, citing the findings of a qualitative study on the situation of disabled women in the Middle East concluded, "disability acts to further increase the vulnerability of women and reinforce their subordinate position in society" (1997, p. 73). The oppression of disabled women is amplified due to their gender and disability, and their situation further deteriorates because of their poverty and their lack of opportunities for health care, education, employment, and rehabilitation.

The Bangladeshi state is constitutionally committed to protecting women's rights to equality in all spheres, and thereby to ensuring equal participation of all men and women in the overall development process. However, as the Government of Bangladesh (N. D.) in chapter nine (Women in Development and Child Development Issues) of The Fifth Five Year Plan 1997-2002 confesses, the obvious and ongoing discrepancies between men and women in terms of life expectancy, health and nutrition status, education, employment and income opportunities, control over assets, social and personal security, and participation in the political process–all clearly show that development initiatives, investments and interventions in Bangladesh have not been sufficient to benefit women equitably.

At present, Bangladeshi NGOs seem to be more trusted and celebrated than the government, both by general, grass roots people and by aid agencies, for their innovative and down-to earth-programs and services. Currently, NGOs are estimated to be operating in nearly 80% of all Bangladeshi villages (Brazier 2001). In 1997, there were 848 registered NGOs in Bangladesh (Brazier 2001). But less than 12% of the NGOs operate in the field of disability, and only a few work for disabled women.

Wahab (1997) notes that even though some of the developmenf projects at the global, regional, national, and community levels are "gender neutral" and even "female biased" in traditional terms, most of the beneficiaries are still men. Given the patriarchal nature of Bangladesh society and the overall uneven power relations between men and women that create gender differences in the discrimination and disadvantages faced by disabled people, development policy or projects targeting disabled population in general will fail to benefit disabled men and women equally. In other words, without adequate consideration of the gender dimension of disability, along with other forms of social inequalities, development plans and social policies for people with disabilities will continue to marginalize disabled women, particularly in the rural areas, in both the public and private spheres.

BEYOND PATRIARCHY: GENDER AS A CONTESTED IMAGE

The term patriarchy has been defined and understood differently by different feminists. Radical feminists tend to conceptualize patriarchy as a universal or single social phenomenon across place and time, within which men are viewed as universal oppressors and women as oppressed (Wilson 2000). Such a conceptualization leaves no room for understanding the oppression of women and/or men at the hands of upper-class women and instead renders all women as equally and completely powerless. Patriarchy is not a transhistorical, unitary or monolithic system, and women's subordination and exploitation cannot be understood or explained without considering the link between patriarchy, colonialism and global capitalism. For example, the separation between private and public spheres, the isolated nature of women's domestic work, and the glorification of women as dependent–all of these were a product of the shift from agriculture to industrial economies during the Victorian era (Wilson 2000). Marilyn French (cited in Wilson 2000) defines patriarchy as

The manifestation and institutionalization of male dominance over women and children in the family and the extension of male dominance over women in society in general. It implies that men hold power in all the important institutions of society and women are deprived of access to such power. It does not imply that women are either totally powerless or totally deprived of rights, influences, and resources (French 1985, p. 239).

Not only does this definition provide a more elaborate understanding of patriarchy, but it also signals the possibility for women's resistance against and negotiation with authority, and for a change in their positions as victims. While feminists still continue to use patriarchy in their analyses, gradually "gender" is becoming a more accepted and popular alternative in comprehending the unequal relationship, both between men and women and among women themselves.

Sarah White (1992), in her classic study on gender and class in a Bangladeshi village, has stressed that viewing gender as a "contested image" can help us better understand women's situation in Bangladeshi society in at least three ways. First, such a perspective focuses on the ways women and men can shift, manipulate and negotiate definitions of identity or gender roles and relations in accordance with their own interests. Second, it opposes the dichotomy of women and men as essentially complementary or contradictory to each other. And third, it resists any identification of women as "passive victims," while still allowing the study of power in gender relations.

Thus, using gender as a contested image for exploring how power is articulated in class and gender identities in Bangladesh society, White found that while women may show submission to the dominant culture of male superiority, they also, despite very limited opportunities for doing so, pursue informal strategies of resistance, express power through informal means such as "personal influence and brokerage," and manipulate the terms by which they negotiate their dependence on men. She also remarks: "Relations between rich and poor or men and women are not simply based in conflict but show complex negotiations of mutual gain and shared interest. Conversely relations between members of the same class or gender group are often characterized by conflict" (White 1992, p. 135).

This paper has presented an overview, based on the available literature, of the situations of Bangladeshi disabled women, rather than a comprehensive picture of the topic. It also attempts to generate inquiries into whether women with disabilities in Bangladesh are completely powerless or passive victims of discrimination based on their gender and disabilities, how the gender roles and relations or identities of real disabled women are defined and negotiated in their real lives, and how they vary by type and severity of disability, age, socio-economic class and religion. Thus, it also reflects the need to fill the vacuum of information about the lives and lived experiences of women with disabilities in Bangladesh through undertaking in-depth empirical and anthropological studies employing various qualitative research methods, particularly representing disabled women's own points of view and using gender and disability as a contested image, as suggested by Sarah White.

Most development planners and organizations, donor agencies, and even disabled people's associations, consider disabled people as a sexless, classless homogenous group with common goals and shared interests and views on disability. But in reality, as Abu-Habib (1997, p. 22) points out, the disability world, in common with any other world, is fraught with power struggles. Therefore, she cautions, any simplistic analysis that focuses on disability in isolation from other social relations like class, race, religion, ethnicity or age must be rejected. In-depth analyses of social and power relations within a group of people are essential in determining the focus of development initiatives and social policy interventions.

REFERENCES

Abu-Habib, L. (Ed.). (1997), Gender and Disability: Women's Experiences in the Middle East. Oxford: Oxfam.

Arsenault, F. (1996), A Global flavor. In D. Driedger, I. Feika & G. Batres (Eds.), Across Borders: Women with Disabilities Working Together (pp. 131-134). Charlottetown, PEI:Gynergy Books.

Asch, A., & M. Fine. (1988), Introduction: Beyond Pedestals. In M. Fine & A. Asch (Eds.), Women with Disabilities: Essays in Psychology, Culture and Politics (pp.1-37). Philadelphia: Temple University.

Asch, A., & M. Fine (1992), Beyond Pedestals: Revisiting the Lives of Women with Disabilities. In M Fine (Ed.), Disruptive Voices: The Possibilities of Feminist Research (pp. 139-171). Ann Arbor: The University of Michigan Press.

Bangladesh Data Sheet (1999), Retrieved Jan. 23, 2003 from *http://www.bangladeshgov.org/mop/nbd/data_sheet/intex.htm*

Banik, B. K. (2003), Rural Health Services: Some Observations. In K.T. Hossain, M.H. Imam & S. E. Habib (Eds.), Women, health and poverty (pp. 11-16). Rajshahi, Bangladesh: Higher Education Link Program, Department of Sociology, University of Rajshahi.

Barnes, C. (1996), Theories of Disability and the Origins of the Oppression of Disabled People in Western Society. In L. Barton (Ed.), Disability and Society: Emerging Issues and Insights (pp. 43-60). Essex, London: Longman.

Begum, N. (1992), Disabled Women and the Feminist Agenda. Feminist Review, 40, 70-84.

Begum, N. (1996), Snow White. In L. Keith (Ed.), What Happened to You? Writing by Disabled Women (pp. 46-51). New York: The New Press.

Boylan, E. (Ed) (1991), Women and Disability. London: Zed Books.

Brazier, C. (2001). Building up the Poor or Reinforcing Inequality? New Internationalist 332, 9-12.

Center for Services and Information on Disability (CSID) (2001), The Feminine Dimension of Disability: A Study on Situation of Adolescent Girls and Women with Disabilities in Bangladesh. Dhaka, Bangladesh: CSID, in association with the Program for Research on Poverty Alleviation (PRPA), and the Grameen Trust, Dhaka, Bangladesh.

Chen, L. C., E. Haque, & S. D'Souza (1981), Sex Bias in the Family Allocation of Food and Health Care in Rural Bangladesh. Population and Development Review 7 (3), 435-474.

Chen, M. (1986), Poverty, Gender, and Work in Bangladesh. Economic and Political Weekly 21 (5), 217-222.

Demas, D. (1993), Triple Jeopardy: Native Women with Disabilities, Canadian Woman Studies, 13 (4), 53-55.

Desmet, M., I. Bashir, H. Rahman; M. Sayeeduzzaman, & Q. Chowdhury (1999a), Can We Provide a More Appropriate Health Care in Bangladesh? In N. Islam (Ed.), Sociology: Health Women and Environment (pp. 103- 113). Dhaka, Bangladesh: Bangladesh Sociological Association.

Desmet, M., Q. Chowdhury, I. Bashir, H. Rahman, & M. Sayeeduzzaman (1999b), Pluralistic Health Care Options in a Rural Village of Bangladesh: Implications for Health Care Reform. In N. Islam (Ed.), Sociology: health women and environment (pp. 94-102). Dhaka, Bangladesh: Bangladesh Sociological Association.

Driedger, D. (1991), Women with Disabilities: Naming Oppression. Resources for Feminist Researchers, 20 (1&2), 5-9.

Driedger, D. (1996), Emerging from the Shadows: Women with Disabilities Organize. In D. Driedger, E. Feika & G. Batres (Eds.), Across Borders: Women with Disabilities Working Together (pp. 10-25). Charlottetown, PEI: Gynergy Books.

Driedger, D., & S. Gray (Eds.) (1992), Imprinting Our Image: An International Anthology by Women with Disabilities. Charlottetown, PEI: Gynergy Books.

Driedger, D., I. Feika, & E. G. Batres (Eds.) (1996), Across Borders: Women with Disabilities working together. Charlottetown, PEI: Gynergy Books.

Elwan, A. (1999), Poverty and Disability: A Survey of the Literature. Paper prepared as a background paper for WDR 2000/2001 and as part of the Social Protection Unit's research on the economic consequences of disability. Retrieved Feb. 16, 2000, from http:// www.worldbank.org /poverty/wdrpoverty/background/ elwan.pdf .

Economic and Social Commission for Asia and the Pacific (ESCAP), Social Development Division. (1995), Hidden Sisters: Women and Girls with Disabilities in Asian and Pacific region. Retrieved Feb. 15, 2000, from *http://www.unescap.org/decade/wwd1.htm.*

Ferri, B. A., & N. Gregg (1998), Women with Disabilities: Missing Voices. Women's Studies International Forum, 21 (40), 429-439.

Fine, M. (Ed.) (1992), Disruptive Voices: The Possibilities of Feminist Research. Ann Arbor: The University of Michigan Press.

Fine, M., & A. Asch (Eds.) (1988), Women with Disabilities: Essays in Psychology, Culture and Politics. Philadelphia: Temple University.

Finkelstein, V. (1980), Attitudes and Disabled People. Geneva: World Health Organization.

French, M. (1985), Beyond Power: On Women, Men, and Morals. New York: Summit.

Friesen, B. J. (1992), Bangladeshi Disabled Women Find Hope. In D. Driedger & S. Gray (Eds.), Imprinting Our Image: An International Anthology by Women with Disabilities (pp. 39-46). Charlottetown, PEI: Gynergy Books.

Ghai, A. (2001), Marginalization and Disability: Experiences from the Third World. In M. Priestley (Ed.), Disability and the Life Course: Global Perspective (pp. 26-37). Cambridge: Cambridge University Press.

Ghai, A. (2002), Disabled Women: An Excluded Agenda of Indian Feminism. Hypatia, 17 (3), 49-66.

Government of Bangladesh (N. D.) The fifth five year plan 1997-2002. Retrieved Jan. 22, 2003 from *http://www.sdnbd.orghttp://www. sdnbd.org/sdi/metadata/fifth5-yesr*-plan/Fifth% 20five % 20year %20plan.htm/sdi/metadata/fifth5-yesr-plan/Fifth% 20five20year%20plan.htm

Hammerman, S., & S. Maikowski (1981), The Economics of Disability: International Perspectives. New York: Rehabilitation International, in Cooperation with the United Nations.

Harris-White, B., & S. Subramaninian (Eds.) (1999), Ill Fare in India. New Delhi, India: Sage Publications.

Hosain, M. G. M., & N. Chatterjee (1998), Health Care Utilization by Disabled Persons: A Survey in Rural Bangladesh. Disability and Rehabilitation: An International Multidisciplinary Journal, 20 (9), 337-345.

Kabeer, N. (1994), Reversed Realities: Gender Hierarchies in Development Thought. London and New York: Verso.

Keith, L. (Ed.). (1996), What Happened to You? Writing by Disabled Women. New York: The New Press.

Khan, N., & M. Durkin (1995), Framework: Prevalence. In P. Zinkin & H. McConachie (Eds.), Disabled Children and Developing Countries (pp. 1-9). London: MacKeith Press.

Khanum, S. M. (1999), Health Promotion Programs in Developing World: Search for an Appropriate Strategy. In N. Islam (Ed.), Sociology: Health Women and Environment (pp. 114- 130). Dhaka, Bangladesh: Bangladesh Sociological Association.

Mahmud, W., & S. Mahmud (1985), Aspects of the Food and Nutritional Problem in Rural Bangladesh. ILO/WEP Research Working Paper 10-6/WP74.

Nancoo, L. (1993), Marriage-able? Cultural Perspectives of Women with Disabilities of South Asian origin. Canadian Woman Studies, 13 (4), 49-51.

Oliver, M. (1996), A Sociology of Disability or a Disablist Sociology? In L. Barton (Ed.), Disability and Society: Emerging Issues and Insights (pp. 18-42). London: Longman.

Ostergaard, L . (1992), Health. In L. Ostergaard (Ed.), Gender and Development: A Practical Guide (pp. 110-134). London: Routledge.

Paul-Majumder, P. (1996), Health Impact of Women's Wage Employment: A Case Study of the Garment Industry of Bangladesh. The Bangladesh Development Studies, 24 (1 & 2), 59-102.

Rahman, A., & P. Ahmed (1993), Women with Disabilities in Bangladesh. Translated by M. Ahmed. Canadian Woman Studies, 13 (4), 47-48.

Sabir, N. I., & G. J. Ebrahim (1984), Are Daughters More at Risk than Sons in Some Societies? Journal of Tropical Paediatrics, 30 (4), 237-239.

Sarder, A. M., & L. C. Chen (1981), Distribution and Characteristics of Non-government Health Practitioners in a Rural Area of Bangladesh. Social Science and Medicine, 15A (5), 543-550.

Sen, A. K. (1981), Poverty and Famines: An Essay on Entitlement and Deprivation. Oxford: Oxford University Press.

Sen, A. K. (1990). Gender and Cooperative Conflicts. In I. Tinker (Ed.), Persistent Inequalities, Women and World Development (pp.123-149). Oxford: Oxford University Press.

Shah, F. (1992), The Blind Woman, Her Family and Participation in the Community (rural). In D. Driedger & S. Gray (Eds.), Imprinting our Image: An International Anthology by Women with Disabilities (pp.19-24). Charlottetown, PEI: Gynergy Books.

Siddiquee, A. (2003), Women, Poverty and Reproductive Health: Reflections on the Rural Scene of Bangladesh. In K. T. Hossain, M. H. Imam & S. E. Habib (Eds.), Women, Health and Poverty (pp. 11-16). Rajshahi, Bangladesh: Higher Education Link Program, Department of Sociology, University of Rajshahi.

Sorcar, N. R., & J. K. Mondal (1992), Mental Retardation: Care and Prognosis. Bangladesh Journal of Psychology, 13, 109-119.

Srinivasan, T. N. (2000), Poverty and Under-nutrition in South Asia. Food Policy, 25, 269-282.

Stuart, H., B. Percival, & E. R. Epperly (Eds.) (1992), The More We Get Together: Women and Disability. Charlottetown, PEI: Gynergy Books.

Sufi, A. H., K. Yamashita, & S. Nazneen (1996), Virgin Village Bandaikhara: Its Women and Mental Handicaps. Rajshahi, Bangladesh: Sivas Institute, and Japan: Makibito kai.

Sultana, N (2003), Health and Sanitation of Rural Women in Bangladesh: Some Observations from Belgharia Village. In K. T. Hossain, M. H. Imam & S. E. Habib (Eds.), Women, health and poverty (pp. 17- 24). Rajshahi, Bangladesh: Higher Education Link Program, Department of Sociology, University of Rajshahi.

Tuckwell, S. (1991), The Hidden 40 Million. In E. Boylan (Ed:) Women and Disability (pp. 11-12). London: Zed Books.

Unnayan Bikalper Nitinirdharoni Gobeshona (UBINIG) (Policy Research for Development Alternatives) (1987), Health and Illness in Two Villages of Commilla: An Interim Report of the on-going Study on Illness Behavior in Rural Bangladesh. Dhaka, Bangladesh: UBINIG.

United Nations Development Program (UNDP) (2003), Human Development Reports 2003. Retrieved Feb. 14, 2003 from *http://www.undp.org/hdr2003/indicator/cty_f_BGD.html*

United Nations Children Education Fund (UNICEF) (2000), The State of the World Children 2000. New York: UNICEF.

Wahab, F. (1997), Empowering the Rural Disabled in Asia and the Pacific: Disabled Women in Rural Areas of the Region. FAO Publications. Retrieved Feb. 14, 2000 from *http://www.fao.org/sd/PPdirect/* Ppre0042.htm

White, S. C (1992), Arguing with the Crocodile: Gender and Class in Bangladesh. London: Zed Books.

Wilson, A. (2000), Patriarchy: Feminist Theory. The Routledge International Encyclopaedia of Women (Vol. 3, pp. 1493-1497). New York and London: Routledge.

World Health Organization (WHO) (1986), Maternal Mortality Rates: A Tabulation of Available Information (pp. 63-87). Geneva: WHO.

Zakir, M., & P. V. Wunnava. (1999), Factors Affecting Infant Mortality Rates: Evidence from Cross-sectional Data. Applied Economics Letters, 6, 271-273.

Zaman, H (1999), Violence Against Women in Bangladesh: Issues and Responses. Women's Studies International Forum, 22 (1), 37-48.

3

THE IMPACT OF GRAMEEN BANK CREDIT PROGRAMS ON THE ROLE OF RURAL WOMEN IN BANGLADESH: AN EMPIRICAL ASSESSMENT

Tahmina Akhtar
M. Omar Faruk
M. Azizur Rahman

INTRODUCTION

Women constitute the single largest group of population in Bangladesh. Any significant reduction of poverty is not possible unless comprehensive strategic plans are taken to expand employment opportunities for the women and removed obstacles to their development. Despite a crucial need, there have been little attempts to uphold the participation of women in development projects for increasing their status in the family, society, and the political system. On the other hand, their perception on the value of children, desire fertility, and the contraceptive usage attitude. Intervention programs run by non-financial institutions and government agencies have been able to reach even the poorest women in the rural areas. Non-financial institutions provide referrals, assist borrowers, and guarantee loans, thereby reducing the costs of formal borrowing and also reducing the risk of lending money to poor women.

Women's right to self-determination is rapidly becoming recognized as one of the key factors for development. With a ' view to modify the role of women by involving them in Grameen Bank development projects, there would have impact on education, health, life style and social progress and this in turn would affect their attitudes towards their family size. Credit program also have impact on the reproductive role of rural women, which is also regulated by the traditions. Customs and practices effectively deny women of Bangladesh to own land and inherit property. A vast majority of Bangladeshi women cannot participate fully in economic, social, community and family life because of socio-cultural barriers. A woman's freedom of movement is severely restricted by the social institution called Samaj, which governs the lives of traditional rural women in various ways. For this reason, Grameen Bank's women in development projects embarked upon a comprehensive basic need, which led to employ into income generating activities, make empowerment of women in decision-making, and educating their children.

There are two types of women's role in a developing society such as achieved and ascribed roles. Ascribed role of woman generally relate to agricultural and domestic work such as tending the animals, storing water, collecting wood, grinding and cooking spinning, making clothes, washing and other formers of taxing labor which amount to drudgery. Improved access to credit by woman could lead to two developments (i) increased employment in income generating activities and (ii) an inventive to adopt unproved technology. In Bangladesh, the economic participation of most women depends on a very few resource base consisting of mainly their unskilled physical labor. Role of women could be enhanced if their resource bases were expanded by the addition of complementary sources (essentially through human capital development and access to credit). It is this context that credit becomes important, if women had improved access to credit they could expand the "expenditure saving" activities of the homestead into "income generating" ones and in the, prices improve their economic status in the society.

Thein (1988), in her recent study, identified factors that contributed to the success and failure of the women in development projects. The participation of women in her projects increased their status in the family as well as in their community. However, there are indications that participation of women in the development activities brings them out of the home and their exposures to different ideas emerge and their interaction with other village women increase. This has a positive effect on the acceptance of contraception. Independent income by women also increases husband-wife communication and helps in family decision with regard to family size and adoption of contraceptive (Kabir, et. al., 1988; Kabir, et. al., 1987; Robinson, 1985; Rahman, 1986; Schaffer, 1986).

Rural poor women in Bangladesh normally do not have access to institutional credit. The nationalized commercial banks do not advance credit for the women borrow except special programs for poverty alleviation such as VGD, VMDP, and Swanirvar. The special programs exhibit on increasing trend in recent past. Up to June 1992, more than thirty thousand women received credit from government institutions (CPD, 1990). According to a study conducted by Ahmed and Islam (1990), the membership participation rate of the females in BRDB and RCS co-operation was 17.3 percent and that of NGO's at that time was 52.2 percent. In the Palli Karma Shayak Foundation (PKSF) sponsored credit programs of 100 indigenous NGO's 82 percent of the borrowers were found to be women (Rahman, 1996). Thus, NGO's paid more attention to include more women in their program. Most of these NGO's utilize group guarantee lending. Peer pressure encourages high repayment rates because group eligibility for future loans depends on group repayment.

It is observed that when women participation rate is higher, recovery rate is also higher. This does not mean that recovery rate depends only on women participation. Other factors such as, intensity of supervision, peer pressure, size and assurance of future loans etc. may also be responsible for higher recovery rate (Haque, 1995). For example, the female participation rate of the rural poor co-operative project (RPCP) in northeastern region of Bangladesh is 82 percent and recovery rate is almost 100 percent. On the other hand, women development project of the BKB with BSCIC collaboration is a program exclusively for women where recovery rate is 64 percent. Grameen Bank's recovery rate was high when the female participation was relatively low. However, many experiences support that women are more sincere in repaying and utilizing loans.

However, an assessment of the activities for which loans were disbursed and the formalities were completed for receiving credit concluded that access of women to formal credit has been limited (Hossain and Afsar, 1988; Ahmed, 1996). It was contended that the bulk of institutional credit has been issued mainly for financing the cost of technological innovation in agriculture, essential inputs (e.g., seeds, fertilizer, and irrigation), and for non-crop activities such as fisheries, tea plantation, rural transport and small-scale industries. Few women entrepreneurs are involved in these activities. Moreover, male members of the household mostly owned collateral requirement, which typically involved land ownership, implied that most women could not qualify as landowners. The Bangladesh Institute of Development Studies (BIDS) has analyzed data on a 1987 survey of 40 villages and identified the causes on the issue of access by women to extend credit in the rural areas (cited in: Hossain and Afsar, 1988). According to this survey, female borrowers accounted for 2.8 percent of total respondents with access to credit and 2.1 percent of total credit made available. These findings, while subject to small sample limitations, support a number of hypotheses relating to unequal access of credit by the poor and women, in particular.

Investment in diversified activities in the previous analysis indicates that credit plays an important role in creating self-employment and increasing income of women. Most of the existing studies support the findings of self-employment (Hossain, 1988; Lovell, 1992; Ray 1087; Rahman and

Khondaker, 1994). An evaluation report of Sawnirvar Credit Program in 1987 indicates that the average family income of the borrowers increased by about 126 percent. While the savings increased by 292 percent with 61 percent other saving being re-invested for profit. The proportion of under employed family labor dropped from 41 percent to 20 percent (CPD, 1995). However, the activities performed by women are mostly traditional in most of the program. The majority of the activities cannot be organized on a large scale due to the fact that the market for these goods is not that big. With these activities it may be difficult for women to further increase their income once they will reach the poverty line. Osmany (1989) feared that the expansion of activities by Grameen Bank type credit would soon saturate as the usual rate of growth, which will not ensure a rising rate of returns from the activities. Hence, the cost of borrowing will be more than return. This fear may not be appropriate or may not be true. Some studies suggest that as the level of income of the poor increases due to higher rate of participation in economic activities, a pattern of demand would be generated which would sustain and even expand the market for the product of such activities (Rahman & Hossain, 1988).

OBJECTIVES OF THE STUDY

This study has been designed to provide in-depth information about poor women in rural area and the assessment of the impact of Grameen Bank to improve their changing pattern of life style, roles socio-economic status and decision-making process. Specially, the objectives of the study includes the following:

- To assess the impact of Grameen Bank Credit Program on social development such as life style, living standard, sanitation systems water use-housing nature, education
- To look how to improve and increase the income, savings employment situation of the respondents after joining the credit program of Government of Bangladesh (GB).

- To identify how the respondents are involving in family decision-making process.

METHODOLOGY OF THE STUDY

This paper attempts to explore the impact of Grameen Bank Credit Program on the role of rural women in Bangladesh. Impact has been defined in this paper as the change in roles of the rural women through Grameen micro credit program. The changes in relation to their income, savings, life style, living standard, occupation, decision-making capability etc. were analyzed in this study, which had indirect impact on the socio-economic status of their families and society as well.

Studies on Grameen Bank have been mostly evaluative in nature. This study tried to examine the impact of Grameen Bank programs, especially on women borrowers of micro credit provided by the Grameen Bank. It collects descriptive data from the field level on gradual changes in the number of Grameen Bank membership, amount of loans taken, income earned from loaned-project, increase in houschold income, investment in development projects, acceptance of dowry, outside participation, and woman's changed changing status of women and role in their families.

RESEARCH AREA

This is a case study on a particular branch of Grameen bank. This study has been conducted on the branch of Lamakazi in Sylhet during October 1999 to July 2000. It was one of oldest branch of Grameen Bank and was working for last 14 years. All the clients of Lamakazi branch of Geameen Bank were considered as the population for this study. There were 1275 clients of the branch. From this population, 110 samples were selected on systematic random sampling and data was collected from the sample clients through interview schedule.

DATA COLLECTION AND ANALYSIS

Data have been collected from the respondent through social survey method. The data have been analyzed by using both descriptive and inferential statistical tools. The tools are simple percentage, measures of central tendency, and measures of dispersion, measurement of inequality - Gini coefficient, Lorenz curve, and path analysis.

MEASUREMENT OF INEQUALITY

A measure that has been very widely used to represent the ext-Mt of inequality is the Gini-coefficient. The Gini-coefficient is the ratio of absolute equality and the Lorenz curve, It was used here both Gini coefficient and Lorenz curve to measure the position the degree of unequaled before joining the Grameen Bank and after joining the Grameen Bank. The inequality is measured by using following formula.

$$G = 1 + {}^{1}/_{n} - 2/_{n^{2}\mu} [Y_1 + 2Y_2 + 3Y_3 + \text{———————} + nY_3]$$

FINDINGS AND DISCUSSION

Among different societies there are different sources of incomes and there are different way to use this income including investment and consumption. Even though these comparisons involve money measure, they are confirmed by the distribution of the labor force among different sectors of the economy. Developed country could up to 20 percent of their Gross Domestic Product and 'invest it in productive equipment yielding increased income. Developing country could save only a smaller proportion of their much smaller income. So their economies could grow only slowly. Earning or income is the best indicator of women's status. Income gives them a position to influence their family members and exercise control over them. Because of income, male counterpart counts them in Lamakazi. As a result, the respondents in Lamakazi can play a vital role in decision-making.

AGE: SOCIAL CHARACTERISTIC OF THE RESPONDENTS

Table 1 shows the age distribution of the respondents. It supports a large number of borrowers of different age group. The result reveals their age range from 20 to 60 years .The highest 32.7% of respondents belong to age group of 40 to 44 years. The respondents' average age is 38.47 years.

Table 1
Age Structure of the Respondents

Age Level	*Frequency*	*Percent*	*Cumulative Percent*
20-24	2	1.8	1.8
25-29	16	14.5	16.4
30-34	15	13.6	30.0
35-39	22	20.0	50.0
40-44	36	32.7	82.7
45-49	7	6.4	89.1
50-54	6	5.5	94.5
54+	6	5.5	100.0
Total	110	100.0	

Educational attainment of the respondents is 12.7% belonging to one to four class and about 5.5%, 1.8%, 18.2%, 61.8% of the respondents belonging to consecutive five to eight class, nine to S.S.C. class, illiterate and literate respectively. Those women are being literate (68%) after joining the bank (Table 2).

Table 2
Educational Qualification of the Respondents

Educational Qualification	*Frequency*	*Percent*	*Cumulative Percent*
One to Four	14	12.7	12.7
Five to Eight	6	5.5	18.2
Nine to S.S.C	2	1.8	20.0
Illiterate	20	18.2	38.2
Literate	68	61.8	100.0
Total	110	100.0	

Table 3 depicts that 69.7% of the sampled women are married, 4.6% are unmarried and 25.7% are widow. Most of married are associated with the association for improving their economic security and safety.

Table 3
Marital Status of Responds

Marital Status	*Frequency*	*Percent*	*Cumulative Percent*
Married	76	69.09	69.09
Unmarried	6	5.4	74.49
Widow	28	25.5	100.0
Total	110	100	

LIFE STYLE

First World and in industrial countries, most people live in house built of brick, stone or concrete, with slate or tiles roof, of wood or cement and usually with a covering for comfort and case of cleaning with electricity and inside water supply to kitchen, bathroom, and flush toilet. In the low or middle-income countries generally, it is usual to find many people living in house built have dried mud, with grass-thatch roof and earth floors. Water may be carried from a well, spring or pond for distances to be measured in kilometers. Only half of the population in these countries had reasonable access to safe water. Housing and sanitary standards are generally much lower in rural areas.

HOUSING CONDITIONS OF THE CLIENTS

It was observed about the house type of the respondents before and after joining Grameen Bank. The past or previous house types of the respondents were about 71.8 % kacha, 24.5% tin made, 9% semi-pucca and 2.7% others. The present house types of the respondents are about 28.2% kacha, 61.8% tin made, 5.5% semi-pucca, and 4.5% others. The condition of the housing of the respondents improved after joining Grameen Bank.

Table 4
Housing Pattern of Responds at Lamakazi, Sylhet

	Previous		*Present*	
House Types	*Frequency*	*Percent*	*Frequency*	*Percent*
Kacha (Build with mud)	79	71.8	31	28.2
Tin	27	24.5	68	61.8
Semi paka (Build with bricks)	1	.9	6	5.5
Others	3	2.7	5	4.5
Total	110	100.0	110	100.0

SANITATION AND WATER SUPPLY SYSTEM

Sanitation system (Table 5) is one of the important variables of life style. Sanitation system is reflected by toilet facilities. Before joining the Grameen bank 86% members use kacha, 1.8% use pucca, 6.4% use sanitary and 5.5% use open place. At present 70.9% members use kacha, 4.5% use pacca, 18.2%-use sanitary and 6.4% use open place.

Table 5
Sanitation System at Lamakazi, Sylhet

	Previous		*Present*	
Sanitation System	*Frequency*	*Percent*	*Frequency*	*Percent*
Kacha (Build with mud)	95	86.4	78	70.9
Paka (Build with bricks)	2	1.8	5	4.5
Sanitary	7	6.4	20	18.2
Open Place	6	5.5	7	6.4
Total	110	100.0	110	100.0

Table 6 shows that the majority of the people (75.5%) use tube well water after taking loan as it increased their awareness about their health followed by ponds water (10.9%), river (11.8%) and boiled water (1.8%). Comparatively now most of the members drink water from tube well (75.5%).

Table 6
Using of Water form Different Sources both Previous and Present

	Previous		*Present*	
Source of Water	*Frequency*	*Percent*	*Frequency*	*Percent*
Ponds	29	26.4	12	10.9
River	20	18.2	13	11.8
Tube well	55	50.0	84	75.5
Boiled Water	6	5.5	1	1.8
Total	110	100.0	110	100.0

Among the respondents 26.6% members drink from own source. 19.1% drink from joint sources, 51.8% drink from other source and 5.5% use public source (Table 7).

Table 7
Ownership of Source of Drinking Water

Ownership of Water Supply	*Frequency*	*Percent*
Own	26	26.6
Joint	21	19.1
Public	6	5.5
Others	57	51.8
Total	110	100.0

ECONOMIC CHARACTERISTICS OF THE RESPONDENTS

INCOME OF THE RESPONDENTS

From the Table 8, we see that the previous monthly income of the respondents was 35.5% belong to group Tk. 300-600. About 16.4%, 14.5%, 2.7%, 5.5% 2.7% and 0.9% consecutively belong to group Tk. 600-900, 900-1200,1200-1500,1500-1800,1800-2100 and 2100-2400. Here 21.8% respondents answered that they didn't know anything about family income.

Table 8
Previous and Present Monthly Incomes of the Respondents

Previous Income (Tk)	*Frequency*	*Percent*	*Cumulative*
300-600	39	35.5	35.5
600-900	18	16.4	51.8
900- 1200	16	14.5	66.4
1200-1500	3	2.7	69.1
1500-1800	6	5.5	74.5
1800-2100	3	2.7	77.3
2100-2400	1	0.9	78.2
Missing	24	21.8	100.0
Total	110	100.0	

Present Monthly Income (Table-8) shows that about 22.7% respondents belong to present monthly income group Tk 300-600. About 14.5%, 7.3%, 10.9%, 13.6%, 2.7%, 1.8%, 3.6%, 9%,.9% and 1.8% respondents group of income are Tk.600-900,900-1200,1200-1500,1500-1800,1800-2100,2100-2400,2400-2700,2700-3000,3000-3300 and 3300+. Also here 19.1% respondents answered that they didn't know anything about family income.

The respondents' average previous income was Tk. 874.9 and present average income is Tk. 1280.72. Previous maximum income was Tk. 2699 and minimum income was Tk. 300. of the respondents on the other hand the present maximum income is Tk. 3300 and minimum income is Tk. 490. This mean income is Tk. 1349. This made a positive impact on their economic condition. Respondents this made them dependent to the bank and most of them became the permanent client, which serves them positively in their social, political and cultural life.

Table 9
Present Monthly Incomes of the Respondents

Present Income (in Tk)	*Frequency*	*Percent*	*Cumulative Percent*
300-600	25	22.7	22.7
600-900	16	14.5	37.3
900-1200	8	7.3	44.5
1200-1500	12	10.9	55.5
1500-1800	15	13.6	69.1
1800-2100	3	2.7	71.8
2100-2400	2	1.8	73.6
2400-2700	4	3.6	77.3
2700-3000	1	.9	78.2
3000-3300	1	.9	79.1
3300+	2	1.8	80.9
Missing	21	19.1	100.0
Total	110	100.0	

SAVINGS AND POVERTY ALLEVIATION IN RURAL WOMEN OF BANGLADESH

Western industrial economies save and invest around 23 percent of their Gross Domestic Product. On the other hand less developed country saving range is 19-22 percent of Gross Domestic Product. The post Independence era of less develop society has experienced the spread of several non-banking financial institution. Their rapid growth over major parts of the country calls for an evaluation of their overall position in our society today. The non banking financial institution help to characterize the non activated liquid household saving and provide such saving alternatives that are an extension of traditional forms of money lending and provide an easy and informal access to credit in comparison with the indifference of official machinery of formal banking system. Most of the respondents of the study area control saving has TK. 7,050.00 in the Branch. This means each client has to deposit some amount of money on a regular basis as savings, which is used in their accidents and other problems.

CHANGING PATTERN OF OCCUPATION OF WOMEN

An occupation is a social role that is determined by the general division of labor within a society. As a specialization of an individual's function in society, it is an important factor defining a person's prestige, class position, and style of life. Before joining the bank the women's occupation were housewife 22.7%, day Laborer 3.6%, handicraft 54.5%, poultry farm 5.5%, mid wife 1.8%, small business 4.5%, and others 7.3%. In the past most of the occupation is handicraft 54.5%. After joining the bank the present occupation of women's are housewife 20.0%, day Laborer 1.8%, handicraft 57.3%, poultry farm 1.8%, small business 5.5% and others 13.6%. We found that majority of the respondent's occupation handicraft, which was 54.5%, in previous time and is 57.3% after joining Grameen Bank (Table 10).

Table 10
Occupational Structure of the Respondents

	Previous		*Present*	
Occupation	*Frequency*	*Percent*	*Frequency*	*Percent*
House Wife	25	22.7	22	20.0
Day Labor	4	3.6	2	1.8
Handicraft	60	54.5	63	57.3
Poultry farm	6	5.5	2	1.8
Family service	2	1.8	0	
Business	5	4.5	6	5.5
Others	8	7.3	15	13.6
Total	110	100.0	110	100.0

PARTICIPATION PROCESS IN THE FAMILY

One of the major indicators of the women in development is their participation in income generation activities. It would exposed to various decision including health, family planning, better marriage for daughters, will look after family business and desired family size. It was observed that, 87.3% respondents said before joining the bank their decision making power accepted to the family positively and 12.7% responded negatively (Table 11). After joining the bank 93.6% respondents mentioned their decision making power increased to the family and 6.4% respondents mentioned did not increase. From this, it is observed that it is a positive impact of changing women role and right.

Table 11
Decision Making Authorities of the Respondents in the Family

	Previous		*Present*	
Decision Making	*Frequency*	*Percent*	*Frequency*	*Percent*
Yes	96	87.3	103	93.6
No	14	12.7	7	6.4
Total	110	100.0		100.0

RESULTS OF INEQUALITY MEASUREMENT

For previous personal income (Table 12), the value of Gini-coefficient, G is 0.695 and for present personal income (Table 12), the Gini-coefficient, G is 0.326. From these two values it can be said that the degree of inequality decreases by 0.369 that is their economic condition improves after joining the Grameen Bank. This result is represented by the Lorenz curve:

Table 12
Percentage of Shared of Income

Family	*Previous Income*	*CF*	*Present Income*	*CF*
20% Lowest fifth	7.35%	7.35	6.69%	6.69
40% Second fifth	9.22%	16.57	10.64%	17.33
60% Third fifth	14.04%	30.61	18.21%	35.54
80% Forth fifth	30.44%	61.05	23.24%	58.83
100% Highest fifth	38.95%	100	41.17%	100

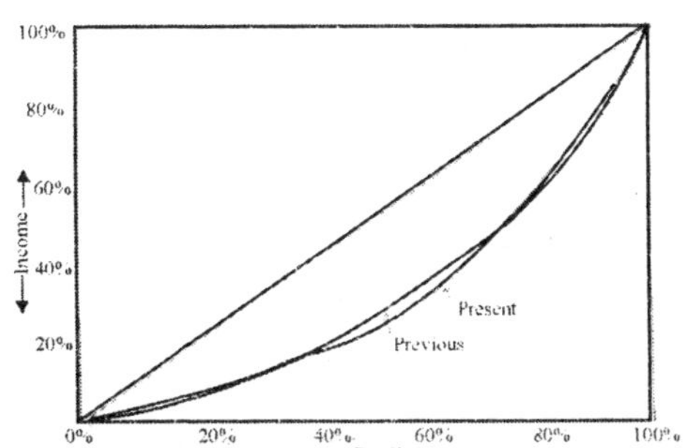

Figure 1: Lorenz Curves for Previous and Present Income

Figure 1 shows that Lorenz curve for present income is closer with 45-Degree lines than for previous family income. This also shows that social inequality decreases after joining the Grameen Bank.

RESULTS OF MULTIPLE ANALYSES

Degree of Freedom	=	2
Parameter	=	8
Free Parameter	=	8
Sample Moment	=	10
X1	=	Present income
X2	=	Loan
X3	=	Saving
U	=	Intervening Variables
V	=	Intervening Variables

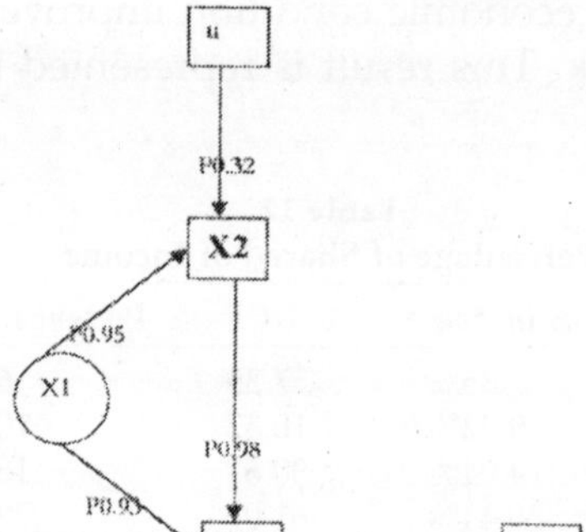

Figure 2 Path Diagram: Direct Effects, Indirect Effects and Path Co-Efficient (Present)

In the path (Figure 2) X1 (Income) is an observed variable. X2 (Loan) is dependent value 0.95 on the XI (income). X3 (Saving) is dependent value 0.98 on the X2 (Loan) and X3 (saving) is dependent value 0.93 on the X1 (Income). Those are direct effects of the variables X1 (Income), X2 (Loan)) and X3 (Saving). The indirect effects intervening variable U is dependent value 0.32 on the X2 (Loan) and intervening variable V is dependent value 0.31 on the X3 (Saving).

Degree of Freedom	=	2
Parameter	=	8
Free Parameter	=	8
Sample Moment	=	10
X1	=	Present income
X2	=	Loan
X3	=	Saving
V	=	Intervening Variables
U	=	Intervening Variables

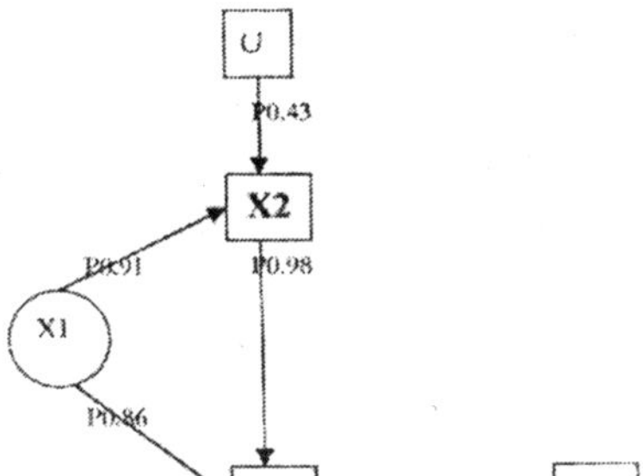

Figure 3: Path Diagram: Direct Effects, Indirect Effects and Path Co-Efficient (Previous)

In the path (Figure 3) X1 (Income) is observed variable. X2 (Loan) is dependent value 0.91 on the XI (Income). X3 (Saving) is dependent', value 0.98 on the X2 (Loan) and X3 (Saving) is dependent value 0.86 on the X1 (income). Those are direct effects of the variables XI (Income), X2 (Lean) and X3 (Saving). The indirect effects intervening variable U is dependent value 0.43 on the X2 (Loan) and intervening variable V is dependent value 0.41 on the X3

Path coefficient is simply beta weight, and the residual paths an per square root of I-R square and the indirect effect are the multiplication of the indirect path coefficient (Nachmias and Nachmias, 1997).

Path analysis needed multiple linear regression analysis among the interval level of variables. In above analysis all variables were at the level of interval. And the result of the regression analysis was included with the put of annexure.

In sum it is observed that now the women can generate more income and more independent movement access because residual effects of their variables are low than the past situation. So they can control more activities than before, which may empower them in their own position.

CONCLUDING REMARKS

The research findings demonstrated changes in life style, occupation, income, saving of the respondents after joining the Grameen Bank. Their socio-economic condition and role is changed. Inequality of women member is decreasing after joining in the Grameen Bank and decision making power in the family. Participation in weekly meetings is increasing. It is also observed that fundamental changes occurred in the lives of the women, in their self-perceptions, their positions within the family and community. The women go against traditional norms, to meetings weekly in public place, interacting with men outside the community. They become, in most cases for the first time in their lives, involved in financial transactions and are encouraged and enabled to conduct independent economic activities and acquire assets in their own names. The study analyzed the effects of Grameen Bank women's contribution to family support and a composite empowerment indicator (which aggregates eight different indicators of women's empowerment including, among others, physical mobility, economic security, participation in important decisions). Membership status had a significant effect on both women's contribution and the composite empowerment measure. The study on reproductive behavior also showed that duration of participation in a credit program had a significant effect on current contraceptive use. It is thus evident that there is significant impact of the Grameen Bank credit program on its clients-rural women in terms of income, saving, housing conditions, water and sanitation, and family decisions.

REFERENCES

Abubakar, Md. (1996), "Experiences of Some Special Credit Programs in Bangladesh Targeting Women", *Bank parikrama*, Volume XXl (September)

Afser Rita (1987), "Women's Roles: The Achievement Versus Ascription Dialectic" *The Bangladesh Development Studies,* Volume XV (June).

Anderson R.J and Shrrock W.W. (1984), "Applied Sociological Perspectives"(London: George Allen and Unwin Publishers Ltd).

Bhuyan Md.Daniel (1996), "Unnan Bichoon"(Dhaka:Homuyra Yesmin)

Chowdhury Nuimuddin (1990), "Labour Use in Rural Bangladesh", *The Bangladesh Development Studies,* Volume -XVIII (June).

Cook, R. (1994), "Human Right of Women" *National and International Perspectives* (Pennsylvania: University of Pennsylvania press).

D.Wood Geoffrey and Sharif Iffath (1997), "Poverty and Finance in Bangladesh" *Who Need Credit,(*Dhaka: The University Press Limited).

Frankfort Chava-Nachmias and Nachmias David (1996), "Research Method in the Social Sciences"(New York: St Martin's Press, Inc).

Goldthorpe, J, E. (1984), "Disparity and Development" *The Sociology of Third World* (Cambridge University Press).

Haque, Md. Z. (1991), *"Unnan Apthoniti O Parikalpana"* (Dhaka: Book Society).

Haynes Jeff (1996), "Third World Politics (UK: Black well publishers Ltd)

Hoogvelt M.M Ankie (1988), "The Sociology of Development Societies"(London: Macmillan Education Ltd).

Kabir, M. K. (1994), "Sarbik Gramm Unnan Marmashuchi" (Comilla:BARD).

Kabir M, Khaun Rokey and Ahmed Israt (1993), *Impact of Women in Development Projects on Women's Status and Fertility in Bangladesh* (Dhaka: Development Resources and Associates.)

Khan Shakeeb Adnan (1989), " The State and Village Society" (Dhaka: University Press Ltd.).

Lensiki Gerhard, Lenski Jean and Nolan Patrick (1991), "An Introduction to Macro Sociology" *Human Societies* (New York: McGraw. Inc).

Mizan Nahar Ainon (1990), "In Quest of Empowerment" (Dhaka: University Press Limited).

Rahaman Jowshen A (1992), "The Role of NGOs in Development" *From crisis to Development* (Dhaka: University Press Limited).

Rahaman. R. I and Khandker. S.R (1994), *Role of Targeted Credit Programs in Promoting Employment and Productivity of the Poor in Bangladesh.* (Dhaka: The Bangladesh Development Studies, Vol. 22).

R.Catton Willium (1996), "From Animistic to Naturalistic Sociology"(New York, Mc Grow-Hill).

Salahuddin, K., and Insrat, S., (1992), "Employment Pattern Activity Types and Problems" *Women in Urban Informal Section* (Dhaka: Women for Women)

Sen Amartya (1993), "On Economic Inequality"(Oxford: Clarendon Press)

Stoll M.S, (1990), "Social Formation in Dhaka City"(Dhaka: University Press Limited)

Therese Bakerl (1994), "Doing Social Research" (Delhi: McGraw Hill Iaah).

V. Young Pauline and F. Schmid Calvin (1994), "Scientific Social Surveys and Research."(New Delhi: Prentice-Hill of India Private Limited).

Wallerstein N. (1994), "Empowerment in Practice" Health Action.

W.Elifson Kirk, P.Runyon Richard and HarberAudrey(1990), "Fundamental of Social Statistics"(New York: McGraw Hill).

4

WOMEN'S POLITICAL PARTICIPATION IN BANGLADESH AND INDIA: SYMBOLIC OR REAL?

Pranab Kumar Panday

INTRODUCTION

Let us start by quoting from Landman (2003) "making comparison[1] is a natural human activity. From antiquity to the present generations, humans have sought to understand and explain the similarities and differences they perceive between themselves and others. At the turn of the new millennium, citizens in all countries compare their position in society to those of others in terms of their regional, ethnic, linguistic, religious, familial and cultural allegiances and identities, material possessions, economic, Social and political positions and relative locations in systems of power and authority". So comparison gives us knowledge about cross countries and cross cultural issues.

Women's lives in South Asia very often are affected by various socio-cultural and ethnic populations, a range of religious faiths, legal frameworks and economic and political forces. Despite diversities across countries, women of South Asian region face similar conditions on various fronts (Rustagi,

2004:1). Patriarchy characterizes South Asian countries (Caldwell, 1982) where women are dominated by a kin-ordered social structure (Mathema, 1998). They low status, little or no access to property and land (Bardhan, 1986) and suffer from non-recognition of their largely unpaid home based labour (Rustagi, 2004:1).

Socio-cultural practices based on strong patriarchal traditions have served to curtail mobility of women in this region. Disproportionate dealing in the areas of labour marker, socio cultural influences on education, nutrition, health and political participation, are evident towards women in most of the South Asian Countries although it is not always possible to measure gender discrimination in all spheres (Rustagi, 2004:1). The present study will be significance as it is one of the few studies that attempt at linking gender issue with that of local governance. The study gains further importance due to the fact that it is a comparative study of two similar neighboring countries and yet encrusted with significant differentials. Since our main objective is to highlight the issue of political participation of women in Bangladesh and India, other aspects of gender inequalities will not be taken into consideration in this paper.

This paper attempts to explore the dimension of women's participation in the local governance in Bangladesh and India, while doing so special emphasis will be given on the following components: (a) the issue of women and local governance in South Asia (b) determinants of women's participation and their role in Bangladesh and India (c) challenges that women are facing in regards to their participation in local governance in both the countries (d) are they (women) able to participate fully in the local government decision making in both the countries? (e) suggest ways to overcome persistent barriers of women's participation and (f) conclusion

GENDER AND DEMOCRACY: WHY?

'Democracy' which is a much debated issue in modern times, has become an objective that needs to be achieved for every individual and nation around the world. Democracy generally falls within the traditional definition of politics which includes domination of male in the public sphere. Due to these traditional orientations of democracy, it is widely argued that democracy is not women friendly (Karim, 1998:7). Despite having these limitation there has been increasing popularity of the concept and practice of democracy in recent times. In this context, an important question draws the attention of the academics and practitioners why gender should be interlinked with democracy? Some of the important argument in this regard has been put forward by (Karim (1998).

First, while broadly defined 'politics' include every body concerns. In these regard, women's political right is an integral part of human rights which in turn is a fundamental aspects of democratic framework. *The second* argument is that while formulating any decision or carrying out any strategy in democracy it is essential to take into accounts the views of all involved groups. In other words, it can be said that opinions and perceptions of men and women must be included alike. This argument is also important to justify the usefulness of bringing minorities in the decision making processes. *Final and strongest* contributing factor is that half of the total population of each and every single country in today's world is women. That is why it is quite unreasonable to treat women as minority. So, while making any policies on citizens lives the policy makers should bear the fact in mind that their policy will no longer be credible unless and until they ensure equal participation of both men and women in the policy processes.

So it can be said that sound democratic framework requires equal participation and account of gendered governance in decision making process as democracy strives towards equality and representation of women and men in decision making process.

WOMEN AND LOCAL GOVERNANCE IN SOUTH ASIA

Certain common features like centralized government, socio-economic inequalities based on class, gender and caste and nationalistic divisive claims on grounds of ethnicity has characterized South Asian Countries. For more than 50 years

India and Sri Lanka have been experiencing democracy but Pakistan and Bangladesh have been in fluctuation between democracy, militarism and autocracy. Nepal is passing through a turmoil situation. It has passed from democracy to absolute monarchy and back to democracy and later on again back to absolute monarchy. (Kabir, 2003:1).

It is universal in case of South Asia that formal political system is dominated by male but the degree of domination varies from country to country or region to region. The sign of domination is evident when we see that women are assigned to soft portfolios 'appropriate' for women's concerns even though they become a part of the formal political process as members of elite political groups. Usually, women in entire Indian Subcontinent are viewed with distrust if they interact outside given relations. Ingrained social values consider protection necessary for women as they are weak and also expect women to remain outside politics as it is a 'dirty game' (Kabir, 2003:1).

One of the significant characteristic of South Asian Politics is that highest positions in government of several South Asian Countries had or have been occupied by women. Some of the classic examples are Indira Gandhi and Sonia Gandhi in India, Sheikh Hasina and Khakeda Zia in Bangladesh, Benozir Bhutto in Pakistan and Sirimavo Bandaranaike and Chandrika Kumaratunga in Sri Lanka. Even though these women had occupied the highest positions in government statistics of the larger picture tell a different story. The vast majorities of South Asian women are illiterate, in poor health, invisible in the system of national accounts, and suffer legal, political, economic and social discrimination in all walks of life. Another noticeable fact is that women in South Asia have the lowest rates of participation in their governance structures as compared to many developed nations (Mahbub Ul Haq, Human Development Centre, 2000).

The Fourth World Conference on women which took place in Beijing advocated in favour of ensuring adequate representation of women in all decision making bodies (Beijing Platform for Action, 1995). It was suggested that in order to ensure the voice of the concerns of the society in equal terms it was necessary to have 'logical balance' of men and women in public life. Participation, accountability, predictability and transparency are the basic characteristics of good governance. In these contexts, good governance generally calls for gender balance in political decision making. Very often, it is argued that overall decision making process can be enriched if women's insights and values of governance is reflected in these process. It has been also established that women at the local level are more responsive to community issues. (Shamim and Kumari, 2002:2).

In recent times, each of the South Asian Country apprehends the fact that for ensuring good governance in a country it is essential to establish a strong and effective local government. It is generally established that the success of any democratic nations depends on the strength of an empowered local government. Keeping this realization in consideration, South Asian Governments have amended their laws for fair representation of gender in the local government institutions because organization at the grassroots level allows people to contribute significantly to the governance of their communities. For women, successful grassroots experience has meant a chance to form coherent voice, to be heard and to make a difference in their communities. Across South Asia, the experience of women in local governance has been varied, with some being more successful that others in attaining greater women's participation.

CURRENT STATE OF WOMEN'S POLITICAL PARTICIPATION IN BANGLADESH AND INDIA

Women's representation in the South Asian region is at two levels, in national and provincial/state legislatures and in local governments. In the former they can play a role as law and policy makers and in the latter in development-related implementation. The experience in different countries in the region reveals that collectively the number of women in legislatures has been lower than 9 percent over the last five years. This was despite the 1995 Beijing Platform for Action's goal of adequate representation of women in all decision making bodies and the recommendation of creating a "critical mass" and "gender balance" in political decision making. In this paper our main concern is to highlight the state of women's participation in the local governance in Bangladesh and India.[2] That is why, we would restrict our discussion within the local governance of two countries only.

INDIA

The scope for women's participation in politics in India is wider due to its federal nature.[3] Women have increasingly become active in informal politics too. The historic opening for women in India came in 1993 with the enactment of the 73rd amendment (*Panchayati Raj*) and 74th amendment (the Municipalities Act for urban local government) to the Constitution of India. These amendments came against the backdrop of the campaigns of the women's movement in India that gained momentum in the eighties — defining its movement's identity, finding a base in "issues being articulated by poor women at the grassroots" and their absorption into the "movement's range of concerns" (Mazumder and Agnihorti,1999:229). Earlier in 1975 the Committee on the Status of Women had recommended the establishment of statutory women's *panchayats* at the local level but the recommendations had been shelved (Mumtaz, 2005:12).

The amendments provided for not less than one third membership (33 percent) to women in the three tier system of Panchayati Raj[4] in rural areas. One -third of the prescribed women's seats are for women of Scheduled Castes and Scheduled Tribes. At least one-third of the office bearers are also reserved for women. The term of the *panchayats*, their re-election and the conditions for their suspension were also laid out in the amendments. These were followed by states enacting conformity legislations by 1996, with some variations in details (Gala, 1996). For instance, the Orissa government made it mandatory for the vice-chairperson to be a woman if the chairperson is a man. Rajasthan, Haryana and Orissa debarred candidates with two children to contest elections and some have special provisions for conflict resolution at all levels (Mumtaz, 2005:12).

The *Panchayati Raj* brought more than one million women as members and chairpersons of local bodies. However the performance and election of women in different states varies: Madhya Pradesh and Himachal Pradesh elected 38 percent women in the elections of 1996, Punjab 29.6 percent and Karnataka a little over 43 percent (Mohanty, 1999:23).

While the Acts per se do not provide for all-women *panchayats*, their subsequent emergence has been an interesting development. It needs to be pointed out that as early as 1989 nine villages in the western state of Maharashtra had elected all-women *gram panchayats* reportedly an outcome of the campaign of an independent farmers' organization, Shetkari Sanghatana. West Bengal got its all women *gram panchayat* in May 1993 under the Left Front Government (Gala, 1996). Earlier, an all woman *panchayat* was elected in Andhra Pradesh in the seventies and another in the eighties (Kaushik, 2000:16). One other reason for all women *panchayats* was that higher caste men did not want to work under a lower caste woman (Mumtaz, 2005:13).

BANGLADESH

The scope for women's participation in politics in Bangladesh is not so wide like India due to its unitary nature.[5] Since independence in 1971, local government system[6] has been central to policy makers concerns. With a view to secure a minimum representation of women at local level government bodies, in 1976, the government promulgated the Local Government Ordinance and introduces three-tier local government system. In this Ordinance the structure of local government system underwent changes and the provision was made to select two women members in the union council (Ahmed: 2001:3). For the first time women were considered to be included in the local government. With the passage of time, every government tried to incorporate more women in local government bodies. In 1983, the changes were brought in the structure of union parishad promulgating the local government (Union Parishad) ordinance. The earlier system (1976) remain unchanged; one chairman and 9 members were to be elected directly, 3 female members, 1 from each ward had been added in the new ordinance. In 1993, Local Government (Union Parishad) Act (Amendment) was passed in the Parliament to secure the minimum representation of women in local government. According to this act, provision was made that each union parishad would be divided into 9 wards. Moreover, three seats were reserved for women; accordingly, they were elected by elected chairman and members of the Union Parishad rather directly elected by the voters (Ahmed: 2001:3).

The Local Government (Union Parishad) Second amendment Act, 1997 is a milestone in the history of women's participation in Bangladesh. In this act, provision was made for three reserved seats for women in each Union Parishad. In addition, they would be elected by direct election based on universal adult franchise. This was a major initiative taken by the government of Bangladesh for ensuring women's participation in political decision making (Sultana, 2000: 14).

The union council is made up of thirteen members including the Chairman and three women. Each woman however represents three wards and is elected by the combined voters of these wards thus serving three times the number of constituents than her male counterparts. The Chairman is elected by the entire union council. Various functions of the union council are executed through 13 standing committees and women are to head one third of them with the mandate to head the committees on women's children's welfare, culture and sports, however in reality women are often excluded from committees (Cited in Mumtaz, 2005:20).

Getting the right to participate in governance through reserved seats is the proverbial first step for women in Bangladesh. In the Union Parishad election 2003, 39419 female candidates contested for 12669 reserved women's seats. On an average, 3.1 women contested for one seat in union parishad. Although rate of participation of women candidates in reserve seats is quite satisfactory, but the participation rate of women in general seats and for the post of chairmanship is quite low. 21376 candidates contested for chairman posts. Among them 21, 144 were male and 617 female. On the other hand 137909 candidates competed for general member posts among them 137292 are male and 617 are female (Bangladesh Election Commission, visit: *www.bd-ec.org/election.php3).*

DETERMINANTS OF WOMEN'S POLITICAL PARTICIPATION IN BOTH COUNTRIES

In the preceding section, an effort was made to highlight the current state of women's participation in the local governance in Bangladesh and India. It has been observed that due to initiation of several amendments of the Constitution by both governments to increase women's participation in the political process, the presence of women in local governments has increased by a considerable extent. Now the important question that need to be answered what are the determinants of women's participation in both the countries? In the following section an effort will be made to identify those determinants and analyze their role for women's participation in both countries.

NON GOVERNMENTAL ORGANIZATIONS (NGOS)

Both the Government have been influenced to a large extent by ever growing contribution of Non Governmental Organizations (NGOs) in furthering the cause of equal rights of women in every sphere in life. Over the last few decades in India and last few years in Bangladesh, along with advocating for women's equal rights, NGOs are carrying out several training program for women.

In India, NGOs have been actively involved in training over a half million Panchayats members in the state, a majority of whom are poor, uneducated and helpless. It is a complex task. NGOs have a key role in generating consciousness and mobilizing the people (Sharan, 1998). Whilst there are a large number of NGOs in India having the goal of their capacity building in training varies greatly. Whilst there are a large number of NGOs in India, serving the goal of helping women to win confidence and to give them more knowledge about their role as Panchayats members, their capacity in training varies greatly (Matland, 1998(b):66-67). One successful example is that of Confederation of Voluntary Organizations (COVA), a network of 750 organizations in Hyderabad, India. COVA works for communal harmony through community empowerment. It began its intervention with the objective of establishing the legitimacy of women political representatives to address the concern that women's reserved seats had been captured by male politicians who in fact performed the duties of elected women ((Mukhopadhyay, 2005:92). Once they became self reliant, women members would also raise their demands upon the Government.

The case of Bangladesh is slightly different from India. Along with advocating for equal rights for women, some times these NGOs extended a direct role in politics. Some NGOs through their umbrella organization, Association of Development Agencies of Bangladesh (ADAB)[7], indeed played a proactive role in national politics during the mass movement[8] which emerged against the Khaleda Zia regime in the mid 1990s. In the election of 1996, ADAB coordinated a Democracy Awareness Education Programme through which 15000 trainers ran awareness raising workshop across the whole country, contributing to an impressive voter turn out of 74% (Ashman, 1997). These activities have inspired both men and women to involve themselves in the electoral politics, especially women members gained immense knowledge from these programmmes. Another example is the efforts of Gono Shahajjo Sangstha (GSS)[9] to encourage its landless group members as candidates in local union parishad election in Nilphamari[10] was met with brutal confrontation by local landlords, who burnt down the NGO's schools, attacked staff and members and conducted a house to house search to seize books and publications (Hashemi, 1995). All these activities of NGOs build awareness among its women members in regards to their involvement in the political process on the one hand and create immense pressure on the government to make necessary changes in their policies regarding women's participation.

INTERNATIONAL POLITICS

Recent shifts in the international politics in favour of equality of women in all spheres of human life also partially account for the changes made by the government in the national as well as local levels. The government of Bangladesh approved both the Programme of Action of the international conference on Population and Development (1994) and the Beijing Platform for Action (PFA) without any reservation (Karim, 2000:55). Apart from these conferences, various donor agencies like World Bank, International Monetary Fund (IMF) and so on have taken the issue of gendered governance as their priority objectives. For instance, although World Bank is mainly an economic institution that has to maintain political impartiality, the issue that 'good governance is essential for development' is gaining importance within it. Studies by World Bank have confirmed that (1) worldwide women are under represented in parliaments: the best performing region has less that 20% while the worst performing region has less those 5% representatives in their parliaments; (2) governments are less corrupt where women and men have more equal rights and more equal participation. Although this finding is very controversial as regards causality it is nevertheless a positive finding (Mukhopadhyay, 2003). Based on the findings World Bank always laid importance to ensure women's equal participation in the political process within its aid recipient's countries which might have an effect on the government of Bangladesh in regards to bringing necessary changes in their policies towards women.

This factor may not have any direct effect on the Government of India as the economic base of India is much stronger so that they are not dependant on several donor agencies, but they do exist within the world. To some extent, the government of India responds firmly with the slogans of the international communities.

WOMEN'S ORGANIZATIONS

Women's own agencies which are fighting for ensuring equal social and political rights for women, has been an important factor that led both the governments of India and Bangladesh to bring changes in policies regarding women's participation in politics. The experience in India and Bangladesh demonstrates that women's activism gained them the space that they now have and in many instances have also to defend and protect. In India, the debates around women's seats carried into the post independence period. Women members of the 1949 Constituent Assembly opposed special concessions for women and hence reserved seats were not considered in the Constitution. Similarly, the Committee on the Status of Women in India rejected the idea of women's reserved seats in 1975 (there was a dissenting note on the issue by two members, activist/academics Vina Mazumder and Lotika Sarker who saw reservations as a necessary affirmative action for women). However, the Committee did make a strong recommendation for institutionalization of women's participation in local government through special quotas (Mumtaz, 2005:10). If we look at the role of women's agencies, there would be thousands of examples. The emergence of a countrywide women's movement on a mass scale in 1979-80 was sparked off by a case of police rape- a common but no means unique form a police brutality. The massive demonstrations and agitations by women which followed the Supreme Court acquittal of a policeman who had raped a young woman can be seen as a crucial element in the human and civil rights movement to protect citizens from arbitrary violence of state functionaries. Many of the women's organizations formed in the course of that campaign survived and grew subsequently, extending their concerns to various other forms of violence against women as well as more general social control over and discrimination against women(Hensman, 1996:56).

In Bangladesh, towards the end of the year 2001 when the provision of reservation of 30 seats in the National Parliaments was lapsed, the movement by several women organizations mounted a concerted effort to mobilize opinion and create the necessary political will to provide for a quota system that reflected their stand. Before the impending dissolution of Parliament in 2001, some 20 women's groups mobilized by

Mohila Parishad (Women's council- the largest movement oriented women's organization) lobbied the government, political parties and parliamentarians. Women activists carried on street activities, formed human chains, and staged rallies and symbolic protests advocating for increasing the number of reserved seats in the Parliament as well as introduction of the system of direct election for women in those seats. However, this heightened level of advocacy failed to have enough impact of the Government of Bangladesh (Chowdhury, 2002). Although the government increased the number of reserved seats from 30 to 45, but the system of election remained the same. When the government passed the bill for reservation of 45 seats for women in the parliament, those women's agencies went to the Court challenging the acts of the government, specially the provision of indirect election, although the Court had rejected their challenge. Along with advocating for ensuring women's equal rights, these women's organization always remains active to organize various training programme through which they can train women leadership. For instance, Bangladesh Mahila Parishad (BMP), a mass-based organization was established in 1970. Committed to a society based on gender equality, democracy and peace, it has played a key role in promoting women's formal participation and has worked on training programmes for women political representatives. Identifying the latter's main problem as isolation and hostility and disregard from male colleagues, BMP decided to intervene in three constituencies to address these problems. The BMP strategy was of developing support groups for three women representatives-one from an urban council and two from union parishad. Each support group was made up of 15 women from the representatives' constituency and included BMP members. The members were trained by BMP to enable them to provide support to the elected representative. They organized constituency meetings, built alliances with influential political leaders and linked the representatives with government officials. They also built the capacity of elected women and organized joint training for women and male elected members of the councils. The result was that elected women attended council meetings and questioned procedures thus developing transparency; became more active and succeeded in getting development projects for their areas; took up gender specific issue; and set up an autonomous women's cell (Mukhopadyay and Meer, 2004: 94-98). Thus, women's organization not only create pressure on the government to initiate policy in favour of ensuring equal participation but also organize several training progammes for women members with a view to crating awareness among them so that they may realize what is good for them and what are their rights and what they should do?

STATE

The different courses and roots political development took place in both the countries have determined the nature of the each state. India has institutionalized democratic system, however, with aberrations of emergency rule in the country. Bangladesh has moved from Parliamentary to military rule to the presidential system and sought integration into the regional and global economy. The state is however similarly seen in both countries as the agent for socio-political transformation. Given the privileged classes and groups inherited political power any opportunities that women got were through the benevolence of the state (Mumtaz 2005, 8-9). The turmoil that accompanied independence, in case of India opened spaces for women and legitimized their participation at the public level (Mumtaz, 2005: 8). It took the final shape when the Government of India passed 73rd and 74th amendments of the Constitution ensuring 33% reservation of seats for women in the local level.

The emerging democracy of Bangladesh had its drive begun in the end of 1990 with the overthrows of autocratic rule by a mass movement. Since then democratization of local government units, has become a priority for the government. That is why in 1993, the Local Government Ordinance, 1983 was amended to recognize the UP wards from existing three to nine new wards. Moreover, doing a way with the nomination system of women members the amendment provided for indirect election of three women members- by the chairman and members of the respective UPs. Again, in 1997, by the amendment of the ordinance, direct election for women members was introduced. Therefore, the changes in UP structure have been partially accounted for by the democratic transition in the country.

CONSTITUTION

Constitution plays a vital role for ensuring women's political participation in both the countries. The Indian Constitution has been committed to introduce socio-economic and political transformation. The initiatives of empowering women and the marginalized sections are the reflection of its democratic spirit of Indian Constitution and can be noticed from a number of amendments in these fields. Especially, the 73rd and 74th Constitutional Amendment Acts provide for an opportunity for women's entry into political sphere (Shamim and Kumari, 2002: 7).

Like the Indian Constitution, the Constitution of Bangladesh also provides for equality of men and women. There is no legal barrier to women contesting or voting for any elective office, including that of head of the state. Article 9 of the Constitution promotes the special representation of women in local government (Constitution of the People's Republic of Bangladesh, 1972, Shamim and Kumari, 5). These constitutional declarations to some extent compel the government to take necessary initiatives for implementation of constitutional declaration.

POLITICAL PARITIES

In recent times, opposition political parties make for a powerful engine for enforcing government to initiate several changes for increasing women's participation. The party in power all too often has strong incentives to evade accountability, but opposition parties have their own incentives to uncover wrongdoings of the government and publicly hound incumbents of their misdeeds. In case of India, over the decades, political parties played a crucial role in furthering the issue of women's equal participation. If we look at the formation of political parties in India, we will find a good number of women political leaders[11] in every political party. Most of the political parties in India are committed towards the betterment of women. Another important factor is that in India, local government election is conducted on party basis. In this regard, political parties play an important role from candidate selection to election.

But, the case of Bangladesh is quite different. In the circumstance of the unstable political situation, opposition parities always remain busy in criticizing the government. They have hardly any time to raise their voice or create pressure on the government to initiative affirmative changes in regards to women. But, there are some leftist political parties who are more vocal in these issues, but they have no representation in parliament. As a result, their voices are not taken into consideration by the government. Another factor is that local government election in Bangladesh is not conducted on party basis. That is why, political parties show little or no interest in the process of women's participation at the local level. Moreover, both the leading political parties in Bangladesh are headed by women chairperson but it is a matter of regret that nothing is still encouraging for women.[12]

CIVIL SOCIETY

Civil society is usually defined as organizational activity between the individual (or the family) and the state. Its democratic roles are to advocate for constituents, to act as watch dog over the state, and to support political competition generally (Hansen, 1996, cited in Blair, 2000). According to USAID and several donor agencies, civil society is essential for Democratic Local Government (Blair, 2000:28). And for ensuring democratic local government, it is essential to ensure equal participation of women in the decision making process. In this context, civil society plays a strong role to ensure women's participation as well as ensures DLG. India is the most startling case because DLG has been in place there the longest. One would assume that civil society has at least gotten off to a good start. It has at the national and state (and to some extent the district) levels, where organizations of women, environmentalists, Professionals, farmers, and others have been a prominent part of the political landscape for some time.

But the case of Civil Society Organizations in Bangladesh is different from India. Before 1990, there were hardly any civil society organization existed in Bangladesh. After the restoration of Democracy in 1991, several civil society organizations have been in operation. But, these organizations are not successful in furthering women's issue. The possible reasons might be that the number of civil society organizations that deals with women's issue is few on the one hand and the partisan characteristics of these organizations on the other hand. The civil society organizations are clearly divided in two political streams. One type of organization is inclined to Bangladesh Awami League (AL) and other type is oriented to Bangladesh Nationalist Party (BNP). That is why; they failed to capture the confidence of the general public as well as government.

MEDIA

In recent times, media plays a crucial role for furthering women's issues in front of the government. Actually, media's role is two fold. It brings several women's issue in government's notion on the one hand. On the other, it informs the general mass about government's decision on a particular issue. In India, both print and broadcast media are free from government control. These media highlight the issues of women's equal rights and demand government decisions in this regard. But, media in Bangladesh till 1990 were totally controlled by the government. After, 1991, there were emerged several private TV and radio channels. Along with the broadcast media, there are more that 170 daily news papers published from various corners of Bangladesh. In these news papers and broadcast media, women's issues are highlighted with greater importance. Sometimes, they build public opinion which compelled the government to accept changes.

CHALLENGES TO WOMEN'S PARTICIPATION

In the above section, effort was made to analyze several determinants and their role for women's participation in Bangladesh and India. Above discussion substantiates that the overall extent of women's participation in the local governance in both the countries is much lower that its male counterpart has. A question may be raised why is the situation despite having several efforts by the governments to increase participation of women in the process of local governance? Actually, there are several challenges that women are facing while participating in political process. This section explores these challenges of women's participation in local governance in both the countries.

EDUCATIONAL BACKWARDNESS AND LACK OF ECONOMIC RESOURCES:

Education is perhaps the single strongest influence on women's control on their own future. To make them knowledgeable, skilled and self-confident for their full participation in the ongoing development process of the country, one of the most important means is education (Villaluz: 2000). It creates awareness among women. However, it is unfortunate that the World's largest numbers of illiterate women are in India. According to the 2001 census, there is rampant illiteracy among women, it being around 46 per cent as against 24 percent to men. Among scheduled Castes and Scheduled Tribes, women's illiteracy is as high as 76 per cent and 81 percent (Mohon et.al, 2003:53). The case of Bangladesh is similar. According to Human Development in South Asia, 2003, the illiteracy is about 38% percent. But even beyond basic illiteracy, information about political process-for example, which levels of government to access for policies that respond to women's interests, or even how and where to vote- is often difficult for women to obtain (Kabir, 2003). Women of both countries are not conscious about their rights. Unequal access to information impairs the recognition and enjoyment of the right of women to contest elections, become members of political parties and social networks. That is why they are not interested in participating in political activities (Vijaylakshmi 2002, cited in Mukhopdhyay, 2005). On the other hand, women in both countries are mostly concentrated in the informal economy, the subsistence sector, where many are engaged in low wage or unpaid, low skilled or unskilled labour. Much of their work remains invisible, unrecognized and devaluated and is therefore unprotected by laws and legislations. The incomes they earn, however meager are still seen by them and their families as an income to be paid on the family. Therefore the expense required for political participation such as election campaign, expenditure or resources required to attend meetings, visit and interact with government officials, became an additional burden that women can ill afford, thus impeding their full participation. The following example will substantiate to what extent literacy has a strong impact on women's capacity to perform in political institutions:

"Manavva from Beldadi village, Gadag Taluk, Karnataka State of India, was elected to the position of Gram Panchayati (GP) president, which was reserved for Scheduled Tribe women. Because she was aware and articulate, her family encouraged her to stand for elections. The secretary of GP appointed by the Government was an upper caste urban woman, who gave Mannave papers and ledgers to sign without explaining to her its content. Manavva was unaware that the secretary was appropriating funds. In time, Manavva became suspicious and reported the secretary's action, which were investigated and resulted in the secretary's replacement. If Manavva were literate she would probably have been able to stop the secretary at an early stage" (Narasimhan, (1998), cited in Mohan2003: 54-55).

MOBILITY

The cultural norms operate both as a restriction on a woman's mobility as well as an impediment for women's participation in the public sphere in both Bangladesh and India. These cultural norms are perpetuated and sustained by powerful institutions of family, caste and religion. The location of polling booths and their relative distances from their homes and workplace often deter women from exercising their right as voters. The demands of contestants right from filling nominations to canvassing for elections, requires them to be mobile. The inconvenient timings, location distance and the lack of escort are impediments for women elected representatives to attend meetings. Along with these problems, family of women members is also an impediment to their mobility. Mokhopadhyay (2003) in his studies pointed out that, "in Bangladesh, as one husband said, this is a Muslim country; she (a women member) is a women so she could not go out in the evening. He (the husband) saw his wife's responsibility is caring for the children". Thus, it becomes very difficult for a woman to move out from house and involve herself in other activities.

In case of local government in India, the situation is more severe than Bangladesh. Along with several social, religious and economic constraints, women face violence against them too. And violence against women has increased a greater extent after the introduction of 73rd Constitutional Amendment Act in India. Violence in the form of beating up those women and their family members who contested for election, sexual harassment in public are more frequent during elections. In protest of this violence, women remain silent (Shamim and Kumari, 2002).

STRUCTURAL DEFICIENCIES

In Bangladesh women representatives are disadvantaged by structural constraints arising from the way in which quotas for women are incorporated within the electoral system. For instance, the union parishad (the local government institution in Bangladesh) is made up of nine wards and the electorate in each of these wards elects a general member-usually a man although women are not barred as candidates to general seats within each general seats. The quotas for women were instituted by providing three additional seats within each union parishad, and potential women representatives to these seats are elected by and responsible for three wards. This meant that women candidates had to canvass across and be responsible for an area three times the size of the area covered by a general (male) member. Women were further disadvantaged by resource constraints because they received the same budgetary and other resources received by a general member, even though women covered a wide area. There was also role confusion, as the role of the one woman representative who operates in a constituency which also has three general members, was not clear (Mukhopadhyay & Meer, 2004, cited Mukhopadhyay, 2005:14).

In India where there is 33% reservation for women at all levels of the local government institutions (three tier system), the seats reserved for women rotate in every election. Thus a ward reserved for all female competition becomes a general ward (in which women and men can compete) in the next election. As a result political parties simply do not take women's candidacy seriously nor do they invest in the elected woman candidate knowing very well that in the next round of elections these women are of no use to their electoral prospects. The selection of female candidates by parties for reserved seats is thus to a large extent determined by the calculation as to which women are the most 'useful' either because they are related to powerful men or because they can be easily bypassed in everyday political decision making (Mukhopadhyay, 2005:1). Goetz (2004) and Beall (2004) noted that in many countries where affirmative action for women exist in local government elections, these measures were introduced as an afterthought(late edition, extra) thus detracting (pessimistic) from the credibility(reliability) and legitimacy of women as political actors (Mukhopadhyay, 2005:14).

RELIGION

Religion also plays a very crucial role to keep women stays at home rather than going outside and participate in political decision process in the both countries. The only point of difference is the type of religion that impedes women's participation. As all knows, more than 90% people of Bangladesh are Muslim and their religion is Islam. Islam represents a strong apology for patriarchy and is explicit about the sexual division of labour and responsibility and in effect, sanctifies male dominance. According to numerous illustrators of Islam, man is the earner and woman is the server of man. Being the server of man, it has been indicated that woman should be kept into the house. Restriction has been imposed by the religion on the movement of women outside their house. Women are instructed to have used 'purdha'[13] while they will be outside their home so that they might be able to hide themselves from others. Once woman are habituated to restrict them within 'purdha' they would virtually loose their interest to go out and be participate in political activities.

Unlike Bangladesh, the majority of Indian population is Hindu although there is a considerable number of Muslims in India. The Hindus by religion suffers from different class and caste. Upper class Hindus always dominate the lower class Hindus and they generally do not allow lower caste people to come forward to go for elections in political institutions although there are reservations for tribal people in different levels. But the problem lies in the fact that it has been rooted in the mentality of millions of population which will need decades to come out from these trauma.

CULTURAL FACTOR

There are socio-cultural norms and outlooks that have significant impacts on gender related issues. It is noted by the Center for Asia Pacific Women in Politics (CAPWIP) that the empowerment of women in terms of their decision making position is considerably affected by cultural stereotypes that exists in most societies. In the Asia-pacific region, which covers East Asian countries, the major forms of cultural stereotypes include: (a) women's primary responsibility is to take care of family and children, and it is only their secondary obligation to get involved in social and political institutions; (b) women do not have experience, and thus are not capable to assume leadership positions; (c) the public domain is mainly for men while the private household domain is for women; and (d) women's involvement in the public sphere (politics, administration and business) should be an extension of their roles in the privately family sphere (Center for Asia-Pacific

Women in Politics, 2000, cited in Haque, 2003:580-81). Such gender stereotypes, which constrain women's representation and participation, are rooted in social and cultural norms of Bangladesh and India. Bangladeshi women always put priorities in taking care of her families rather than involving themselves in the process of politics. There is a myth in the Bangladeshi culture that 'a woman's paradise is at the feet of her husband'. Many women believe that myth and bear any violence hoping to attain their paradise.

In India, the age old patriarchal system gives primacy to males and perpetuates deep rooted values within society that discriminate against women of all ages. Men are privileged access to the economic, educational, political and social spheres. Patriarchal norms typically relegate women to the private sphere, place restrictions on her mobility, and perpetuate the view that the girl child is an economic liability. When women do believe the confidence to articulate their needs and demands, their voice often go unheard, or they become targets for further violence (Mohan, 2003:65). In such a situation women do not show any interest in getting involved in any activities outsides their home.

PARTICIPATION OF WOMEN IN POLITICAL DECISION MAKING

Now an important questions needs to be addressed whether reservation of seats for women in the Local government institutions in both the countries ensures their active participation in the political decision making process? The situation is perhaps not satisfactory as male members are more dominant and use their patronage networks to function as elected representatives because their role in the public world of politics is taken for granted. However, this is not so for women and herein lies the gender dimension of political representation. There is no getting way from the fact that affirmative action taken by various government has given rise to what has been termed as de facto politics (Vijaylakshmi 2002, cited in Mukhopadhyay, 2005: 31).

Affirmative action does ensure that more women come into politics but it does not ensure that elected women will be seen as legitimate political actors. This situation is obvious in case of women in the Union Parishad as well as women members in the Panchayati Raj. But, it does not mean that all women in all circumstances are subsumed in de facto politics[14]. There are few women in local government bodies in both the countries who have been effective in discharging their duties and responsibilities. But there number is so few that it does not represent the whole women community.

Several research had been undertaken on women participation in political process in order to assess their role in the decision making process. According to an assessment carried out by the Asian Development Bank (ADB, 2004) more than 70% of women councilors interviewed in Bangladesh were not aware of their rights and responsibilities as representatives, even higher percentages- more than 80%- expressed their lack of confidence in their ability to conduct meetings (Mukhopadhyay, 2005:32). Actually patriarchal society offers little or no space for women's authority and agency. As a result women became handicapped and play symbolic role in the decision making. Goetz (2004) offers the argument that decentralization process tend to bolster and ingrain existing traditional institutions and local elites. These institutions tend to be deeply patriarchal, offering little or no space for women's authority and agency. In other words, society do not accept them in a way where women are dominating the process of decision making or play a positive role or more vocal in any where. We can quote here a speech of an ex-parliament Member of Bangladesh whose name is Tasnima Hossain. She is the wife of Anowar Hossain Munju[15]. Tasnima Hossain in her address in a goal table meeting in Dhaka on 'Role of Civil Society and New Media to Prevent Violence against Women' told that:

'I was not treated as a colleague by other Parliament Members in the Parliament. Rather I was mostly treated as 'bhavi'[16] or the wife of Anowar Hossain Munju although I was an elected MP. While I was entering into the Parliament session I had to hear that why I

was alone? Why I had not come with my Husband? The situation was like that I would have to come with my husband in the Parliament every time' The Prothom Alo, dated: March 13, 2006.

Actually it is a question of identity. The male counterparts as part of society do not accept women parallel to them. Sufferings of the women members do not restrict within the problems of identity only. Some times they are given wrong treatment if they speak for their rights. In the local governance level, women's marginalization is reinforced by paternalistic and discriminatory attitudes of male representatives and male chairmen, and their beliefs that women should not get involved in local politics, and that while men get into office on merit, women get in through government favours in the form of quotas (Mukhopadhya, 2003: 44). The following few cases will substantiate the above observation:

CASE 1

Hasnehena: A Case of Neglect

Hasnehena, Union Parishad Member told that "After my oath I went to the chairman and asked him to assign me some work. The chairman become annoyed and said that the government has brought out the women from their houses to create unnecessary trouble in the union Parishad. [He said] 'What will you do in the Union Parishad?' Go upstairs and sit with my wife and spend your time. I do not find any work for you. No specific work is mentioned in the manual for women' (Mukhopadhyay and Meer (2004) Creating Voice and Carving Space, cited in Mukhopadhyay, 2005: 33).

CASE 2

Aparna Rani: Story of Misfortune

Aparna Rani was a Union Parishad member of Moulvibazar. Her husband, who was a Primary School Teacher, encouraged Aparna to compete in the Union Parishad election. She was elected from the reserved seat. During the early stages of her time in the Union Parishad, Aparna did not face any problem but the situation changed later when she started to be vocal than other women members and often argued with the chairman, which took a serious turn. The chairman did not support of her active participation in the meetings and tried to teach her a lesson. A friendly male colleague used to help Aparna in performing different Union Parishad activities. The chairman spread rumors using Aparna's friendly relationship with her male colleague. This horrified Aparna's married life. She was almost hated in the society. Finally she had to leave the Union Parishad (Shamim and Kumari, 2002:55).

Above cases substantiates that how women have been accepted by their male counterparts at all levels. They are not only neglected but also face serious challenges which may destroy their family life. Under these circumstances, women loose interest to take part in political process.

The next question which need further elaboration that what is the case for Indian women in the Panchayati Raj System? Sen (2000:52-53) in her studies pointed out that reservation of seats for women in local government bodies has definitely opened the scope for women representation. She also noted that Indian women fall behind men in all social and economic indexes. But she emphasized the fact that it is the women who will promote the interest of women in the process of national growth and development. The inference is that men cannot (for social or political reasons) or do not (to protect patriarchal authority) represent women's true interest. Now the concern is to analyze to what extent these women are in a position to contribute in the local government decision making process? Are they cordially accepted by their male counterparts in the local body? Do they face any problem while participation in the activities of the local government?

While finding the answers of these type of questions, Shamim and Kumari (2002:52-54) explained that there are two kinds of women representatives in the Panchayats; those who are facing problems and those who have had a smooth entry. Women representatives faced problems when she did not have any political or organizational affiliations, did not have any family members in politics and fought independently without any party support for which she had to contest election. On the other hand, women who were associated with political parties, accepted party ticket for election and was elected without contesting and did not even made any promises had hardly any problems. One important point here is that party affiliation. Party affiliation plays a vital role in assuring good treatment for women. The situation may be favourable for the upper class women but the lower class women are still the victims of negligence by their male counterparts. One such case of negligence is worth mentioning:

Smt. Dhan Devi, a panchayat member of Bahadurpur Luhiya Gram Panchayat, basrehar Block of Etawah District said, "In our Nyaya Panchayat the Pradhan and other officials work according to their personal whims fancies. Though we attend the meeting but deliberately keep quite. In my locality not even a brick lane has been made and the common passage that existed earlier has been closed down independently. We women have been made Panchayat members only to behave as passive 'yes' people sans respect and importance whatsoever' (Source: Shamim and Kumari, 2002:52).

Another aspect that needs to be mentioned here that there is a trend of exclusion of lower class women (dalit[17]) from the public office by council practice and procedures (Mukhopadhya, 2005: 34). There are several studies pointed to how dalit men and women are excluded from public office through the manipulation of official rules of procedure governing local government institutions. I may refer to case of Chaggibai that was studied by Goetz (2004).

CHAGGIBAI: A STORY OF VICTIM

'Chaggibai was elected sarpanch of Rasulpura Panchayat, Rajasthan, India, in 1995, a chair reserved not just for a woman, but for a Dalit. Chaggibai, a member of the tiny Bhil group, part of the Dalit community there, was encouraged to run for the sarpanch position by members of the Rawat caste group, the elite class that made up over 60% of the residents of the area. As an independent-minded woman, she was not an obvious choice for an uppercaste proxy candidate, as she was literate, known in the area as a woman's rights activist, a participant in the national level Mahila Samakhya programme, and had worked as a school administrator. But she had long ago separated from her husband, and she was seen therefore as more easy to manipulate than a married woman would be. At the first village assembly after her election, the local Rawat strong man

who had always rung the local council, Charan Singh, conducted the meeting and refused to allow Chaggibai to speak. She had assembled over 400 women and Dalits from the area to attend, but Charan Singh, who was accustomed to conducting all council meeting in secret and from his own house, order them all to go home. Chaggibai mobilized the local Dalit and female community in the subsequent month to support her efforts to change council practices. She held open meetings to discuss local development plans, initiated projects to cover local drains, repair the school building and some raods, and she completed the Panchayat buildings so as to accommodate open sessions. When she led local women in demonstrations against the illegal liquor store run by the deputy sarpanch, Charan Singh and the Rawat community counter attacked, locking the Panchayat doors agaist her, hiding files containing illicitly transactions, and attempting to assault Chaggibai. Subsequently, nine of twelve panchayat members, including two women, convened a secret meeting and passed a vote of no-confidence against her. Chaggibai's case was taken up by the People's Union of Civil Liberties and by Rajasthan's vibrant Women's movement, and a petition was filed against her removal in the Jaipur High Court. In the end she did not succeed in getting reinstated. As she commented to a journalist several years later: 'they simple couldn't tolerate a woman. And above and beyond that, the panchayat is dominated by non-Dalits, so they couldn't tolerate me doubly. If I had been their puppet, as they expected me to be, none of this would have happened' (Goetz, 2002, cited in Mukhopadhya, 2005:35).

If we analyze the case of Chaggibai, two characteristics of Indian society will be evident. One would be that the Indian society is still suffered from caste struggle. Other would be the neglecting the situation of women. But on the other hand a number of studies find that women councilors and residents manage to articulate priorities in local planning and decision making differently from men. Basu (Nussnaum et al 2003, cited in Mukhopadhyay,2005:350 reports evidence from villages in Maharashtra, women led Panchayats placed greater emphasis on construction of wells, playgrounds, roads, public toilets and non-polluting stoves. Topalova (2003) found that drinking water supply services tend to be better in Panchayats led by women rather than men and that the local residents agreed that women were less likely to demand bribes. Chattopadhyay and Duflo (2004) in their study on 165 viallge councils in West Bengal and Rajasthan found that women's leadership has indeed had positive impacts on policy decisions. On the other hand Vijayalakshmi (2002) argues that a number of factors such as the way in which women are brought into the political process in local government institutions (as de jure and not de facto representatives), the fact that most women elected to reserved sears have no prior experience of politics or of contact with constituencies, that elected women have little communication with each other, that they belong to different social groups which divides them, limit the possibility of developing shared gender specific agendas. The above discussion substantiates that the situation of women in India in comparison to Bangladesh, is slightly better. Although they are the victims of several societal values but in some context they have been successful to play positive role in the local government decision making whatever might be the percentage is.

Thus it is obvious that creating scope for participation of women through affirmative actions by the government does not ensure their active participation in the decision making process. For ensuring full participation in the decision making it is necessary to overcome the rigid social and cultural barriers that women face and which disallow their participation in the public sphere.

WHAT SHOULD BE DONE?

Despite having adapted new legal and institutional measurer, in the form of reservation of seats in local government institutions by the government of Bangladesh and India to ensure grater participation of women in political process, the discussion of preceding section clearly demonstrated that such representation remains below the average line and their representation has been restricted mostly in the reserved seats. The major causes of such lower representation of women have been socio-cultural, political, structural, educational and regional factors. In such a situation, it is therefore necessary to intensify existing measures and initiate new ones so that greater female representation in governance may be ensured.

First: One of the major obstacles to women's participation in politics is the cultural norms and perception that has stereotyped women's role on the family domain only. That is why, it is essential to bring changes in such cultural norms by initiating appropriate cultural, educational and informational policies. Both men and women should have taught the lesson that there is no difference between men and women and women should be treated fairly and equally to make sure that discrimination against women is not acceptable. In doing so, first step should be redesigning educational curricula in a way that highlights the significance of women's participation in national development at all levels (Economic and Social Commission for Asia and the Pacific, 1993). Another mechanism would be to involve various media sources, like television, radio and newspapers, with a view to making policy makers and administrators realize the issue of problems of gender inequality and also to stimulate women to reorganize their roles and affirm themselves as equal partners of men in every sphere (Center for Asia-Pacific Women in politics, 2000 and Haque, 2003:586).

Second: It is obligatory to have taken the initiative by the government to bring effective constitutional and legal provision in regards to gender equality in every spheres of governance. Besides, it is always essential to pass few additional legal measures in order to implement legislation effective. For instance, the Local Government (Union Parishad) Second Amendment Act 1997 does not have any clause where the duties and responsibilities of the women members have been clearly spelt out. In case of India, the provision of raising no confidence motion against the Sarpanch (the president) sometimes offers opportunity to the upper class powerful Panchaayat member to remove the president who belongs to the schedule caste. This case is evident in case of Chaggibai in Rajasthan, India. Taking in considerations these mistakes, specific and well spelt out laws in favour of enhancing women's representation in governing institutions needs to be passed in the parliament.

Third: since women's representation in the legislative and executive bodies greatly depends on their representation in political parties, there is need for the major political parties to take appropriate initiatives to expand such party representation. In this regard, they may at least practice the female quota in political parties as well. This system of female quota of political parties does exist in cases such as Denmark, Germany, Norway and Sweden (Women Around the World, 2000). In addition, it is the political will or commitment of top leaders that remains most critical to adopt and implement all the above measures suggested for ending gender based discrimination and expanding female representation and participation in various domains of governance (Center for Asia-Pacific Women in politics, 2000). In case of Bangladesh, it is easier to bring such reforms in political parties as both largest political parties are headed by women chairperson and it is no avoiding the fact that these two parties are heading for by the directions of two women heads.

Finally: Government that does not consider women's empowerment a priority will more likely channel their budget to defense and trade promotion. Yet without adequate budget for implementation, government initiated policy measures to empower women can not possibly go beyond rhetoric. Political will must translate into both policies and resources if they are to be effective at all. At the same time, government policies must address the need to give women access to career patterns to develop and strengthen their capacity as political leaders, develop media relations, and generate their own resources (Villaluz, 2000:5).

CONCLUSION

The long history of struggles in South Asia-from women's suffrage to women's participation in electoral politics at national and provincial levels- is an ongoing process. The state's initiatives of granting quotas or reservation for women have proved to be a mixed bag. Still women of both Bangladesh and India have been facing numerous social, religion and political hindrances while participating in the process of governance at the local level. Local government decision making process is still dominated by male and women are neglected in that process.

The essence of good governance lies, on one hand, the inclusion of local level planning in the national government and on the other hand, the success of a local government depends on peoples' participation. It is the grassroots level people who could contribute significantly to the governance of their communities. However, unequal participation of women and men in the government planning works as a barrier to ensure good governance in both Bangladesh and India (Shamim and Kumari, 2002: 63). From the above analysis it is clear that there is a crucial need for a gender-specific development paradigm into all areas of policy making and planning so that women's needs can be met and their participation ensured.

The present study was an attempt to review the participation of women at grassroots level democracy in Bangladesh and India. The study examined the role of government of Bangladesh and India to ensure gender balance at local level policy planning. In Bangladesh women's participation at local level politics has been recently ensured through the constitutional reform, while in India it had been for sometimes. It has been found in both the countries that although a large number of women were elected as local representatives, obstacles related to women's gender identity refrained them to play their roles effectively. It was evident that lack of effective and timely planning, lack of political background, absence of proper socio-economic and political environment, lack of appropriate organizational framework, placed women behind to prove their competencies compared to their men counterparts. It had been identified that women have limited scope to exercise political rights, lack of control over resources and limited choice in decision-making. However, women had been trying to overcome the barriers through their active participation in the local level policy-making.

REFERENCES

Ahmed, Shafi and et.al, (2001), 'One Decade of Bangladesh under Women Leadership', *Alochona Magazine*, October, p-3. (www. magazine. alochona.org/).

Ashman, Darcy (1997), 'The Democracy Awareness Education Program of Association of Development Agencies in Bangladesh (ADAB)', *Discourse, A Journal of Policy Studies*, Dhaka, Institute for Development Policy Analysis and Advocacy (IDPAA), Proshika.

Bardhan, Kalpana (1986), Women: Work, Welfare, and Status: Forces of Tradition and Change in India, South Asia Bulletin, 1986, Vol. 6(1), pp.3-16.

Beall, J. (2004), *'Decentralization and Engendering Democracy: Lessons from Local Government Reform in South Africa'*, Working Paper No. 54, November, Crisis States Programme, Development Research Centre, Canada.

Beijing Platform for Action and Declaration (1995), Beijing, China, United Nations, Fourth World Conference on women.

Blair, H. (2000), Participation and Accountability at the Periphery: Democratic Local Governance in Six Countries, World Development, Vol.28, No.1, pp.21-39.

Caldwell, John (1982), Theory of Fertility Decline, London, Academic Press.

Center for Asia-Pacific Women in Politics (2000), Women in Legislative Chambers: Asia-Pacific Region; (Retrieved from: *http://www.capwip.org/participation/womenchambers.html).*

Chattopadhyay, Raghabendra and Esther Duflo (2004), Impact of Reservation in Panchayati Raj: Evidence from a Nationwide Randomized Experiment, Economic and Political Weekly, Vo. 39, No. 9, pp.979-986.

Chowdhury, Dr. Nazma (2002), The Implementation of Quotas: Bangladesh Experience-Dependence and Marginality in Politics, Paper presented in Regional Workshop on the Implementation of Quotas: Asian Experiences, Organized by International Institute for Democracy and Electoral Assistance, Held on 25 September, 2002 in Jakarta, Indonesia.

Constitution of the People's Republic of Bangladesh (1992).

Economic and Social Commission for Asia and the Pacific (1993), Women in Politics in Asia and the Pacific, United Nations, New York, pp-10-11.

Gala, Chetna (1996), "Empowering Women in Villages: All Women Village Councils in Maharastra", Seminar report on "Decentralization and Devolution of Powers in Panchayati Raj System in India". 22-23 March, New Delhi, Centre for Development Studies and Action and FES (mimeo).

Goetz, Anne Marie (2004), 'Decentralization and Gender Equality", Chapter 12 in UNDP's *Striving for Gender Equality in an Unequal World*, UNDP Report for Beijing +10.

Haque, M. Shamsul (2003), 'Citizen Participation in Governance Through Representation: Issue of Gender in East Asia', *International Journal of Public Administration*, Vol. 26, no. 5, pp. 569-590, Marcel Dekker, Ins. USA.

Hensman, Rohini (1996), The Role of Women in the Resistance to Political Authoritarianism in Latin America and South Asia, in Afshar, Haleh (ed) Women and Politics in the Third World, Routledge, London and New York.

Hashemi, S.M. (1995), 'NGO Accountability in Bangladesh: NGOs, State and Donors', in M. Edwards and D. Lewis (eds.) *NGO Performance and Accountability: Beyond the Magic Bullet*, Pp. 103-110, London, Earthscan.

Jayal, Nirja Gopal (1997), 'The Governance Agenda: Making Democratic Development Dispensable', *Economic and Political Weekly*, Vol. XXXII, No.8, February 22.

Kabir, Farah (2003), Political Participation of Women in South Asia (Retrieved from *http://www.dawnorg.org/publications/docs/prstkabir2003.doc.*

Karim, Anwarul (2000), *Recent Changes in the Structure of the Union Parishad in Bangladesh: Scope for Participation of Women*, An Unpublished M.Phil Thesis, Department of Administration and Organization Theory, University of Bergen, Norway.

Karin, Azza Et, al, (Eds) (1998), *Women in Parliaments: Beyond Numbers*, International Institute for Democracy and Electoral Assistance, Stockholm, Sweden.

Kaushik, Susheela (2000), Panchayat Raj and Women: A Profile, New Delhi, Centre for Development Studies and Action.

Landman, Tood (2003), Issues and Methods in Comparative Politics: An Introduction (2nd Edition), London; New York: Routledge.

Mathema, Madhuri (1998), Women in South Asia: Pakis, Bangladesh and Nepal, in Stromquist (ed.).

Matland, Richard E. (1998(b)), Enhancing Women's Political Participation: Legislative Recruitment and Electoral Systems, in Women in Parliament: Beyond Numbers, Karim, Azza (Ed), International IDEA, Handbook Series 2.

Mazumder, Vina and Indu Agnihorti (1999), "The Women's Movement in India, Emergence of a New Perspective", in Bharati Ray and Aparna Basu (Eds.) From Independence to Freedom, New Delhi:OUP.

Mohanty, Bidyut (1999), 'Panchyat Raj Institutions and Women" in in Bharati Ray and Aparna Basu (Eds.) From Independence to Freedom, New Delhi:OUP.

Mohon, Shantha et.al., (2003), "Women and Political Participation in India, Base Line Report, National Institute of Advance Studies-Gender Studies Unit (NIAS), International Women's Rights Action Watch Asia Pacific, Kuala Lumpur, Malaysia.

Mukhopadhyay, Maitrayee (Ed.) (2003), *Governing for Equity: Gender, Citizenship and Governance,* Conference Proceedings, Royal Tropical Institute, KIT Development Policy and Practice, Amsterdam, The Netherlands.

Mukhopadhyay, Maitrayee and Sharmin Meer (2004), *Creative Voice and Carving Space, Redefining Governance from a Gender perspective,* KIT Publishers, Amsterdam, Netherlands.

Mukhopadhyay, Maitrayee (2005), Decentralization and Gender Equity in South Asia: An Issue Paper, The Onternational Development of Research centre, Canada.

Mumtaz, Khawar (2005), Women's Representation, Effectiveness and Leadership in South Asia, paper presented in Fifth South Asia Regional Ministerial Conference: Celebrating Beijing Plus Ten, Islamabad, Pakistan, 3-5, May.

Narasimhan, Shakuntala (1998), "Gusty Rustic", *Decent Herald,* August 16.

Nussbaum, M et, al (eds.) (2003), *Essays on Gender and Governance,* Human Development Resource Centre, United Nations development Programme, New Delhi, India.

Rustagi, Dr. Preet (2004), Women and Development in South Asia, South Asian Journal, Vol.4, South Asia Media Net, Lahore, Pakistan, April-June.

Shamim, Prof. Ishrat and Dr. Ranjana Kumar (2002), *Gender and Local Governance: A New Discourse in Development*, South Asia Network of Economic Research Institutes, Islamabad, Pakistan.

Shamim, Professor Ishrat (2004), "Women and Local Governance: Has it Empowered Women", Paper presented at Regional Conference on Gender and Governance, 16-18 December, Islamabad.

Sultana, Abeda (2000), 'The Role of Training in the Empowerment of Women in Union Parishad: An Analysis', *Lok Proshashon Samoyke*, No 17, December, Dhaka.

Tambiah, Yasmin (2002), Women and Governance in South Asia: Re-imaging the State, Colombo, ICES.

The Prothom Alo (2006), A Widely Circulated National Bengali Dailies, Dhaka, Bangladesh, dated: March 13.

UNDP (2000), *Women's Political Participation and Good Governance: Twenty First Century Challenges*, New York.

Vijayalakshmi, V (2002), *Gender, Accountability and Political Representation in Local Government*, Working Paper No. 102, Institute for Social and Economic Change, Bangalore, India.

Villaluz, Sheila Espine (ed) (2000), *Women Around the World Fact Sheet, A Quarterly Fact Sheet of the Center for Legislative Development*, Dhaka, June, Vol.1, No-4.

Women Around the World (2000), Quota System: Women's Boon or Bane? Vol.1(3

NOTES

1. For more details about comparative politics, see Landman, Tood (2003) *Issues and Methods in Comparative Politics: An Introduction* (2nd Edition), London; New York: Routledge.
2. One may ask a question why 'local government' of both India and Bangladesh has been selected as unit of analysis or why not national level. The answer lies in the fact that local government organizations are the main means through which women enter into the arena of politics. A vast majority of local level women do not have access to national level politics. Besides, it would have been a very difficult task to shed light on the state of women's political participation at the local as well as national level in a comparative perspective in a single paper.

3. India's bi-cameral legislature consists of a 545 strong lower house (Lok Sabha) and a 250 member upper house (Rajya Sabha). Women in the two houses largely belong to the relatively privileged middle class, are educated and in professions. Some women enter through the caste quotas. Despite the constant low number of women having returned as legislators (though they doubled in the first fifty years) some have reached positions of power in mainstream political parties and in governance like Sonia Gandhi, president of the ruling Congress party, Jayalalitha, Chief Minister (CM) of Tamil Nadu and Mayawati, the former CM of Uttar Pradesh who also happened to be a dalit. Religious extremist party, Visha Hindu Parishad (VHP) too has a few militant and activist women among its leadership. Notwithstanding their standing these women have failed to push for gender balance in the decision making bodies within their parties. Women's representation in State Assemblies at an average of four percent is even more dismal. Analysis and studies of women's effectiveness in legislatures reveal that their presence has hardly made any difference despite the fact that women moved private members bills and resolutions relevant to women and managed support form other women members regardless of party lines. Most of these it turns out did not come up for discussions and lapsed (Mumtaz, 2005:11).
4. The system of local self government in rural areas in India is called Panchayati Raj. The system consists of the village (gram), block (taluka) and district (zila) levels.
5. Bangladesh's unicameral legislature consists of a parliament (Jaityo Songhsod) with 300 members. The constitution provided for 15 reserved seats for women (Clause 65), these were doubled to 30 in the second national assembly (1979-1982). The seats lapsed in 2001. In the year 2005, legislation has passed for restoration of reserved seats and increase in the quota to 45 seats. The women are indirectly elected by the members of the house. The quota does not prevent women from contesting on general seats. Currently there are 7 directly elected women in parliament. Unusual in the case of Bangladesh is that both, the head of government and leader of opposition are women (Mumtaz, 2005:19).
6. A fours tier local government system is now in operation in Bangladesh. Among these four tiers, the top tier is the district council (zilla parishad); followed by the upazilla parishad which is the lowest level of operation for the bureaucracy and line ministries; the third tier is the union council (union parishad); and the fourth, village level gram sarker. Union parishad is the only local self government bodies in operation. So we would restrict our discussion of women's participation within the Union Parishad only.
7. ADAB was the leading umbrella organizations of NGOs in Bangladesh.
8. In 1996, there was a political turmoil took place in Bangladesh politics in regards to the controversial election that took place in 15th February, 1996. All opposition political parties boycotted the election and was advocating for passing the bill of 'Non-partisan Care taker Government' to conduct a free and fair election in Bangladesh. Ignoring opposition's

demand, the then Government led by Prime Minster Begum Khaleda Zia went for contested the election alone but the continuous mass movement compelled the Government to resign accepting the opposition demand for 'Non-partisan Care Taker Government'.

9. GSS is the name of a NGO in Bangladesh.
10. Nilphamari is the name of a district in Bangladesh.
11. The prominent women leaders include Sonia Gandhi, president of ruling Congress Party, Kumari Jayalalitha, Chief Minister of Tamil Nadu, Mayawati, the former Chief Minister of Uttar Pradesh and Rabri Devi, the former Chief Minister of Bihar.
12. One possible explanation might be that both leaders do not want to be gender biased by advocating for women or by initiating several affirmative actions designed for the improvement women in Bangladesh.
13. 'Purdha' is a sort of veil used by the Muslim Women in Bangladesh for physical exclusion from the males.
14. 'De facto politics' refers to a political situation where despite being the elected representatives the person elected does not actively participate in the functions of governance. In case of women, the male family members and/or elites who were political active managed the functions of the union parishad on behalf of women members (Vijaylakshmi 2002, cited in Mukhopadhyay, 2005: 31).
15. Anowar Hossain Munju is the Chairman of Jatio Party (Munju group) and also the existing Member of Parliament of Bangladesh.
16. In Bangladesh culture, wife of brother is generally called as 'bhavi'.
17. Dalit is the name of a caste belongs to Schedule Tribes.

5

WIDOWHOOD IN RURAL PURULIA OF INDIA

Prafulla Chakrabarti

Everywhere widowhood is a tragic incident in human life. This is more evident in a woman's life, as in a male dominated world, she has hardly any existence of her own. Perhaps, that is why in all cultures widowhood has been regarded as a distinctly critical period in a woman's life. Spinsterhood, divorce and marital separation are also unfortunate events. But widowhood has no comparison in view of its nature and intensity. The prime reason is that it offers no choice to the person except an unfortunate dismal future.

Widowhood undoubtedly depends on several demographic factors of which mortality has been considered the most important one though the roles of age distribution of marriage, age at marriage, incidence of remarriage, rate of growth of population, etc, cannot be ignored (Kamat 1963 18; Malaker 1981:165). Many of these factors in their turn, however, are conditioned by socio-economic, cultural, hygienic and other factors. During the last few decades the death rates in both the sexes have shown a declining trend almost everywhere in the world and the difference in the age of husbands and wives has, more or less been, narrowed down especially in the developed countries. But even then it is surprising to find that there are more widows than widowers in general population (Goode 1964). In America for instance, there were 12 million widows in the seventies of the last century and the ratio of widows to widowers was 12:1(Lindsay 1977:1). The problem of widowhood has become so acute in the United States that it is being tackled separately as a geriatric problem. A number of voluntary organizations have come forward to offer counsel, advice and marital help to the helpless lonely widows. To understand the problem of widowhood precisely and more comprehensively, many scholars have made attempts to study the psycho-social and role relational situations of. widows. For example, Maries (1958) in his survey of 72 young widows in East London discusses the socio-economic consequences of bereavement, Clayton and others (1972) and Schoenberg and others (1975) studied the psychiatric problems associated with widowhood, Lopata (1973) raised the question of identity crisis and role-conflict among the American widows, Reed (1973) discussed the widows' possibility of getting second marriage, and Lindsay (1977) also made her personal observations over the living strategies of some recent widows in north America.

In the less developed countries also, such as India, widows continue to be in larger numbers than widowers. This happens to be so even when the female has shorter expectation of life than the male (Ruzicka 1984: 14). However, the incidence of widow remarriages has all along been very low in India and that too is confined chiefly to certain castes and sub-groups in some parts of the country as mentioned by Lancelet (1941), Goods (1963). Dubey (1965), Narain (1975) and many others. That legal values and popular customs do not always suggest a positive relationship can be borne out by the fact that people by and large discourage widow remarriage even today. Since the beginning of the last century, many social reformers and philanthropists have made various moves to change the miserable condition of Indian widows, particularly of those belonging to the Hindus, by raising the consciousness of the people (see, for instance, Vidyasagar 1981, Kacker 1930) but very little success has been attained so far.

Widowhood as a general problem has not, therefore, gained as much importance in India as it did in the West. This may be partly because of our excessive concern ever many other urgent problems like over-population, poverty, unemployment, illiteracy, etc that need immediate attention. It may also be one of the reasons that we seem to be less inclined to consider the problem of widows in isolation from that of women.

Nevertheless, some scholars found interest in the issue and examined the census data and other secondary source-materials for tracing the relationships of widowhood with other societal phenomena. For example, Dutta (1956) attributed the slow growth rate of Bengali Hindus to widowhood, Kamat (1963) examined the regional variations in the widowhood upon family structure. A descriptive account of life and living conditions of the late nineteenth century Bengali widows can be had from Chakraborty (1963) who emphasizes the caste-wise differences in their life-styles. Similarly, Ghurye (1963) also points out the differential living conditions of a sample of middle class widows in Maharashtra. But with the exception of Bose and Sen's (1965) study of widows from rural households in Rajasthan and Saraswati's (1985) work on 500 Kashivasi widows, there seems to be no information about the characteristics of the contemporary widows. The extent to which the incidence of widowhood varies in terms of caste and class and their implications for family and society are yet to be known. In the context of the fast changing nature of socio-economic and cultural situations due to the advent of Industrialization, urbanization and increased self-centeredness, it is not unlikely that the problem of widowhood may become more complex in future. This requires a proper assessment of the trend of widowhood, its variations by religion, caste, etc and examination of the conditions of the contemporary widows. The present study makes an attempt in that direction.

OBJECTIVES OF THE STUDY

This paper examines the pattern of widowhood in rural Purulia, an economically backward district in West Bengal,

India. The main objectives of the study were: (1) to make comparative analysis of the trend of widowhood between the rural and urban locations of Purulia and West Bengal, (2) to examine the nature and extent of variations, if any, in the ratio of widowhood by religion, caste, class and education dimensions of households, and (3) to study the socio-economic characteristics of widows in the households.

The scope of the present research is confined to the selected villages only rather than rural Purulia, as a whole. However, with regard to the trend of widowhood, the findings may be taken for the entire universe.

MATERIALS AND METHODS

Data for the present study was collected from households spread over 12 different villages in Purulia. For obtaining the enumerated figures for married and widowed females in each location of Purulia and West Bengal, the Census Reports of 1961, 1971 and 1981 were consulted. The choice of the district was guided by the criteria of its relatively static socio-economic conditions, cultural heterogeneity and poor educational attainment. In order to get a maximum spread of rural population, four out of twenty development blocks in the district were selected at random: Raghunathpur in the north, Santuri in the east, Jhalda in the west, and Manbazar in the south. From the northern blocks three villages, namely Bero, Bundla and Gopinathpur were selected after considering their ethnicity, level of economic development, and exposure to urban centre. Muradi and Dumdumi represented the eastern block while from the western block, four villiages, namely Ichag, Ketya, Murguma and Raghunathpur were chosen in the same manner. The three villages from the southern block were Kashipur, Golapara and Panra. For collecting information, pre-tested questionnaire schedules were used. Household level data were collected from the heads of households which covered religion, caste, kinship composition, age, sex, marital status, duration and place of marriage, education, and occupation of household members. Widows were interviewed to record their status and position in the families. In same cases, case-histories were taken to appraise the problem of widows.

The following indices and attributes were used to study the incidence of widowhood in rural Purulia:

(i) widowhood ratio per 1,000 females,

(ii) percentage of households containing widows, and

(iii) proportion of married females per 100 females.

LOCATION OF STUDY

Purulia is situated in the western most part of West Bengal. As per Census of 1981, Purulia has a total population of 1,85,380 accounting for 3.62 percent of the State population. The density is 256 persons per sq km. the district is vastly rural for only 9 percent of the population lives in urban areas which spread over seven towns. The surface of the district consists generally of a succession of rolling uplands. The soil is lataritic and infertile with a tendency of continual deterioration. The rainfall is scanty and sporadic, averaging only 365 mm per year. Cyclical drought is the perennial feature of the district. Only 45 percent of the land is under cultivation of which only one-fifth has irrigational facilities. The lands are mostly mono-cropped producing paddy once a year which also is dependent on rainfall. The per-capita income of the district was Rs. 402 in 1970-71 as against Rs. 735 for the state as a whole. The dependency ratio, as defined by the ratio between the population below 15 years and 60 years and above, and the population in the age-group 15-59, is 86. Lack of required quantity and low intake of good quality food results in under nourishment which adversely affects the fertility and enhances mortality of many poor peasants and wage-laborers in the district.

Compared to the State as a whole, Purulia recorded a low literacy rate. For instance, while the proportion of literates in West Bengal was 33.2 percent in 1971, it was only 21.5 percent in Purulia. The corresponding figures for the two regions in 1981 were 40.9 percent and 29.8 percent, respectively. The picture is more dismal in the case of females. The female literacy rates were 8.3 percent and 13.3 percent in 1971 and 1981 respectively as against the State figures of 23.4 percent and 30.3 percent. Poverty, lack of educational facilities and higher concentration of tribal and ritually lower caste population in the district may be responsible for the poor literacy rate.

RESULT AND DISCUSSION

TREND OF WIDOWHOOD

In order to get a comparative picture of the trend of widowhood in Purulia and West Bengal for the last three census decades, Table 1 has been prepared which shows the ratios of widows per 1,000 females in 1961, 1971 and 1981 by rural, urban, and combined locations.

It appears from the table that Purulia and West Bengal are more or less differentiated with one another not only in terms of the relative incidence of widowhood but also with regard to the changing ratios of widows. In 1961, for instance, Purulia Registered relatively a lower ratio of widowhood (111) than West Bengal (123). For the next two decades, a contrary picture became apparent as West Bengal registered consistently a declining trend of widowhood over the decades both in its urban and rural locations while Purulia, with the exception of its urban location, showed a fluctuating trend. Urban Purulia, however, registered a decline in the ratio of widows by contrasting even with that of urban West Bengal. The decline was of a much faster pace in the former.

This dissimilar trend of widowhood in Purulia and in West Bengal cannot perhaps, be explained simply by the difference in their population size. For, while the fluctuating trend of widowhood in Purulia may devote a possibility of operating influence of intense socio-cultural factors, in the case of wider heterogenous canvas such as in West Bengal, factors like the decline in mortality rates in both sexes, the improvement in health and hygienic measures over the years, the relatively easy availability of medical service, the increased health consciousness among the people due to influence of education and so on seemed to be responsible for the declining incidence of widowhood. The particular geo-climatic condition, economic backwardness, unequal distribution of the gains of development, and above all people's greater reliance upon age-old customs and values (Chakrabarti 1984) seem to have given the district its separate entity of which a part has only been reflected in the pattern of widowhood.

Table 1
Trend of Widowhood (Production of Widows per 1000 Females) in Purulia and West Bengal, 1961-81

District/State	*Location*	*1961a*	*1971b*	*1981c*
Purulia	Rural	111	127	113
	Urban	122	110	86
	All	111	125	110
West Bengal	Rural	130	102	95
	Urban	101	83	83
	All	123	98	92

Source:
(a) Census of India 1961, Vol. XVI: West Bengal and Sikkim, Part IIC (i) Table CII, Pages 32,33,68,69.
(b) Census of India 1971, Series 22: West Bengal, Part II-C, Table C-II, Pages 64,65,102,103.
(c) Census of India 1981, Serious 23: West Bengal, Part IVA, Table C-1, Pages 50-53, 92-95.

Our examination of the 2,974 households from the sample villages in connection with the search for widowed females also corroborated the above view. For, we noticed a higher ratio of widowhood compared to what was noted for rural Purulia from the census data of 1981. For example, the ratio of widows, as calculated from the survey came to as high as 130 per 1,000 females against the 1981 census figure of 113 (Table 1). Was the smallness of the sample responsible for this difference? Alternatively, could it be plausible that under estimation, which is reported to be the usual phenomenon of census enumeration in India (Hill 1982:16-17) gave a much lower ratio of widowhood in Purulia? Whatever be the reasons, it is certain that aggregated data do not always reveal the dynamics of the problem.

WIDOWHOOD BY RELIGION AND CASTE

In order to examine the variations in the incidence of widowhood by religion and caste, the households were first classified into three groups namely, Hindu, Tribal and Muslim including the rest in terms of their religious affiliation. Numerically, the Hindu households comprised the majority (74.88 percent) followed by the tribal and the Muslim households the respective percentages of which were 18.46 and 6.66. The Hindu group included 34 different castes while the tribal group consisted of six different communities among which the Santals accounted for the majority. The Hindu households were further classified into three categories namely, high, middle and low on the basis of ritual hierarchical position of caste to which they belonged.[2] The Hindu high category had 14.59 percent households belonging to Brahmin, Baidya, and Kayastha castes which represent conventionally the top of the social hierarchy among the Hindus of West Bengal. Although the Saraks were regarded historically as the followers of the Jaina faith (Risley 1891) they were included under the Hindu high group because of their highly sanskritised social behavior and thereby close cultural resemblance to the Brahmins of Purulia (Chakrabarti 1984). Included in the middle category (29.35 percent) were the households belonging to such castes from whose members an orthodox Brahmin may accept water. These castes have been represented mostly by the peasant, artisan and professional people. The Mahatos, a peasant caste, formed the dominant majority in the middle caste group. The low caste category (30.94 percent) comprised such castes from whose members of the orthodox Brahmin would not usually accept water and were regarded to represent the bottom of social hierarchy. In this category, the Bauri households accounted for the majority.

Table 2 shows the ratio of widowhood in terms of number of widows per 1.000 females and the percentage of households containing widows by religion and caste. It is seen from the table that the Hindu group is clearly distinguished from the rest as having the highest ratio of widowhood (134 per 1,000 females) and the largest proportion of households containing widows (34.17 percent). The Muslims, on the other hand, showed the lowest ratio of widowhood, i.e., 105 per 1,000 females and least number of widows per household (0.298). The tribal group, however, remained in an intermediate position by revealing an even ratio of widowhood namely, 124 and lesser proportion of households having widows (31.33 percent). Thus by having a relatively lesser number of widows in their households, the married women belonging to the Muslim and the tribal households seemed to enjoy the privilege of stable marital union more than those coming from the Hindu households. In other words, the findings tend to suggest that the Hindu households in rural Purulia endured the social drag of unproductive load of females more than those belonging to other communities.

The reason for the differential incidence of widowhood in the different religious groups appeared to be mainly cultural. For, widowhood among the Hindus, especially in certain castes, is considered as a way of life as mentioned in the ancient texts (Kane 1941). Apart from the considerations to religious texts prohibiting widow remarriage and the great concern among women for preserving the high ideals of chastity and single-mined devotion to the husband, there are some pragmatic reasons also which explain why there would be more widows among the Hindus. Many a Hindu feel that each girl having been given one chance of marriage, it is her ill-luck if she becomes a widow. She should not be allowed to compete with unmarried girls in the marriage market which is already over-crowded. This feeling, however, appears to be less apparent among the Muslim and tribal population where a widowed female, if young, has a fair chance to be remarried. Since the Muslim women enjoy certain property rights, they stand a better chance to be married again compared to the Hindu women who still recently enjoyed only the rights of maintenance. The tribal widows, unlike the Muslims, are not debarred from working outside to supplement the family income. This gives them additional advantage in the marriage. While this causes a reduction in the incidence of widowhood

Table 2
Widowhood Ratio (Widows Per 1000 Females), Percentage of Households containing Widows, and Proportion of Married Women by Religion and Caste affiliation of households

Classifying Attributes and Indices	*Religious Affiliation of Households*						
	Hindu						
	High Caste	*Middle Caste*	*Low Caste*	*Total*	*Tribal*	*Muslim*	*Total*
Widowed Women	203	304	254	761	172	59	992
Married Women	488	1030	1042	2560	648	257	3456
Total Females	1285	2124	2269	5678	1385	563	7626
Total Households	434	873	920	2227	549	198	2974
Proportion of Widows Per 1,000 Females	158	143	112	134	124	105	130
Percentage of Households Containing Widows	46.77	34.82	27.61	34.17	31.32	29.80	33.36
Proportion of Married Women Per 100 Females	38	48	46	45	47	46	45

among them, the excessive work outside also affects their longevity to some extent.

So far as the caste categories of the Hindu households are concerned, the variations in the incidence of widowhood could be marked more clearly than what was noted in the case of religious groups. The households belonging to the high caste category, for example, showed the highest ratio of widowhood, namely 158 indicating thereby that for every six females one was a widow. The percentage of households containing widows was also as high as 46.77. This being the case, it seems no wonder that only 38 out of 100 married women among the high caste households could enjoy a stable union or conjugal life.

The middle caste Hindu households also showed a relatively higher ratio of widowhood (143) compared to the low caste Hindu households which, however, showed the minimum ratio of widowhood among them (112). The percentage of households containing widows was very low (34:82) but it is certainly higher than those of the low caste which possessed the least number of widows (27.61 percent). So far as the proportion of married women is concerned, the Hindu middle caste households in Purulia seemed to enjoy a better position.

Evidently, therefore, it was the low caste Hindu households in rural Purulia which seemed to be least burdened with the problem of widowhood as they registered the lowest ratio of widows per 1,000 married women, contained the least number of widows and suffered the least from the crisis of unstable conjugal life.

The reasons for the larger incidence of widowhood among the high and middle caste Hindus are not far to seek. For these are the people who have been traditionally oriented to attach much importance to the Hindu manners and customs. Widow remarriage or subsequent marriage of female is socially banned among them and their widows are forced to accept their life as such without any protest. This becomes more inevitable because they have little economic freedom and minimum mobility. But, in certain castes, such as, the Sarak, for instance, widows are rarely looked down upon by their family members. They receive their widowed females as a symbol of wealth and prosperity by calling them dhan-kudra meaning return of their widows in the family farm. Among the Mahato, however, taboos regarding second marriage of women and difference in the age at marriage of husband and wife may be responsible for the higher incidence of widowhood.

The lower extent of widowhood among the low caste Hindus may be indicative of the fact that widow remarriage is socially permissible in their midst and it is economic necessity which discourages many a widow to prolong her widowhood forever except, of course, if age is not an obstacle.

WIDOWHOOD AND CLASS

For exploring the class-wise variations in the incidence of widowhood, the households were initially classified into all possible categories on the basis of their relations to the means of production and main or only occupation. From an observation of the ratios of widowhood it appeared that the relationship between widowhood and class was not so clear as to suggest a pattern. This prompted us to pool certain categories together keeping in view their mutually exclusive and inter-related character, as far as possible. The relative incidence of widowhood under there categories was tested for statistical significance and those categories which did not register any significant difference were pooled together. The process yielded ultimately five derived categories: (1) agricultural laborer (including marginal peasants and unproductive dependants such as beggars, those living on doles etc.), (2) small peasants (including petty-traders and rural artisans), (3) middle and rich peasants (including owner-tenants), (4) salaried class, and (5) factory laborers.

Table 3 presents the ratios of widowhood, percentages of households containing widows and proportions of married women among the different classes of households. It appears from the table that like religion and caste, class also plays some role in shaping the structure of widowhood as there are certain categories of households which tend to show higher ratios of widowhood than others. But how it influences the relative incidence of widowhood is not clear from our empirical observation. It may be that different classes have different chances of survival which ultimately caused a variation in the incidence of widowhood among them. However, it is seen that the proportion of widows per 1,000 females is as high as 151 among the agricultural laborers who are generally regarded as "rural proletariats". An equally poorer class represented by the small peasants also displayed a higher ratio of widowhood (126) while the middle and rich peasants along with the salaried class registered lower ratios of widowhood, namely 112 and 114, respectively. The case of factory laborers is somewhat confusing for even through having more or less similar economic position as the agricultural laborers they showed the lowest ratio of widowhood (106). Whether this is a local phenomenon or has wider relevance needs further investigation.

Table 3
Widowhood Ratio, Percentage of Households Containing Widows and Proportions of Married Women by Household Class

	Class Categories of Households				
Classifying Attrtbutes and Indices	*Agricultural Laborer*	*Small Peasant*	*Middle-rich Peasant*	*Salaried class*	*Factory Laborer*
Widowed women	432	251	164	88	57
Married woman	1283	924	712	318	228
Total females	2865	1996	1441	784	540
Total households	1251	811	473	265	174
Proportion of widows per 1,000 females	151	126	114	112	106
Percentage of households containing widows	34.53	30.94	34.67	33.21	32.76
Proportion of married women per 100 females	45	46	49	41	42

So far as the percentage of households containing widows are concerned, the different classes in rural Purulia did not show much difference with each other except, of course, the middle and rich peasants who possessed a few more widows (about 35 percent) in their households. In that respect, the small peasant class behaved a little differently as having relatively lesser proportion of widows (30.94 percent) in their households.

The proportion of married women is distinctly higher in the category of middle and rich peasants and lower in the factory laborer category indicating thereby that the former class enjoys the fortune of stable marital life more than the latter possibly due to their unequal life styles.

Table4
Widowhood Ratio by Class and Caste/Community

	Caste/Community				
Class	*Hindu High*	*Hindu Middle*	*Hindu Low*	*Tribal*	*Muslim*
Agricultural Laborer	254	180	122	137	164
Small peasant	158	128	116	131	71
Middle-rich peasant	123	136	96	84	70
Salaried class	129	96	85	167	63
Factory Laborer	191	217	71	102	102

Value of H for caste / community = 10.2498 with df.6p < .05

To ascertain the relative importance of cultural vis-à-vis economic factors in the differential incidence of widowhood, we examined the distribution of widowhood ratios by caste/ communities and class in Table 4. It is noticed from the table that in almost all the class-categories the Hindu high and middle castes are clearly distinguished as having the higher ratios of widowhood. On the other hand, the Hindu low caste and the Muslim community registered consistently lower ratios of widowhood putting the tribal community in an intermediate position. The indication, therefore, is that for causing a variation in the incidence of widowhood, the cultural factor is more powerful than economic factor. The Kruskal-Wallis test for one-way analysis of variance also corroborated the above assertion.

WIDOWHOOD BY EDUCATION

Since education plays an important role in the formation of different family structures in society (Mukherjee 1977), and as it broadens people's general awareness and thus helps them in comprehending a from of reality beyond immediate experience (Powder-maker 1962), we considered it relevant to examine whether or not the incidence of widowhood varied in terms of household's level of education. For this we classified the households broadly into two categories: non-educated and educated on the basis of maximum level of education attained by any member of a household.

We found that the ratio of widowhood was a little higher among the non-educated households but not significant enough to indicate any pattern. The percentage of households having widows, however, was very high among the latter suggesting that educated households in rural Purulia did not perhaps consider their widows as a burden.

We shall now examine the characteristics of widows in order to explore the variation, if any, in this respect by religion and caste. The characteristics that appear to be relevant in the present context are; different modes of living of widows, their positions in the households, age and nature of occupation followed by them. It is expected that an analysis of widow characteristics will not only provide their social identification and its variation by caste and religion but also indicate the nature and extent of the widowhood problem that is being experienced by the people of rural Purulia.

WIDOWS' MODES OF LIVING

From an examination of the mode of living of widows, it was revealed that as many as 80 percent widows were accommodated in extended families suggesting thereby that so far as their care and maintenance are concerned, they apparently posed no problem to society at large. Concern should, however, be there for 13 percent widows who lived in parental families without the care of any adult male member. The woes and miseries which these widows had to suffer as a consequence of widowhood cannot be dismissed with simple words of sympathy. Because we noticed that as surviving mothers many of these women bore the dual responsibility of homemaker and child-care in addition to playing the father role while facing severe economic crisis. Some of them even carried the heavy burden of child-supporting in a poor home with a meager source of subsistence. It was also not uncommon, especially for younger widows, to face injustice and sexual exploitation due to their insecure state of existence. These were the women who were held in a very low esteem in rural society and people usually referred to them as raand meaning, prostitute. The heads of mother-child(ren) familities in rural Purulia, therefore, appeared to be worst hit by bereavement crisis even if the conditions of widows living alone were taken into account.

For example, lonely widows living in the single-member households accounted for only 6.53 percent of the total and they were mostly aged women. Mere death of husband cannot perhaps explain their lone existence as more than half of these widows reported that they opted for an independent life in order to look after the family, home and property while their sons were away, earning elsewhere and settled there temporarily with their own families. One-fifth of these widows did not have any male issue and they felt ashamed to move to their daughter's family because of social criticism. In spite of this a few, however, were not able to adjust themselves in their brothers' families, nevertheless they were not completely deprived of having occasional help and assistance from them. If this is the condition of lonely widows, can it be said that destitution resulting from widowhood is not an emergent problem in rural Purulis?

From the distribution of various categories of widows among the households of different societal groups, it appears that culture has little to do in shaping the characteristics of widows. For what categories of widows would occur in which sort of households seemed to be dependent more upon specific situational and economic factors than on religion or caste.

TYPES OF WIDOWS

In order to classify the widows into various types, we made an attempt to trace their membership rights through kinship relations and grouped them into two categories: stock and adhesion. The stock category includes such widows who hold a right of existence in the families as per patri-virilocal norm of residence. They comprise mother, father's mother, son's wife, father's brothers wife, brother's wife, etc. The widows under the adhesion category usually hold no formal right to live in the families, but as they are related either by blood or through marriage with the heads of families they can have some customary right to justify their existence in them. They include daughter, sister, father's sister, mother's mother, mother's sister, mother's brother's wife, daughter's daughter and so on.

Table 5 shows the mode of existence of widows and their relationship with heads of families by caste and community. It is seen from the table that widows as stock-member outnumbered the adhesions by more than twice in almost all the societal groups. An overwhelming majority of the widows were mothers (54.4 percent) while the proportions of widowed son's wife, father's mother and head's collateral kin, namely, widowed brother's wife, father's brother's wife and brother's son's wife were 1.11 percent, 0.60 percent and 2.93 percent, respectively. The relatively lower incidence of widows in the families as head's collateral kin may be indicative of the fact that many of their counterparts could already have been accommodated as consanguineal kin elsewhere. Moreover, most of the families being poor, they could not possibly afford to provide their secondary kin with shelter and sustenance after fulfilling their immediate obligations to primary kin. A little deviation in this regard could be seen in the high caste category which possessed a little over 7 percent of these widows. Considering the uniformly larger occurrence of widowed stock-members in the families, can it be said that people in the same villages are not so much concerned with the problem of their widowed womem?

Kinship-wise, the widows belonging to the adhesion category can again be divided into two sub-categories: lineal and affinal. Females who were once married out but came back later to parental families after losing their husbands such as, father's sister and daughter could be regarded as lineal adhesion. Rankwise, these widows reported to have somewhat

Table 5
Percentage Distribution of Widows by their Modes of Existence, Relationships with Heads of Families and Caste/Community

Widowsm Modes of Existence in Households	*Widowsm relationships with heads of families*	*Caste/community*					
		Hindu					
		High	*Middle*	*Low*	*Tribal*	*Muslim*	*Total*
As Head	Self	7.88	5.92	7.87	5.23		6.35
	Mother	10.84	15.46	15.35	15.11	11.86	14.21
As stock member	Mother	52.71	54.83	53.15	52.91	67.80	54.45
	Sonns wife	0.49	0.33	2.36	1.74		1.11
	Fatherns mother	0.99	0.76	0.39	0.58		0.60
	Brotherns wife Brotherns sonns wife, Fatherns brotherns wife	7.39	2.30	2.76			2.93
As adhesion member							
Lineal	Sister	10.84	7.57	5.91	6.40	5.09	7.46
Affinal	Daughter	5.91	7.57	3.94	8.72	6.78	6.45
	Fatherns sister	0.49	1.32	1.97	0.58	1.69	1.20
	Wifens mother, Wifens sister, Motherns brotherns wife, Daughterns daughter	2.46	3.94	6.30	8.72	6.78	5.2
	Total	100.00	100.00	100.00	100.00	100.00	100.00
	(Number)	(203)	(304)	(254)	(172)	(59)	(992)

an inferior position compared to those mentioned above. The widows under the affinal adhesion sub-category include mother's mother, mother's sister, mother's brother's wife, wife's mother and wife's sister. In rural Purulia, this type of widows hold a very low esteem in society because of their parasitic existence. The proportion of widows in the first category accounted for 15.11 percent while if was only 5.24 percent in the second sub-category.

This tends to suggest that very few widows are thrown out of their original residence because of widowhood and, irrespective of religion and caste, people in rural Purulia seem to attach much value to accommodating their widowed kin and affine. This is clearly evident from the table which shows that relationships of widows with heads of families varied insignificantly by community affiliation of households. In other words, the position of widows in families seems to be uniformly balanced over the societal groups.

STATUS OF WIDOWS

The status of widows, however, can be different from one position to another. For example, a widowed sister in her parental home is quite unlikely to enjoy the same status which she used to have during her premarital or even during marital life. We gathered from many a people that a widowed sister enjoyed an inferior status in her brother's family and was often treated as a burden. The inter-personal relationships between a widowed sister (nanad) and her brother's wife did not appear to be congenial in many families. Quarrel, tension and misunderstanding were reported to be the usual events in families where widowed sisters lived and most of these incidents seemed to occur out of personality conflict. Even after rendering her untiring services to the family, a widowed sister seldom received appreciation from the members of brother's family and as a result suffered from acute frustration. It appears, therefore, that very few women in this position can maintain sound mental health which depends upon self esteem and a sense of social location. Glassner's (1980) observation of two working class women who lost their primary social roles and ultimately reached the level of maniac depression through several stages of depression, also seems to hold good at least in case of some widowed sisters in rural Purulia.

Culture-wise, however, the attitudes and behaviors of the family towards a widowed sister were found to be quite different. For, while the high caste Hindu families tend to impose excessive control and repression upon the widowed sisters by restricting their mobility beyond the immediate initiation, ceremonial rice-taking etc., prescribing certain dress and food (namely, white garments, and sundried rice, with strict vegetarian dish) and debarring them from taking an active role in the decision-making process of the family and so on, no such discriminatory behavior could usually be shown to widowed sisters by the people belonging to Hindu low caste, tribal and Muslim communities possibly because of their relative economic independence which will be evident later.

The position of widowed daughters, in that respect, seemed to be somewhat better. For barring a few cases of maladjusted ones, many a widowed daughter was of the opinion that widowhood had little impact upon their face to face relationships with the members of natal families. During the early years of widowhood, they did spend their lives under severe stress. The members of husband's family, particularly, mother-in-law, sisters-in-law or even the neighbors used to blame them for premature death of their sons frequently calling them as bhatar-khaki (i.e., a women who has killed her husband). Sometimes, charges of witchcraft were also framed against them. Hence, in order to get relief from this kind of inhuman behavior, the majority of the young-age widows returned to their parental home so that they could share their grief with their own people. Almost every one of these widows reported that they enjoyed more freedom and mobility at their parental home than what they used to have in their husband's family. In their parental home, they had never been discriminated against in receiving family privileges and in taking active roles in domestic matters. Even in respect of widowhood observance, deviations could pronouncedly be marked among them. The majory of them being young, nobody seemed to observe the rules so meticulously, the only exception being a few upper caste Hindu widows who voluntarily accepted the customary rules. On further scrutiny, it was revealed that these women belonged to orthodox priestly families. Generally, no parents would like to see their widowed daughters clad in white dress, taking strict vegetarian food, going out bare foot, and spending time in religious rituals. Relaxation was also apparent in the participation of widowed daughters in wedding ceremonies, and village festivals as other women members in the family. In short widowed daughters in rural Purulia seemed to face minimum cirrisis in life due to widowhood.

From the parental side, however, the presence of a childless young, widowed daughter in the family may not always be a happy situation. Because economic pressure apart, they are constantly worried about protecting these women from moral degradation. As in many other parts of rural India, young widows from weaker communities are also liable to be easy prey for sexuall exploitation in this part of rural Bengal. Poverty and hunger compel many families to send their women folk to work as domestic maids, attached laborers, and cowherds in the houses of wealthy peasants, money lenders and grocers. It is this section of village population who usually exploit the weaker people along with their womenfolk. This being the condition, it is no wonder that the parents or for that matter, every head of households having young widows would be constantly worried.

We mentioned earlier that the occurrence of widows as second subcategory of adhesion was very low in the rural households of Purulia. This may be due to the fact that people usually do not feel like living permanently in their daughter's family, possibly apprehending that presence of affinal relatives can generate tension. But in exigencies such as for instance, if a daughter seeks maternal help during childbirth, ailment, or when she is away for wage-employment outside the home, her mother can go to her place. Under other life-situations also, deviations can take place. For instance, we noticed eight widows who opted for living at daughter's place because they

Table 6
Percentage Distribution of Widows by their Relationships with Heads of Families and Age-Groups

Widow's Relationships with Heads of Families	*Age-group of Widows (years)*					
	< 24	*25-34*	*35-44*	*45-54*	*> 55*	*Total*
Mother		0.19	12.96	24.63	62.63	100.00 (540)
Self	0.98	8.82	26.47	31.37	32.26	100.00 (204)
Sister, daughter	8.70	58.70	16.67	9.42	6.71	100.00 (138)
Father's sister				25.00	75.00	100.00 (12)
Father's mother					100.00	100.00 (6)
Son's wife	9.09	54.55	27.27	9.09		100.00 (11)
Brother's wife, Father's brother's Wife, Brother's son's wife		20.69	24.14	13.79	41.38	100.00 (29)
Wife's mother, Wife's sister, Mother's mother, Mother's brother's wife, Mother's sister, Daughter's daughter	1.92	3.85	7.69	17.31	69.43	100.00 (52)
Total	1.61	11.49	16.23	22.88	47.79	100.00 (992)

did not have any others to depend upon. In four cases, it was not the wife's mother but the sons-in-law who settled permanently at the instance of their in-laws for supervising the family farm. In all cases, however, these widows were quite aged and economically very poor.

From the foregoing account, it is evident that the conditions of widows in rural Purulia differ markedly in terms of their mode of existence and kinship position in the family. Of the various categories of widows, only those functioning as heads of mother-children families, living as destitutes in single-member households, and widowed sisters who appeared to be greatly distressed due to bereavement crisis numerically accounted for about one-fifth of the total suggesting thereby that an overwhelming majority was not deprived of minimum comfort and bare necessities of life in their respective places of existence. Being related to the family as primary kin-members, most of these widows tended to have minimum crisis in role performance. Widows belonging to ritually lower categories and other religious affiliations appeared to be least affected by widowhood disabilities possibly due to their unrestricted participation in labor-force and that may be the reason why they could enjoy a relatively higher familial position than their counterparts from the upper caste Hindu and Muslim families.

AGE COMPOSITION OF WIDOWS

The average age of widows was 51.76 years. Though a slightly higher average age was apparent among the widows belonging to the Hindu high castes (54.02) compared to those of other societal groups, the difference appeared to be negligible. Since a little over 70 percent of the widows were beyond the age-group of 55-44 years, it seemed quite possible that these widows suffered less from gender-role crisis. These were 13.11 percent widows who remained under their peak reproductive period of 34 years or less while the production of those in the late reproductive period i.e., 35-44 years was 16.23 percent.

Even though the majority of widows were seen to have crossed their reproductive life, it may be interesting to know who among the rest suffered most from sexual deprivation. For exploring this, we examined the kinship positions of widows against their ages. Table 6 summarizes the result. As expected, the table shows that widows who were related with the heads of households as sisters, daughters and son's wives seemed to be the worst sufferers from sex crisis as the dominant majority belonged to the age groups of 35-44 years or less. Those belonging to the heads' preceding generations namely, mothers, father's mothers, father's sisters, wife's mothers, mother's mother and so on obviously posed no concern to society for gender role-crisis. But this might be quite apparent in the case of the relatively younger widows who existed in the families either as surviving mothers or as heads' sisters, daughters, son's wives and so on. It was revealed further from the analysis of family composition that the latter widows were mostly childless suggesting thereby that they could not possibly have experienced their married life long.

In the backdrop of preceding discussions, it is clear that while a majority of the widowed women were insured more or less under family coverage and suffered less agony from bereavement crisis there were some upon whom widowhood seemed to have imposed a status of death in life.

OCCUPATION OF WIDOWS

The proportion of widows at work appeared to be very low in rural Purulia as only 35.23 percent of them had some form of economic activities either as wage-earners or as self-employed persons. This low incidence of widow workers may be due to limited opportunities available to them for economic activities. Lack of formal education as revealed from the survey, also seems to be a factor for this. Since a large segment of the widows interviewed fall in the age-group of 55 and above and had adult children to look after them, they possibly felt very little urge for supplementing the family income by working outside. As the opportunities of widows at work varied considerably in terms of caste and community affiliation of widows, it is equally possible that cultural factor is also responsible for permitting or prohibiting some widows to

Table 7
Proportional Distribution of Widow-Workers by Nature of Occupation and Caste/Community

Nature of Occupation Followed by Widows	*Caste/Community*						
	Hindu						
	High	*Middle*	*Low*	*Total*	*Tribal*	*Muslim*	*Total*
Agricultural labor	1.97	10.20	45.52	18.80	34.88	3.40	20.67
Cultivation	1.97	1.97	0.39	1.44	0.58		1.21
Domestic maid	2.46	0.99	4.33	2.49		1.69	2.02
Paddy husking or making puffed-rice	7.40	5.92	2.36	5.13	0.58	5.08	4.33
Basketry or making leaf-cups		1.97	1.97	1.45	7.55		2.42
Collection of cowdung, wood or coal	0.49	2.30	1.97	1.71	2.91		1.81
Rearing of poultry birds	0.49		0.39	0.26	2.33		0.60
Fish-selling			5.91	1.97			1.51
Cook, midwifery, sewing or pot-making	1.97	0.66	0.39	0.92			0.71
Total	16.75	24.01	60.23	34.17	48.83	10.17	35.28

undertake economic activities. The distribution of widow-workers in terms of their nature of occupations and caste community clearly suggests the pattern. It is seen from Table 7 that the proportions of widows at work are distinctly low among the Hindu high and middle castes and the Muslims while these are quite high among the Hindu low castes and the tribals. Unless otherwise constrained, and with the exception of the Sarak who encourage women's participation in certain types of agricultural work like transplanting, reaping, threshing, husking etc., and allow them to work as wage-earners, most of the high and middle caste Hindus on the other hand consider it a taboo possibly because of social custom and family prestige. That the Muslim widows seem to be averse to employment can be borne out by the fact that only 10.17 percent of them were found to be working either as paddy-husker, food-processor (i.e., making puffed or flattened-rice) or as agricultural laborer. It was learnt that Muslim widows who are brought up under different types of socialization are strongly influenced by their own culture which permits or prohibits them from under-taking certain activities. While employment of women outside the home is taken to be a taboo, employment for wages under the male-earners is something which is totally tabooed not only among the Muslim but also among the Brahmin, Kayastha, Baidya and other castes belonging to the Hindu middle group.

There seem to be no such cultural restrictions among the Bauri, Kora Mudi, Sunri, Kaibarta, and similar other low castes and the tribal to the participation of widows in gainfull occupantions. Poverty apart, every adult woman belonging to these people tends to take part in economic activities,in the status of a casual, seasonal or attached laborer. We found that the Ghunia widows supplemented their family income by selling fish in the nearby urban centers while the tribal widows, through basketry or selling forest products. The widows belonging to the Hindu high and middle categories and to the Muslim group seem to prefer such occupations which involve less movement outside the village such as paddy husking, food processing, cooking, domestic maid, sewing, etc. suggesting perhaps that they are more dependent on the village and household economy than those belonging to the Hindu low caste and the Muslim category.

Economically, therefore, the status of widows belonging to the Hindu low caste, the tribal and the Muslim community appeared to be relatively higher than the widows of other categories.

SUMMARY AND CONCLUSION

Throughout the preceding sections, we have tried to describe the widowhood phenomenon in terms of its temporal and social structural variation with reference to some select areas in rural Purulia, and economically backward district in West Bengal. We have also shown how the consequences of the death of husband are related with one another and influence the living conditions and status of widows.

The study began with an analysis of the locational and temporal variations in widowhood. It revealed that compared to the state of West Bengal as a whole, the Purulia district registered consistently a higher ratio and a fluctuating trend of widowhood over the last three census decades. This may be indicative of the fact that Purulia is passing through a transitional phase before attaining any concrete shape in its widowhood pattern. From the consistently lower incidence of widowhood in its urban location since 1961 it tends to suggest that with the betterment of living conditions and improvement in the health and hygienic conditions of the people in rural Purulia, the ratio of widowhood among the female population would show a sign of decline in near future.

At present, however, one in every third household had a female widow and the proportion of widows per 1,000 female population was found to be 130 which is much higher than the state's figure of 95. but not all people tended to share the burden of widowhood equally as there is a significant variation in this regard by religion and caste. The Hindu households, for instance, have been clearly distinguished from the rest as having the highest ratio of widowhood and having the largest volume of widows possibly due to widow-remarriage being less pronounced among them. The restriction against widow-remarriage being absent among the tribal and the Muslim, and the instance of subsequent marriage more, the frequency of widows per household and the ratio of widowhood are quite low among them.

Again within the Hindu religious group, the relative incidence of widowhood is maximum among those belonging to the high and middle castes who happened to be the propagator and the preserver of the Sanskritic tradition. Widowhood as a way of life has all through been considered to be the ideal for their widows banning therefore practice of widow remarriage. Among the Hindu low castes no such ideals seem to prevail and since their women are relatively free to work to supplement the family income, it is for this economic advantage also, widowers get an incentive to marry a widow (Dubey 1965). The Muslim women, however, are forbidden to work outside home but even then the widows can expect to have a second marriage because of their ownership of property rights.

Widowhood tends to be weakly associated with class or economic position of a household. Even then, there is an indication that the rural proletariat class, comprised mainly by the mendicants, landless or near landless laborers and poor peasant, registers a higher ratio of widowhood than those which are relatively well-off. This may lead us to believe that different classes or at least those who are poor and not so poor, have different chances of survival which, in their turn could have resulted in differential male mortality among them. Or, could it be that it is not the class but the culture which has regulated the extent of widowhood among the people of rural Purulia? For, it was noticed while examining the relationships between the incidence of widowhood and caste/community after controlling the class that certain castes remained consistently on the top irrespective of their class affiliation with regard to the possession of widows, while others behaved on the contrary.

In terms of education also, widowhood showed a little difference between the educated or non-educated sections. But a slight indication is there which tends to suggest that compared to the educated section, the illiterate or semi-literate section of rural Purulia possess more widows.

There seems to be very little problem centering round the widowhood in rural Purulia especially in regard to the care and maintenance of widows. For as many as 10 percent of the widows lived in extended families under the headship of adult males. The occurrence of such a high proportion of widows in extended families seems to be not the exclusive feature of rural Purulia as similar pattern has also been noted in other parts of India, for instance, in rural Rajasthan (Bose and Sen 1965) and at Varanasi in Uttar Pradesh (Saraswati 1985). Most of these widows, however, were quite old and dissociated with any economic pursuits and, hence, largely depended on their own children, borhters, and other relatives for sustenance. While this may be indicative of the unrestricted attachment of the rural people towards old-age values, at the some time it clears out the apprehension that our widows would gradually be left uncared for. To be widowed may be to be twice-stricken, both by grief and by loneliness in other civilizations, but in India, particularly in its rural section, widowhood seldom generates loneliness because of informal nature of social relations imbued with traditional values.

One of the reasons why widowhood as a district problem has not emerged in the rural Purulia may be that very few households do suffer the crisis which normally follow bereavement. Most of the widows interviewed were attached to the families as stock-members, i.e., those who were supposed to live in them as per patri-virilocal norm of residence. Among them, widows as mother comprised the majority followed by father's mother, son's wife, brother's wife and so on. Widows grafted to the families as adhesion were there but in a small proportion compared to the former. These widows comprised sister, daughter and such other members who were related to the women members of the family like mother's mother, mother's sister, wife's mother, wife's sister and so on. The existence of relatively less number of affinally related female widows tends to suggest that people generally do not approve of living permanently in daughter's or sister's house because of social taboo.

As in other societies, widows having separate households with minor children in rural Purulia, too, seemed to be the worst hit by bereavement crisis. Numerically, they accounted for about 13 percent of the total and were mostly young women. As surviving mothers they had to bear the dual responsibility of home making and child-care in addition to performing the role of a father while facing severe economic crisis. As in the case of young widows from North America (Lindsay 1977) or from East London (Marris 1958) these women in rural Purulia also tended to lead an isolated life owing to their self-withdrawal and apathy which might have arisen out of bereavement. Widowhood has not only put them under severe mental stress but also made them economically unstable. For many of these women reported to have no regular income of their own and those who had some, earned less because a women cannot earn a man's wage. However independent they seemed to be, they were found to be the target of social exploitation and oppression in rural Purulia.

Destitution resulting from widowhood does not seem to occur much in rural Purulia as there were only 7 percent widows who lived alone in single member households. Their role state of existence was mainly due to practical needs which arose for looking after the home and husbands property while their sons were out for work elsewhere. However, there were some who could not adjust themselves with the member of husbands' family after the severance of the marital ties. These widows were mostly old women and being so, the consequences of widowhood in their present life seemed to have been confused with those of age and infirmity.

Women who were married out once but returned to the natal families after being widowed were also found to be relatively young and mostly childless. It was learnt that they could not live in their husband's family because of uncongenial and strained relations there. This tends to indicate that a childless woman rarely gets adjusted in her husband's family when he is dead and comes closer to her parental family than to her husband's.

The status of widows tends to be different from one position to another. A widow sister, for instance, is quite likely to have an inferior status in her brother's family because she is often treated as an outsider. The inter-personal relationships between a widowed sister and other members of the family seem to be not so congenial in many families possibly due to personality clash. In the Hindu high and some middle caste families, the young widowed sisters tend to suffer greater hardships and severe family oppression because of their helpless position. Since there is always something in misfortune-a sense of being pitied or patronized (marries 1958:126), it is possible that this type of widows are endowed with a sense of inferiority complex when they lose their husbands and become dependent on others.

Barring grief and its other related consequences that follow bereavement, the widows in general and younger ones particular from the Hindu low caste and tribal families seem to be relatively free from the crisis of loss of status. They enjoy greater mobility and less family oppression because widowhood has not put them under any restriction. Perhaps, hunger is more powerful than grief and mourning and compels many a widow of this section to resume her normal life soon.

Just as deadwood wears out with time so do rituals, but forced change never lasts. Much has been shed in widowhood rituals even in this rural area of Purulia. The social attitudes towards the widows are also undergoing a change due to mass communication and advancement of learning. But even then the ideals of widowhood that are so deep-rooted in the Hindu culture seem still to be active in the minds of Indian women. The recent Roop kanwar incident in Rajasthan which upheld the Sati ideals is only a pointer to this.

ACKNOWLEDGEMENT

The author is grateful to Professor Donald von-Eschen of the Department of Sociology, McGill University, Canada and his colleagues, Dr. Suraj Bandyopadhyay and Mr.Kumarananda Chattopadhyay for their valued comments and suggestions on an earlier version of the paper. Particular thanks are due to

Mr.Debashish Bhattacharya who assisted in the collection of field-data and rendered technical assistance. Sincere thanks are also due to Mr.L.Ramchandra Bhattaru and Mr.Asit Banerjee of Purulia for their help and assistance during the field-work. For secretarial assistance, the author expresses his thanks to Mr.Narayan Ch.Saha and Mr.Ramendra Nath Biswas of the Sociological Research Unit, Indian Statistical Institute, Calcutta.

NOTES

1. That the problem is gradually becoming apparent can be evident from the various articles that are being published in the dailies and regional magazines all over India which deal mainly with the miserable life led by the widows. In an article by Ms.Bolan Gangopadhyay in the Ananda Bazar Patrika (dated 27 March 1988), it has been stressed as to how the particular value-orientation of the Hindu widows towards upkeeping the widowhood ideals made them socially isolated from the mainstream of life, and unless they come out of the bondage of tradition in order to change their status from widow to woman, their sufferings and exploitation will continue to remain as before. The article raised so much sensation that many people, mostly women, congratulated the author for her thought-provoking article.
2. The list of castes and communities included under each category of Hindu households is given below with the number of households in parentheses. Hindu high caste: Mahato (331), Kumbhakar (121), Teli (70), Swarnakar (67), Tanti (52), Baisnab (46), Karmakar (43), Bene (39), Rajput Kshatriya (37), Napit (35), Modak (9), Koiri (8), Sutradhar (7), Baishya (6), Barui (1), and Mahishya (1); Hindu low caste: Bauri (436), Ghunia/Kaibarta (160), Mal (70), Sunri (62), Dom (60), Dhopa (43), Koramudi (26), Sahis (26), Harijan (23), Muchi (8), Bagdi (3), Bhagat (1), Namasudra (1) and Pasi (1).
3. Initially, the households were classified into 11 class categories: (1) Landless agricultural laborer (969), (2)

Factory Laborer (174), (3) Owner-tenant (163), (4) Marginal peasant (241), (5)Small peasant (527), (6) Middle and rich peasant (310), (7) Petty trader (120), (8)White-collar job (144), (9) Other salaried job (144), (10) Artisan (164) and unproductive dependent (41).

4. Out of 992 widows surveyed, only 12 had some formal education: 7 read upto the level of primary, 4 continued upto the secondary level and the remaining solitary widow, whom we found at Bero as an immigrant teacher, reported to have passed the Intermediate examination.

REFERENCES

Bosc, A.B. and M.L.A. Sen (1966), Some Characteristics of the Widows in Rural Society. Man in India, 46: 226-232.

Census of India

1961 Vol. XVI: West Bengal and Sikkim Part-IIC (1): Social and Cultural Tables, Table, C-II, Pages 32-33, 68-69.

1971 Series 22, West Bengal Part IIC: Social and Cultural Tables, Table C-II, Pages 64-65, 102, 133.

1981 Series 23, West Bengal, Part IVA: Social and Cultural Tables. Table-C-I, Pages 50-53, 92-95, Delhi: Controller of Publications.

Chakrabarti, Prafulla (1984), Impact of Rural Development on Some Aspects of Village Life: Report of a Pilot Study in a Multi-ethnic Village in Purulia. (Mimeo) Calcutta: Sociological Research Unit, Indian Statistical Institute.

Chakraborty, Usha (1962), Condition of Bengali Women Around the 2nd Half of the 19th Century. Calcutta: Firma K.L. Mukhopadhyay.

Clayton, P.,J.A. Halikas and W.L. Maurice (1972), The Depression of Widowhood, British, Journal of Psychiatry 120: 71-77.

Dubey, Bhagwant R. (1965), Widow Re-marriage in Madhya Pradesh, Man in India 45:50-56.

Dutta, J.M. (1956), Is Enforced Widowhood the Only Cause of the Slower Growth of the Bengali Hindus? Man in India 36:272-77.

Ghurye, G.S. (1936), Marriage and Widowhood in India: A Study of a Middle Class Sample of 3400 marriages, Marriage Hygiene, 2:258-270.

Glassner, Barry (1980), Role Loss and Manic Depression, in Helenaz Lopata (ed) Research in the Interweave of Social Roles: Women and Men, Vol.1. PP. 265-282. Greenwich: Aijai Press.

Goode, William J

1963 World Revolution and Family Patterns. Glencoe: The Free Press.

1964 The Family. New Jersey: Prentice-Hall.

Hill, Polly (1982), rming Families. Cambridge: Cambridge University Press.

Kacker, Murlidhar (1930), Hindu Shastras on Marriage of Widows. Allahabad.

Kamat, A.K. (1963), The Decline in Death Rate and Its Effect on the Extent of Widowhood Sociological Bulletin. 12:18-31.

Kane, P.V. (1941), History of Dharmashastra. Vol. 2, Part I, Pages 583-607, Poona: Bhandarkar Oriental Research Institute.

Lancelot, Wilkinson (1841), Introduction to an Essay on the Second Marriage of Widows, by a Learned Brahmin of Nagpore. Sehore.

Lindsay, Rae (1977), Alone and Surviving: A Guide for Today's Widows. New York: Walker and Co.

Lopata, Helena Z. (1973), Widowhood in an American City. Cambridge Mass.: Schenkmaun.

Malakar, Chitta Ranjan (1981), Evaluation of Widowhood Data in Indian Censuscs A Life Table Investigation. Genus 37: 165-177.

Marris, Peter (1958), Widows and Their Families. London: Routledge and kegan Paul.

Mukherjec, R (1977), West Bengal Family Structures: 1946-66. New Delhi: Macmillan and Company.

Narain, Dhirendra (1975), Family Disorganization in India. In Dhirendra Narain (ed), Explorations in the Family and Other Essays. PP. 81-106. Bombay: Thacker&Co.Ltd.

Pakrashi, Kanti (1966), A Study on Widowhood in India, 1951. Bulletin of the Cultural Research Institute. 5: 67-74.

Powdermaker, H. (1977), Copper Town: Changing Africa New York: Harper and Row.

Reed, Angela (1973), The Challenge of Second Marriage. London: The Plume Press Limited.

Risley, H.H. (1891), Tribes and Castes of Bengal, Vol.2, Calcutta: Bengal Secretariat Press.

Ruzicka, Lado T (1984), Mortality in India: Past Trends and Future Prospects, in Tim Dyson and Nigel Cook (eds) India's Demopraphy: Essay on the Contemporary Population. PP. 13-26. New Delhi: South Asian Publishers Pvt.Ltd.

Saraswati. Baidya Nath (1985), The Kashivasi Widows, Man in India. 65: 107-120.

Schoenberg, Bernard, Irwin Gerber, Alfred Wiener, Austin H Kutcher, David Peretz and Arther C Carr (1975), Bereavement: Its Psychological Aspects. Columbia University Press.

Subramanyam, M. (1909), The Tonsure of Hindu Widows Madras: G.A. Natesan & Co.

Vidyasagar, Iswar Chandra (1881), Marriage of Hindu Widows. Calcutta: Sanskrit Press.

6

WOMEN JOURNALISTS IN THE PRINT MEDIA OF BANGLADESH AND THEIR PROFESSIONAL CHALLENGES

Pradip Kumar Panday

INTRODUCTION

Women are the victims of all types of discrimination in all parts of the world. They are also deprived of their right to education, diet, health and so on. In Bangladesh, women constitute almost half of the total population but the status of women is deplorable. The equal right of women in all spheres of life is ensured in the Constitution of Bangladesh. However, women are being discriminated in employment, payment of emoluments, right to inheritance, marriage and divorce laws etc. In Bangladesh the scenario has improved significantly during the past two decades. The enrolment of girls in the Primary Schools is increasing. For more than one decade, the Prime Minister and the Leader of the Opposition are women. Women have been working in the Cabinet, Judges of The Supreme Court, Teaching Staffs in the Universities and Colleges as well as in public and private sectors. This picture depicts the sunny side of women of Bangladesh. But there is also a steamy side in this picture in reality. In the male-dominated society of Bangladesh women are still being subjected to all kinds of indignities and repression. Most of the women living in the countryside are not conscious about their rights, status and responsibilities and they are coming mostly from disadvantaged section of society and they become the victims of oppression, physical torture and harassment. It has been observed that the status of Women Journalists in Bangladesh is not satisfactory.

Although women participation in journalism is increasing globally, but they have not gained much parity with men. Top management is still largely male dominated although a few women hold senior positions in media organizations. In some of the countries like South Korea and Cambodia, women's participation in media institutions is gradually deteriorating. Stereotyped attitudes, sexual harassment, salary differences, unfair treatment in assignments and promotions, traditional gender hierarchies, lack of support mechanisms for working women and low education are the main impediments for the participation of women in journalism (Khan 2004:12).

It should be mentioned that the women enrolment and achievements at the educational institutions are improving in different dimensions. They are also proving their qualities in different job sectors in developed countries like the USA, UK, Canada etc. Moreover, women are doing exceptionally well as journalists in the Western media. Particularly in the age of electronic mail, worldwide web and fax, they can contribute to journalism as journalists of newspapers with their immense energy and talent. But the past experience shows that the status of Women Journalists in Bangladesh is not satisfactory. The main focus of this paper is to examine the extent of devaluation of Women Journalists in newspapers in connection with wage and salary, access to information and employment and gender discrimination.

TREND OF PARTICIPATION OF WOMEN JOURNALISTS

Those who engaged with the process of news collection, news making and news presentation, are called journalist. In most of the time the profession of journalism is risky and dangerous. The male journalists always assume that they have the skill and capacity to overcome the risk behind the profession. On the other hand the idea of female journalists do not consider this profession as their own. Consequently, they show their less interest in this profession. Although women journalists are found in seminars, conferences and in investigative reporting, but the number is not quite satisfactory. This section deals with the trends of participation of Women in Journalism in Bangladesh.

The age of Bangla Newspapers in this sub-continent (the newspapers that are published in the country's national language) are not more than two hundred years. The first newspaper was introduced in 1780 under the initiative of Marsman (Razi, 2003:9). Women issue was focused in 'Sambad Koumodi' and 'Bangodutt' both were published by Raja Rammohan Roy (Ibid). These two newspapers played an important role in shaping public opinion in favour of women.

The 'Anadabazar' and the 'Azad' were published in 1878 and 1936 respectively from Kolkata. These two newspapers were prominent during that time in the unseparated Bengal. During mid 50's. 'the Sangbad' and 'The Ittefaq' were published from Dhaka. These four newspapers played an important role in the development of Bangla newspaper. Up to 1971, about ten daily Bangla newspapers were published. The expansion of publication of newspapers increased rapidly in early 1980's. This increasing rate of publication of newspaper is associated with the application of computer (Razi 2003:8).

On the other hand, women's participation in newspapers began in 1870 in this subcontinent (Razi, 2003:9). Henceforth, many women personalities have been trying their best to raise the female cause in the media almost on a regular basis. Still women participation in the existing Bangladeshi newspapers as journalists, editors, reporters and writers, are very insignificant. 'Bangobani' was the first bi-weekly newspaper that was edited by a woman. After that 'Anathini' was published in 1875. The 'Begum' was the first weekly newspaper that was published under the editorship of Nurzahan Begun in 1947. In 1949, weekly 'Sultana' was published. It was edited by Begum Sufia Kamal and Jahanara Arju. Before 1950s' women were engaged in editing magazines. But after that women were engaged in sub-editing and reporting. In 50s', Laila Samad and Mafruha Chowdhury were engaged in reporting in 'Sangbad' and 'Millat' respectively. They both were part time reporters. In 60s' Hasina Asraf, Nishat Sadani and Baby Moudud were engaged in reporting. Besides these, Nargis Rafique and Shirin Shahida were in reporting in 'The Purbodesh' and 'The people' respectively. During this period, there were 150 journalists working in the newspaper industry in the country. Among them only four percent were women. This scenario of women participation in newspapers is insignificant in number (Razi 2003:9-10).

Although the number of newspapers in Bangladesh expanded rapidly during 80's and 90's, the number of women journalists did not expand as well. In an article entitled "Reporting: Why are Women not Coming?" Baby Moudud reported that there was only one woman journalist in the newspapers of Bangladesh in 1970. In 1972, the number increased from one to two. In 1990 the number was also confined within only two (Moudud, 1990). According to a report published in 1996, among 1500 journalists working in Dhaka-based Bangla and English newspapers, the number of women journalists were sixty. It was below 4 percent among the journalists working in the newspapers in Bangladesh (Ahmed 1998:7-8).

STATUS OF WOMEN JOURNALISTS

The women in Bangladesh are victims of gender discrimination in every sphere of their life cycle. They are identified by kinship relations rather than individual. For example, the girl is identified as a daughter of a father during childhood, a wife is identified by husband in her adulthood and the mother is identified by her children in her old age. The women are satisfied with less of everything, which may be food, education, health care etc. The women devalued in terms of their gender identity in every aspect in the patriarchal social system.

In his article (Hossain 1998:33), "What does Prevent Bangladeshi Women from Journalism?" published in 'Women and Media' issue of Bangladesh Journalism Review (BJR), (August, 1998, Vol.2, No.2), Farid Hossain, The Associated Press (AP) representative in Dhaka , Bangladesh stated "In Bangladesh women journalists are as few as stars on a cloudy night. They can be head-counted. Among more than 470 members of the National Press Club only about 15 are women. If this is not enough to show the disparity then have a glance at the list of members of Reporters' Unity, an exclusive club of Dhaka city based reporters. Their recently published members' telephone directory reveals only three women among 366 reporters. True, there are some women working at newspapers and news agencies in Dhaka and elsewhere in country. But almost all of them are on the soft side of the industry. The women work mostly as sub-editors at desks or look after the specialized feature sections of the newspapers. Some of them have their eyes on other jobs. They leave journalism as soon as better job offers come. Back in 1988, I was involved in hiring journalist for news agency that was about to be launched. A good number of women university graduates applied to join the news organization. At least six of the women were recruited. Given a choice none of them, however, had opted to become reporters. They preferred deskwork to reporting. A decade later none of the women is in the profession. Two of them got married and were happy to become housewives. One left journalism to be a banker. Another took an airline job and never returned to journalism" (Hossain 1998:33).

Although the situation has been changing very slowly, this is the real scenario of women journalists in the newspapers. Bangladesh Centre for Development Journalism and Communication (BCDJC) conducted a survey during 1997-98 under their "Women in Journalism" programme. Their survey findings show the appropriate picture of women working in the print media in Bangladesh. They surveyed 20 daily newspapers, three periodicals and five news agencies[1] (Khan 2004: 8). The following picture depicts the actual figure of women in the newspapers of Bangladesh.

It has been found in this survey that there were only 7 percent women employees in the news organizations and just about 4 percent were reporters. Among the women Reporters, highest 17 percent were feature writers, 13 percent in subbing, 6 percent in editing and only 2 percent in reporting. They found only one women press photographer in Dhaka among those leading news organizations. The gender ration is far beyond imagination.

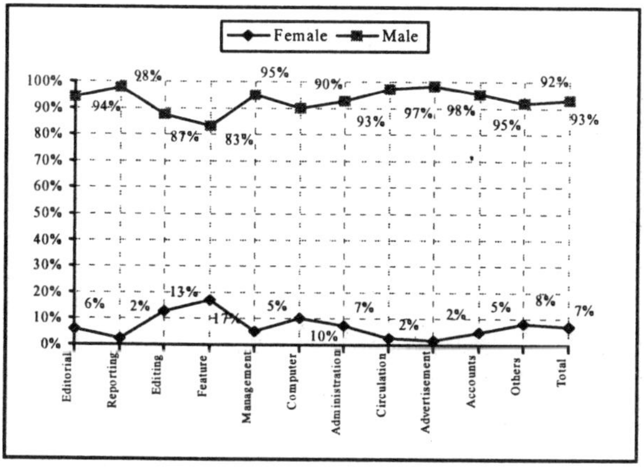

Graph 1: Percentage of Women Journalists in the Newspaper Industry of Bangladesh
(Khan 2004:8)

A survey conducted by Mass Line Media Centre (MMC) in November 2000 on "What is the Realities of the Condition and Position of Women Journalists in Newspapers" surveyed nine districts of costal zone of the country. They found only one woman journalist in Laxmipur, Feni and Noakhali districts and found six others in Barisal, Jalkhathi, Pautakhali, Pirozpur, Borguna and Bhola districts (Ferdous, 2001:11).

Most of the women graduating in Journalism from three universities (Dhaka, Rajshahi and Chittagong) of the country have not pursued it as a profession. According to statistics released by Dhaka University, of the 838 students who obtained degrees from its Mass Communication and Journalism Department from 1990 to 1999, 227 were women (more than one in four). Chittagong University, which is one of the three public universities offering a journalism degree, has seen its women's enrollment steadily increased since its inception in 1995. During the first academic year, three students were women and that number increased to ten in 2003-04 session. The same is also true for University of Rajshahi where women's enrollment has increased since its founding in 1992. During the session 1991-92, the number of women students was seven and it increased to 18 in 2004-05 session.

However, even for these graduates, few had enrolled in journalism to become reporters. In Dhaka, there are 116 daily, 370 weekly, 129 fortnightly and 270 monthly newspapers. Out of 4 percent of journalists who were women (Ahmed, 1998:7), there were almost none working as reporters. As indicated in another survey (Kabir 1998:18), 85 percent of the working women journalists are assistant editors, ten percent recruited as reporters and the rest worked in the editorial department. Similar result were reported in a survey by the Press Institute of Bangladesh (PIB) in Dhaka which revealed that of the 120 women working on 86 Bangladeshi Newspapers, 62 work as Editors, but only ten (eight percent of the total) work as Reporters. In Chittagong there are 3 women sub-editors working at daily newspapers (Chepesiuk 2004:5). But There is no sub-editor working at daily newspapers published from Rajshahi. Nowadays a few women are getting interested to come to journalism profession (interview with the editors of four daily newspapers published from Rajshahi).

A report entitled "In Bangladesh, women are not encouraged to take up journalism as career" published by a news agency named 'News Network' stated that according to DFP, there were 397 daily, 752 weekly, 346 monthly and 45 quarterly newspapers in 2001 in the country. But excluding the apprentices, among the staffs of these newspapers, only 6 percent were women. In this report it was remarked that "The figures indicate the number of newspapers and magazines is rising in the country. But the number of participation of women in newspapers is not rising at the same pace (Sadia 2001).

PROFESSIONAL CHALLENGES

A report by UNESCO addressing gender discrimination in media employment in more than 40 countries shows that in the Asian countries studied, the percentage of women employed in the media is among the lowest in the world. With women comprising only eight percent of employees in the media, Japan has the lowest proportion of all countries included in the report. In India, women do not fare much better, constituting only 12 percent of the workforce in media organizations. Even for those women who do hold positions in the news media, the situation is not always favourable. The 1996 IWMF (International Women's Media Foundation) report 'Women in the Media: Facing Obstacles ....Changing Attitudes' with data from women journalists in 40 countries, shows that 93 percent of the respondents felt that they encountered obstacles in their career development that their male counterparts did not. Balancing family obligation with work responsibilities and different types of discrimination were the most commonly cited challenges (Johnson 1996). Women journalists of Bangladesh are not the exception in the circumstances. They have been facing the following professional challenges in their working place.

SOCIETAL PROBLEM

Bangladesh is the world's eighth largest country with a population about 141 million (BBS 2004). Educated Bangladeshis invariably describe their nation as a 'Liberal Muslim Country'. Bangladesh is one of the few countries in the Islamic World with a free press, and its contribution is not written specifically according to the strict tenants of Islamic law. However, Bangladesh's culture is conservative, especially in its attitude towards the role of women within the home and society. Women are primarily expected to be wives and mothers engaged in undervalued work like reproducing and rearing children and caring the elderly, cooking, cleaning and looking after the household. Otherwise, they are expected to work in areas considered suitable for women: in the agricultural sector, this includes sowing, plantation, husking, reaping etc. and in the non-agricultural sector, teaching, sewing, knitting, crafts and embroidery etc. But, as Bhattacharya points out, it is in the non-traditional sector of manufacturing that women may expect changes in the sexual division of labour, higher incomes and a concomitant change in social attitudes (Bhattacharya 1994:13-14).

The subordination of the majority of women in Bangladesh is illustrated by the attitudes of men derived from socially and culturally determined concepts of gender roles which prevent women from becoming self-reliant, for example, observance of seclusion reduces female mobility and the scope for full participation in national life, such as in education and employment; hence it enhances dependence. Most men, in professions like journalism, consider women inferior. Women's work is undervalued both in terms of pay and status (Nahid, 1994:319-21).

To women the job of a journalist is hazardous, especially in Bangladesh. It involves outdoor assignments covering such topics as political riots, natural disasters (such as cyclones and floods) and gunfights etc. In addition, working at odd hours is one of the factors that discourages women from taking journalism as a career. If a woman is put on the night shift that lasts until the wee hours, she would feel uncomfortable. A woman working even in the early hours of the night requires a male escort to return home, even if the employer provides her with transport. This puts her at a clear disadvantages vis-à-vis man, as she is seen as a liability to her company. The case of Bulbul can be sited here:

Aroza Bulbul worked as a reporter for Press Institute of Bangladesh (PIB), Dhaka, Bangladesh before joining the Communication and Journalism Department of Chittagong University in 2002 as a Lecturer. She says that while Bangladeshi women are entering professions like law, nursing, social work and teaching in increasingly larger numbers, journalism still remains an unacceptable career choice for many families. Bulbul concedes that she would not want her daughter to follow in her career path. She also explains candidly that she would want her daughter to work in a profession that had regular hours and where security is not an issue" (Chepesiuk, 2004:5).

BALANCING WORK AND FAMILY

Balancing work and family is a major obstacle for women journalists. In the society, the responsibility of taking care of children still rests solely with women. In order to delegate more time for home, women often pass up the 'essential extras' – working long hours, networking with colleagues, and participating in after-hours training, in which (like their male counterparts) they need to participate to advance in their careers. Eventually, this places them at a disadvantage in competing for the best jobs and the best assignments. When they do attempt to take advantage of more professional opportunities, the repercussions on their other priorities cause further stain on their work, resulting in tension that can have a profound impact on women's careers, their families, and the companies for which they work. A case of Shabiha and Nilufar can be sited:

Both Shabiha Shobnom and Nilufar Yeasmin were interested to take up journalism as their profession after the completion of their Master's degree from Mass Communication Department of the University of Rajshahi. But, like many female students they discarded the idea of being journalists in consideration of their families' disapproval. They both said that reporting the lively part of journalism needs a vast tract of mobility, to mingle with various types of people and no specific time of working that their conservative society did not permit to women to do so. They also said that their conservative society still discourages women to go out at night, as it is not safe at all for them, it did not even think that women might work at night. The dual role of women's in home and office is really hard to carry together (Interview with them by the writer).

DISCRIMINATION

Simply stated, discrimination is still a common feature in the newspapers of Bangladesh. The following categories indicate a perception of being denied the same benefits and opportunities for women journalists in Bangladesh.

(a) *Salary:* Salary is a problem to become a journalist of a newspaper of the country. The pay packet for an experienced journalist in Bangladesh is not a very attractive deal. However, many women are often forced to accept lower wages out of necessity or as a survival tactic in hard competition. Furthermore, most of the newspapers are not regular in paying salary to the journalists. But this is not the case in other sectors of the country.

(b) *Access to Information:* Women journalists are frequently denied access to information in the workplace. Against the usual mentorship between men, the lack of women's alliances and networking groups remarkably limit the kind of critical information for stories, assignments and special opportunities to which women in the newspapers have access. Ultimately, all these produce a negative effect on women's careers.

(c) *Access to Jobs:* Being denied access to job is another form of discrimination. Internationally, women hold an average of between 20 and 24 percent of all editorial positions in the news media (Uritus and Rockey, 1998:68). Whereas, in Bangladesh women holds only 8 percent and more likely women are to be found in as sub-editors rather than reporters, anchors and technicians or in management. Sometimes, despite there areas of expertise and interests, their skills are not put to use: too often women are assigned to covering 'soft topics' such as fashion and entertainment, instead of the more challenging news issues in science, technology, politics, and business. It is their male colleagues who cover the most visible, controversial and newsworthy stories. A seminar jointly organized by Nepal based NGO 'MANUSHI' and Singapore based 'Asian Mass Communication Research and Information Centre (AMIC)' entitled 'Editorial Management for Women Journalists' held in Katmandu, Nepal during 7-14 December, 1994 where 25 women journalists from India, Bangladesh, Nepal, Pakistan, Srilanka were present. A survey was conducted among these 25 journalists and found that they all were interested in investigative reporting, but the scenario was quite different in case of Bangladesh (Ferdous, 2001:11). Thus women journalists are denied access to information that could further their careers.

(d) *Sexual Harassment:* Women journalists frequently experience verbal or physical harassment in their working environment. Sexual harassment may come from their own bosses or colleagues, or even from people they interview (Ferdous 2001:11). However, if the female journalist raises formal complaint against the transgressor, she may be viewed as overreacting or the fault may even be placed upon her. And to be sure, there will be more bumps along the way in her career as a newswoman.

PREJUDICE

Negative social attitudes extend far and deep as causes for discrimination. Although not as visible, they weigh women down, nonetheless rendering them victims of harassment and exclusion from the "old-boys' network" (Ferdous 2001:11).

STEREOTYPE ATTITUDE

Despite of the accomplishments of a woman journalist, her professional qualifications are often ignored due to stereotypes. For example, when a woman journalist becomes successful, people begin to assume that a special relationship exists between her and her superior, or her and the interviewee, especially when the journalist is covering social or political subject matters. Since most of the time these superiors and the interviewees are men, society rather believe that woman journalists carry out sexual favors in order to obtain exclusive news than to believe in their professionalism (Ferdous 2001:12).

Another way women journalists are stereotyped is the belief that women are only good for embellishment. The fact is, some media put more weight on the women journalist's appearance than her qualifications, especially on the television news. These women who often appear on the television because they are pretty but not because of the quality of the material they cover. More like movie stars, their private lives become the subject of review on entertainment columns. This type of attention sometimes misleads these women journalists to confuse the responsibilities. Their job is to do the interview, but is not to be the subject of the interview.

In most newspaper offices, the environment is not women friendly. Since women are dwarfed by the huge male presence they feel intimidated by their male colleagues, even though some of them are decent and helpful. In a male dominated industry, women liken themselves with fish out of water. This the atmosphere becomes suffocating for them. For example, some newspaper offices do not offer a separate toilet for women. Women complaint that the newspaper offices are biased against them. If a male apprentice fails to perform a job it may go unnoticed with the hope that he will improve one day. But the same failure for a woman will earn humiliating remarks, making them feel unsuitable for the job. Most management blame non-professional attitude of women as an excuse to create a barrier to their leadership advancement, insinuating that journalism is a full-time job with which women simply can not cope. A case of Daisy Moudud can be put here:

Daisy Moudud joined the staff of the Dainik Purbokone in 1986 and become the fist woman journalist in Chittagong (the port city of Bangladesh). Today, she is a sub-editor at the newspaper, supervising a staff of six and overseeing the editing of the city news. Her family was supportive of her career choice but establishing herself in the profession wasn't easy. She says that she had to prove herself constantly and be better at her job than her male colleagues. Moudud explains that many of her male colleagues did not think that she could do the job as well as they (male colleagues) could. Moudud had to be tough to survive; otherwise the challenges would have discouraged her (Chepesiuk 2004: 5).

CONCLUSIONS AND RECOMMENDATIONS

Women are gradually coming up in different sectors including newspaper industry. But still they are dreadful in many sectors compared to their counterpart man. In order to lure women to the country's newspapers, the employers must demonstrate their sincerity. At present they are doing nothing beyond lip service. Working atmosphere for women must improve. Since women have many misconceptions about journalism, extra efforts are required to make the industry attractive to them. To overcome this situation, especially in newspaper sector following recommendations are made.

(a) Nowadays, women have become a force in the media. There are women sub-editors. Even there are some editors of women magazines with a reasonably good standard. Even many female journalists work in night shifts, i.e. from 8 p.m. to 2 a.m. in some newspapers. They should be given two-way transport facilities so that they do not feel a sense of insecurity.

(b) Same wage for both male and female working in the same position in the newspaper industry is a right for both male and female. Any sort of discrepancy regarding wages should be removed.

(c) Because of time constraint, women journalists often find it difficult to get training and education – "key to success" in the ever-evolving mass media realm. Training programs need to be developed that help women in job skills, management skills, and how to locate and capitalize on resources to overcome the barriers.

(d) Women should keep in mind that nearly 90 percent of the country's garment workers are woman. They come to work early in the morning and return home even late in the night, many of them simply walk. The case is almost the same in case of NGO workers. But women have shown the way they have overcome whatever obstacles they face. So, women journalists should follow this path and take journalism as their permanent profession. When those who come to the profession taste the excitement associated with it, they are likely to stay and inspire others to follow them.

REFERENCES

Ahmed, Alfaz (1998), "Mass Media and Women", a chapter of the book *"Women andMedia"* edited by Nayeemul Islam Khan, Bangladesh Centre for Development Journalism and Communication (BCDJC), Vol 2, No. 2, August, Dhaka, Bangladesh.

Bangladesh Bureau of Statistics (BBS) (2004), *Statistical Year Book of Bangladesh,* Bangladesh Bureau of Statistics, Dhaka, Bangladesh.

Chepesiuk, Ron (2004), "Tough Assignment: Working as a Woman Journalists in Bangladesh", *The Daily Star,* 14June 2004, Vol. XIV, no. 143.

Bhattacharya, Debapriya (1994), "Women and Industrial Employment in Bangladesh: Challenges and Opportunities in the Era of New Technologies" a paper prepared for the United Nations University Institute for New Technologies, July, Dhaka, Bangladesh.

Ferdous, Zannatul (2001), *"Condition and Position of Women Journalists in Newspapers"* Mass Line Media Centre (MMC), Dhaka, Bangladesh.

Haque, Nasimun Ara (2004), "Women Journalists in Newspapers: Is It for Lack of Inexperience or Lack of Help"-A paper presented in the conference on *"Women in Bangladesh Media"* held in 17 August, 2004 organized by BCDJC and MMC, Dhaka, Bangladesh.

Hossain, Farid (1998), "What does Prevent Bangladeshi Women from Journalsim?" *Bangladesh Journalism Review* (Women and Media Issue), Vol.2, No.2, 1998, Dhaka, Bangladesh.

Johnson, Amy (1996), 'Empowering Women in the Asian Media', IWMF report on "Women in the Media: Facing Obstacles ...... Changing Attitudes", *Exchange Bulletin,* Wom-Mcd-Fem-Med, No.1, Autumn 1996, retrieved from *http://alainet.org/mujerers/bull1.html* on 25 January 2005.

Kabir, Farah (1998), 'Women and Media", a chapter of the book *"Women and Media"* edited by Nayeemul Islam Khan, Bangladesh Centre for Development Journalism and Communication (BCDJC), Vol 2, No. 2, August 1998, Dhaka, Bangladesh.

Khan, Nayeemul Islam (eds,) (2004), 'Women in Journalism-brief Report of Survey ", in Media Congress-2004, BCDJC and MMC, Dhaka, Bangladesh.

Moudud, Babi (1990), "Reporting: Why Women not Coming?" *Niriskha*, A Monthly Publication about Mass Media, Press Institute of Bangladesh (PIB), Dhaka, Bangladesh.

Nahid, Bark (1994), "Problems Faced by Women Journalsits in Bangladesh", in Firdous Azam and Niaz Zaman (Eds.), *Infinite Variety*, Dhaka: University Press Ltd.

Razi, Ali R., (2003), "Women Journalists: 30 Years of Experience", *Niriskha*, A Monthly Publication about Mass Media No. 117, December 2003, Press Institute of Bangladesh (PIB), Dhaka, Bangladesh.

Sadia, Kader (2001), Bangladesh: Women are not Encouraged to Take up Journalism as Career, *News Network*, (News Agency), October 29, Dhaka, Bangladesh.

Uritus, Theodore, P. & Rockey Clark (1998), "Women Working in the Print Media" Media issues, Media Awareness Network, Ottawa, Ontario, Canada.

FOOTNOTES

1. Daily Newspapers (20):
   The Bangladesh Observer, The Bangladesh Times, The New Nation, The Daily Star, The Independent, Ittefaq, Inqilab, Sangbad, Janakantha, Ajker Kagoj, Banglar Bani, Banglabazar Patrika, Bhorer Kagoj, Muktakantha, Dinkal, Janata, Khabor, Manavzamin, Meillat and Shakaler Khabor.
   Periodicals (3) :
   Anannya, Prokriti and Robbar
   News Agencies (5) :
   Associated Press of Bangladesh (APB), Bangladesh Sangbad Sangstha (BSS), United News of Bangladesh (UNB Bangla), United News of Bangladesh (UNB English) and Probe.

7

HUMAN RIGHTS AND WOMEN'S HEALTH IN INDIAN SOCIETY

Paramananda Dash Sharma

HUMAN RIGHTS

The scientific foundation of anthropology progressed and was made stronger with the progress of colonization. Levi-Strauss (1975) wrote "Anthropology as we understand the term would not have existed if one vast segment of mankind had not been subjected to another and if, for decades and in some cases for centuries, the dominant portion had not savagely massacred or reduced to a condition of slavery men whose natural resources they also pillaged and whom they exterminated, either deliberately or involuntarily"(p.27).

Anthropologists arrived together with the administrators of the colonial powers and the missionaries when the peoples were struggling for their independence from the yoke of the colonial powers. "The fundamental problem for anthropology was to find a definition of the human condition which had the idea of freedom as its corollary. As it happened after surveying some 4,000 types of society, past and present, anthropology confessed its impotence. It had to admit that the concept of human rights had no universal foundations. Indeed basing the right to freedom on the nature if man as a moral being is always relative to the place and the culture.

"Levi-Strauss, one of the major theorists of structuralism, proposed a solution to this impasse by defining mankind as a species and individuals as micro-species restricted by the right to existence of other species. He contended that real freedom was enshrined in established habits, predilections and customs and that only 'beliefs' could give freedom a content to be defended. In his opinion, this was the basis on which human rights could be founded" (Levi-Strauss, 1977; *cf.* Human Rights Teaching, *UNESCO, vol.VI,1987,p.2*).

The tradition of 'declarations of rights' began when the States of North America declared their independence in 1776. Following the American example, the revolutionary constitutions of France were preceded by declarations of rights, the most prominent being the Declaration of 1789. This Declaration emphasized the concept of natural rights which every individual possessed by virtue of being human. "The constitutions that followed all referred to the principles of 1789 when they included declarations of rights or equivalent provisions"(Unesco,1987, pp.2-3).

The assertion of human rights assumed an international dimension when the Universal Declaration was adopted on 10 December 1948 by the General Assembly of the United Nations, and when the Commission of Human Rights was set up. This expressed the sentiments of the Western nation-states, traumatized by the recent World War. It was not until 1960 that the General Assembly proclaimed "the necessity of bringing to a speedy and unconditional end of colonialism in all its forms and manifestations. "Six years later , the two International Covenants on Human Rights extended human rights to the right of all peoples to self-determination (Unesco,1987, p.3).

ANTHROPOLOGY AND HUMAN RIGHTS

"Given this need to redefine human rights, one might well ask what role anthropology can play in the process. To begin with, moral judgment must be distinguished from objective facts. In this respect, the role of anthropology is not to criticize or justify cultural practices but to account for differences. The problem of accounting for cultural variations —that is, how to relate cultural variations to a universal conception of man— lies at the root of the theory of anthropology. Evolutionism, functionalism, cultural relativism, structuralism, Marxism and neo-evolutionism are all anthropological schools or theories which have sought or are still seeking to answer this question. It might be noted that none of these theories has provided a satisfactory answer to the problem of human rights (Glowczewski and Razon, 1987,p.3). Human rights interest various social sciences covering aspects like economic, political, juridical, social and cultural. Persons concerned about human rights recognize, more than anything, that this is an interdependent world. A universal conscience has been created which acknowledges the need for shared standards of human dignity and the rights of all peoples.

For several years now, cultural minorities have been demanding a just redefinition of human rights. Anthropologists have reacted in different ways to this voicing of claims by the cultural minorities. While there has been much discussion about the relationship between human rights and international law (The International Commission of Jurists,1987), we still need to understand the range of cultural variations and definitions of human rights. The anthropological approach, with its emphasis on understanding non-Western and technologically less developed societies, and indigenous peoples may provide a frame work within which to undertake a broad based definition of the essentials of human rights. Anthropologists in general have mostly spoken about 'duties', 'obligations', 'values', 'codes', 'practices', 'moralities', 'beliefs', 'status' etc. (Srinivas,1966; Karve,1968; Gough,1973,1981; Menscher, 1974; Beteille, 1985; and many others in later years) but have seldom spoken about the existence or absence of rights—the rights of men, women, children, and underprivileged communities and destitute(Davis,1966; Rex, 1981; Kuper, 1981;Banerjee, 1979, and others) with particular reference to the Indian communities.

The paper discusses briefly about the various facets of women's rights and empowerment in India, with particular emphasis on women's health and human rights.

STATUS OF WOMEN

Women has been bestowed a divine status in ancient scriptures. In Indian mythology the *Shakti* i.e. Power, has always been personified in feminine gender whether it is *Durga, Kali, Bhairavi or Laxmi.* Thus the status of women in ancient Indian society was very high as evidenced from the ancient scriptures but the deterioration started in the Indian Hindu society from the medieval period when the girls were forced to marry at their childhood stage and the *'Sati Pratha'* began to be practiced.

In patrilineal societies the process of discrimination between men and women is set in motion of right from the time of birth. It is most perceptible among the caste Hindus. There is generally no discrimination between boys and girls in tribal communities. But as contact with non-tribal values increases, gender discriminatory practices also started making inroads into the tribal societies. However, even today the extent of gender discrimination is far less in tribal societies as compared to what exists in caste Hindu societies (Dash Sharma,1999).In recent years extensive literature have come out on gender studies. Though a large body of knowledge has been generated on gender in the recent past, gender continues to remain a fascinating field for new explorations and new types of analysis (Indira and Behera,1999, p.1). In all societies roles for performance have been assigned to the genders by the society which varies from society to society and from region to region. The subservience of women from ancient past to the present is rooted in the unique sexual functions women perform as child bearers, and rearing children and managing their homes. Socially, politically and economically women were made to accept an inferior and secondary status which was justified and defended with the help of scriptures, customs and traditions.

It is only a recent phenomenon, that we find of gender equality, which has gained prominence during the last decade of the 20th century through the various women's organizations who have marched forward with the banners for women's emancipation. When we look around us, initially we find that the present day women have made a great stride in terms of access to greater employment, better health facilities and improved standard of living. But on a close look we find that the status of women in the field of education, social and economic aspects and in political empowerment have been confined mainly to the urban educated middle and upper class women of the Indian society. Though as individuals, women have been participating essentially in all spheres of human activities, however, as a group, they have been and are being identified with the particular roles ascribed by the society which is naturally linked with child rearing.

The recognition of the special value accorded to male children early while surrounded by affectionate and appreciative parents, grandparents, uncles, and aunts, cannot escape the attention of a little girl, may be his sister. The happiness expressed all around at the birth of a son and the way the parents and close relatives of the new born are congratulated can hardly escape the attention of the little girl. "The desirability of having sons and the undesirability of having more daughters is made explicit often by outsiders: 'Four daughters? Each one will take ten thousand rupees and walkout of the house. Bringing up a daughter is like pouring water in sand.' Parents who have only daughters are pitied. Their future is bleak for they have no support or succor in old age"(Dube, 2001,p.90).

The Indian society and the government have to do a lot if the status of women in the country has to be raised in public perception. The law gives equal rights to the daughter and the son but the former seldom claims her share from her brother. There may be insignificant number of cases where the daughter claims her share of the parental property from her brother. The demand of the equal rights for the daughter has not taken roots in our Indian society.

The proposed 33% seat reservation for women in Parliament and State legislature have not yet come to fruition.

"For some years now we have been hearing a lot of noise regarding the so-called 'empowerment of women'. This is to be achieved by reserving seats for women in the Union and the State legislatures. Demands for reservations have been vigorously voiced by women organizations and their leaders. The government and the political parties were equally prompt in promising such reservation. The government even declared the year 2001 as "Women's Year". But nothing concrete seems to have happened in this direction" (Kashyap, 2001,p.36).

Despite all the persistent demands and promises, it seems unlikely that the Bill on 33 per cent reservation for women in Indian legislatures will have an easy passage in Parliament. "It is a classic example of politicians' doublespeak According to their public declarations, they are all committed to reservations for women. But when it comes to passing the Bill, no party seems to want it. Every party is male dominated. It is difficult to understand why our women activists in different parties do not take up the cudgels and fight their battles within their respective parties first (Kashyap, 2001,p.37).

On November 26,2006, the status on women's bill is— "Left, RJD differ on women's bill" (Saroj Nagi, New Delhi, November 26, Hindustan Times, Ranchi, November 27,2006.) "The Government's plan to bring the women's bill in the winter session of Parliament has run into more trouble with the CPI (Communist Party of India) opposing the RJD (Rashtriya Janata Dal)'s call for an all-party meeting to evolve a consensus— which has proved elusive so far on this issue.

The difference came to the fore on Sunday when CPI General Secretary Mr A. B. Bardhan noted that several all-party meetings had already been held and there was no need for another. "Holding another meeting will become an excuse for delaying the bill and betray the women's cause for political empowerment, he said demanding introduction and passage of the bill that seeks to reserve one-third seats for women in Lok Sabha and state assemblies.

After RJD chief Mr Lalu Prasad Yadav extended his support at the UPA-Left meeting on November 22, 2006, the coalition claimed unanimity on the introduction of the bill. But later, within 24 hours, Lalu and his MP's met Leader of the House Mr Pranab Mukherrjee and demanded a sub-quota for OBCs and minorities as well as all party meeting to hammer out a consensus. Like the Left, the Congress officially supports the bill in its present form, though several of its members privately oppose it."(ibid.).

Neerja Chowdhury writes under the column 'Platform' (Hindustan Times, Ranchi, December 13, 2006)—"Battling for the bitter half"—"No political party dares to oppose Women's Reservation Bill. Yet the sabotage is evident in the number of roadblocks it has faced since the first attempt to introduce it in 1996.This time it is no different. "So the fate of the Indian women for political empowerment through reservation in Lok Sabha is a distant possibility in the present political system in India.

Further women's status in general in Indian society, can be gauged through the law on 'Protection of Women from Domestic Violence Act' which has come into effect from October, 2006. The government has to enact a law to protect the helpless women from abuse in their own house by their own family members and other relatives, which is as follows:

Finally there is a law to make home safe for women, a news item appeared under the heading "Jail term for wife-bashing from today" (news item appeared in Hindustan Times, October 26, 2006, Ranchi Metro Edition). The new law (Protection of Women from Domestic Violence Act 2005, which comes into effect from Thursday October 26, 2006) provides an all-encompassing definition of domestic violence, and the offenders can be jailed for a maximum of one year or fined or both. They can also be charged under other sections of the Indian Penal Code (IPC), if applicable.

"The new law provides an all-encompassing definition of domestic violence including not only physical violence by the husband, such as beating or physically hurting his wife, or sexual violence like forced intercourse, but also verbal or emotional violence such as insulting the wife or preventing her from taking up a job, and even economic violence such as not allowing the wife to use her salary. The definition includes threats of abuse and dowry demands too, said Renuka Chowdhury, Minister for Women and Child Development, Government of India. Mrs Renuka Chowdhury said around 70 per cent of women in India are victims of domestic violence in some form. The enactment of the law is a historic step towards ending gender discrimination", she said. The law addresses sexual abuse of children, or forcing girls to marry against their wishes as well."

According to 1991 Census of India the girl child population (0-14 years) is 36.1% of the total female population in India. Many micro studies and researches have shown that there are biases against children. Approximately 25% of the female children die before they reach 15 years of age due to parental negligence towards them. They are provided with inadequate food thus effecting lower nutritional level and poor medical treatment during illness, further there are cases of female foetacide and infanticide, and these are being done because of the strong preference for the son. According to the national survey of Body Mass Index (BMI) majority of the girls are from lower income families. At the adolescent stage these girls are 12 to 15 cm shorter as compared to girls of well to-do families. There are records of large number of girls from poor families who are not only underweight but majority of them are also anaemic (Chakravarty, 1998).

This brief foregoing account tells about the situation prevailing among the women in India, be they women labourers, girl students, working women in cities or even married women in affluent families. The situation is more or less the same in Indian society irrespective of religious affiliation, caste and community distinction.

REPRODUCTIVE HEALTH STATUS OF WOMEN

The growing realization that the quality of life enjoyed by the women depends upon her reproductive health status, thus it emphasizes the need to examine the issue from different points of view. To perpetuate the family line the preference of son is still extremely pervasive in Indian families. Hence even after the third or fourth serial birth of a girl child in the family, the husband impregnates his wife with the hope that the next child birth will be their long desired son. The social, economic and the cultural cost at which this reproductive role of women is being performed has never been realized, considered or assessed by the Indian families in general and the families in the rural areas of India in particular. Early marriage not only erodes human dignity but also severely damages a woman's normal growth and development chances. Adolescent girls who make up a sizeable portion of the female population in India receive a raw deal from the society. One of the strongest impediments to women's emancipation in India is early marriage.

A National Sample Survey Organization done for the Unicef paints a dismal picture of traditions hampering development in the country. It points out that 80 per cent of women in Tonk district of Rajasthan get married before attaining the legal age of 18 years, while the more literate Dibrugarh district of Assam is a shade better with 13 per cent minor girls getting married. Less than 10 per cent births takes place in health institutes of the backward districts of West Singhbhum of Jharkhand, Dungs in Gujarat and Koraput of Orissa, while the figure is 84 percent in Tiruvellore district of Tamil Nadu. In Bihar's Gaya district only 5 per cent of the children are immunized as compared to 90 per cent in Karnataka's Tumkur district.

AGE AT MARRIAGE

Early marriage has serious medical and social consequences on the well-being of young girls. A major feature determining the health status of women is the age at marriage and this in turn is influenced by several social, economic and cultural practices in Indian communities. In parts of north India there is custom called gauna where a bride though married early do not go to her in-laws' house until she attains puberty. While in south India in the marriages arranged by the parents the girls have to go to their nuptial home immediately after they are married. The absence of customs like *gauna* is responsible for the attainment of early motherhood for young girls in Karnataka (Raman, 1999, p.82).

A women's reproductive health is closely influenced by the age at which she attains motherhood. However, every conception need not necessarily result in motherhood. Spontaneous abortion, miscarriage, still birth, and infant deaths, immensely influence the state of health of married women, particularly if it is a case of early marriage. Extensive literature is available on the study of age at marriage (Shivkumar, 2000; Pandey *et al.*, 2000; Audinarayana, 1986; Sinha, 1987; Visweswara Rao,1994 and many others) in India. It is generally observed that more than 70% of the marriages of the girls in rural India take place between 12 to 15 years of age (Raman, 1999; Chakravarty,1998).

Early motherhood, serial pregnancies burdened with household chores, slowly pushes the woman into a steady depletion of her health . These grinding situation and mental agony of the married women at an early age have a telling effect on the health of the woman which results in the premature ageing impression on her face which makes her look much older than her actual age.

WHAT SHE CAN DO: PLEAD OR BLEED

Her husband does not listen to her pleads to wait for a couple of years for the birth of their first child until she attains the age of a mature adult.. Both are in dilemma in the tradition bound social systems prevailing in rural India particularly. The husband has to prove that he is virile and the married woman has to prove that she is fertile by presenting a grandchild, preferably a son, to her parents-in-law.

Almost all the women's organizations and NGOs defending the cause and rights of women are sounding clarion call for the women in India who comprise half of the country's population, to give equal authority and responsibility to the women, and equal participation of the women in nation building process. Despite their infinite value and contribution in sustenance of the family, shaping the society, the women in India are generally not treated at par in any of the aspects of life, because of the strong patriarchal system of our society. There is a need to understand the focus and functioning of the voluntary organizations—most of them are politically motivated and are insufficiently paying attention and service to the needs of the poor rural women.

There is a need to change the attitude, particularly of those rural patriarchs who are still clinging to the die hard traditional mores, thereby inviting poverty, ill health, unemployment, and illiteracy to the members of the family, specially to the females and to the society in general.

The Indian society is in the turning point at the beginning of the 21st century. This turning point provides an opportunity to introspect for a country like India to take stock of the situation, and our efforts to know, where we have flourished and where we have floundered in emancipating the rural poor women, whom we are still suppressing and subjugating to the wills and whims of our patriarchal society.

As regards the health care facilities in rural areas, we know that three-fourths of the total population in rural areas there are only less than one-fifth of hospitals and less than half of dispensary beds available in India. In rural areas more than 20 per cent of the people have to travel a distance of ten kilometres or more for securing medical care. The percentages of villages having primary health sub-centres and community health workers are only 7 per cent and 18 per cent respectively (Singh,2000;Census of India, 1991).

In May 2000 India crossed 1 billion (100 crore) mark in population figure covering 16 per cent of the world's population and 2.4 per cent of the land area (Chandra, 2000). "Consequently, even after 55 years of India's Independence, very dishearteningly India's fertility and infant mortality rates remain at very high level, and as the findings of a recent study have shown, these are primarily caused due to abject poverty and widespread illiteracy among the people in India, specially among the females" (Mukherji,2000).

The National Population Policy (NPP) has identified 12 strategic themes which should be simultaneously pursued to achieve the national socio-demographic goals by 2010. The important themes which directly concerns the women are; empowering women for improved health and nutritional levels, child survival and child health, special attention for population groups living in urban slums and hill areas, and the tribals, and increased participation of men in planned parenthood (Chandra, 2000).

These policies and programmes are in paper only and it will take several years to see them in action through the government machinery given the prevailing situation in the rural areas of India.

In the last week of December 2002, a family planning campaign was organised by a voluntary organization in some villages near Ranchi city to educate the people of the villages on the importance of small family. The slogans in Nagpuria like, "*Chhot Rahu, Sukhat Rahu*"; and "*Dui Tho Rahu, Hasat Rahu*" were very well taken by the villagers. The day the Indian women will exert, particularly in rural areas and in remote villages, and will carry the conviction with courage telling their husband "*Why don't you understand ? No more baby please*" from that very day onwards the women in India will be emancipated from poverty, humiliation and degenerated mental and physical health status due to the burden of a large family.

REFERENCES

Audinarayana, N. (1986), The Influence of Age at Marriage on Fertility and Family Planning behaviour: A Cross-Cultural Study. *Family Welfare*, XXXIII(1):50-64.

Banerjee, Sumanta (1979), *Child Labour in India*. Child Labour Series Report No.2, Anti-Slavery Society for the Protection of Human Rights: London.

Barbara Glowczewski and Jean-Patrick Razon (1987), Functionalism, Structuralism, Marxism and Human Rights. In: *Human Rights Teaching* By Unesco, pp.1-8, Volume VI.

Census of India (1991), *Availability of Infrastructural Facilities in Rural Areas of India: An Analysis of Village Directory Data*. Office of the Registrar General, India: New Delhi. (Published in 1997)

Chakravarty, Manjula (1998), Neglect, Cruelty and Wastage of Human Resource: The Girl Child. *Indian Anthropologist*, 28(2): 9-20.

Chandra, Girish (2000), New Policy Seeks Stable Population by 2045. *Kurukshetra*, 44(5), May 2000:5-7.

Dash Sharma, P. (1999), Changing Role and Status of Women Among the Parhaiyas of Chotanagpur. In: R.Indira and Deepak Kumar Behera (ed.), *Gender and Society in India*, pp. 181-191. Manak Publications Pvt. Ltd.: New Delhi.

Davis, David Brion (1976), *The Problem of Slavery in Western Culture.* Cornell University Press: Ithaca.

Dube, Leela (2001), *Anthropological Explorations in Gender: Intersecting Fields.* Sage Publications: New Delhi.

Glowczewski, Barbara and Jean-Patrick Razon (1987), Functionalism, Structuralism, Marxism and Human Rights. In: G.B.Kutukdjian (ed.), Unesco, *Human Rights Teaching*, pp.1-8, Vol. VI. Unesco: Paris. (published in 1988).

Gough, Kathleen (1973), Harijan in Thanjavur. In: K.Gough and H. Sharma (ed.), *Imperialism and Revolution in South Asia.* Monthly Review Press : New York.

Gough, Kathleen (1981), *Rural Society in Southeast Asia.* Cambridge University Press: Cambridge.

Indira, R. and Deepak Kumar Behera (1999), *Gender and Society in India*, Vol.II. Manak Publications Pvt. Ltd.: New Delhi.

Karkal, M., M. Gupta and M. Sadgopal (1995), Women Health and Development. *Radical Journal of Health*, 1: 25-26.

Karve, Irawati (1968), *Hindu Society: An Interpretation.* Prakashan: Poona.

Kashyap, C. Subhash (2001), Empowerment of Women Through Reservation. *Vidhanmala*, 4(1 & 2):36-39.

Kuper, Leo (1981), *Genocide: Its Political Use in the Twentieth Century.* Penguin: London.

Levi-Strauss, C. (1977), "Reflections on Liberty". *New Society*, Vol.40, No. 764 (26 May 1977), New Science Publications, London. (Cited from: *Human Rights Teaching*, Unesco, vol.VI,1987.p.6).

Levi-Strauss, C. (1977), *"Reflections on Liberty". New Society*, Vol.40, No. 764 (26 May 1977), New Science Publications, London.

Levi-Strauss, C., (1975), "Anthropologie" (Anthropology), *Diogenes*, vol.90.

Menscher, Joan (1974), The Caste System Upside Down. *Current Anthropology*,15:469-473.

Mukherji, Shekhar (2000), Syndrome of Poverty and Fertility. *Kurukshetra*, 44(5), May 2000:8-9.

Pandey, P.L., D.C. Jain, G.D. Pandey, R. Choubey and R.S. Tiwary (2000), Some Aspects of Social Factors Affecting Fertility Behaviour of Gond Women. *Man in India*, 80(3 & 4): 251-258.

Raman, Premula (1999), Early Marriage and Reproductive Health Status of Women: A Study in Rural Karnataka. In: R. Indira and Deepak Kumar Behera (ed.), *Gender and Society in India*, pp. 78-87.

Rex, John (1981), *Apartheid and Social Research*. Unesco: Paris.

Singh,J.P. (2000), The State of Development in Rural India: An Overview. *Kurukshetra*, 48(9), June 2000:12-18.

Sivakumar, M.N. (2000), Age at First Birth and Fertility Level of Women in Kerala: A Cohort Analysis. *Man in India*, 80(3 & 4): 273-287.

Srinivas, M.N. (1966), Social Change in Modern India. University of California Press: California.

The International Commission of Jurists (1987), Access to Rights and Measures to Promote the Effective Exercise of Human Rights. In: *Human Rights Teaching* By Unesco, pp.49-69, Volume VI.

Unesco (1987), *Human Rights Teaching Bulletin*. Volume VI. Unesco: Paris.

Visweswara Rao, K., N. Balakrishna, B.V.S. Thimmayamma and Veena Shatrugna (1994), *Interrelationship between Health and Nutritional Status of Children and their Mothers. In: K.B.Pathak (ed.),* Biostatistical Aspects of Health, *29-38. B.R.Publishing Co.: Delhi.*

8

ARSENICOSIS AND ITS IMPACT ON DOMESTIC VIOLENCE AGAINST WOMEN AND CHILDREN IN BANGLADESH

Profulla C. Sarker

INTRODUCTION

The family is a place of paradox, an institution for security, sharing love, affection, joy and any misfortune in the kinship network system. The family on accounts of its smallness and intimacy, and the constant demands its members make on each other as whole person's is really a small community within itself, within which relationships are bound to be both intense and ambivalent; involving love but also hate; fulfillment but also restriction; relaxation and confidence but also violence, conflict and enmity (Fletcher, 1981:23, and Sarker, 1997:7). The women and children are in great danger in the place where they should be safest: within their families. They unable to make their own decision, voice their own opinions or protect themselves and their children for fear of further repercussions. The human rights of the women are denied in many times at the household level. Consequently, the domestic violence is instinct and rooted in the family environment throughout the world (Alder, 1992, Bachman and Satzman,1995, and Heise,1993). Violence in the domestic sphere is usually perpetrated by males who are, or who have been, in positions of trust and intimacy and power-husbands, fathers, fathers-in-law, stepfathers. However, determining the accurate prevalence and incidence rates of abuse and neglect is difficult due to the fact that domestic violence is a private event, rarely open to public observation (Ammerman and Hersen,1999). Under the circumstances, the victims are often reluctant to disclose abuse due to fear from perpetrators. But the subordinate status of women in the patriarchal authority structure of family, and unilateral decisions of the husbands are the main mechanisms through which women are victims of domestic violence by their husbands in Bangladesh (Cain et al, 1994, Hartmann and Boyce, 1983 and Jahan, 1994). Patriarchal authority describes a political system ruled by men in which women have inferior social status, including basic human rights (Kottak, 2005). The perceived legitimacy of men's violence against women is often compounded by other factors like absolute poverty and culture of feminization of poverty. Studies show that the poor economic condition of husbands, lack of proper education of wives and their lower socio-economic status, traditional norms and values, failure of commitment of dowry and joint family system are associated with higher risks of domestic violence (Kabeer, 1989 and Koenig et al, (2003). Kantor (1996) found that domestic violence is significantly high in Canada and United States of America where the neo-local residence and nuclear family system are predominant. In Canada, 29 percent of women reported being physically assault by a current or former partner since the age 16 and 62 percent of murdered women are killed by their husband or domestic partner, compared with 50 percent in Pakistan (ibid). In United States, 28 percent of women are being the victims of physical violent by their partners compared to 25 percent in United Kingdom, 20 percent in New Zealand, 60 percent in Russia and 59 percent in Japan. In Asian countries, 45 percent of women in India are being victims of physical violent by their husbands compared to 54 percent in

Bangladesh, 38 percent in Korea, 20 percent in Thailand, and 16 percent in Cambodia (Unicef,200). It is one of the most pervasive of human rights violations, denying women and girls equality, security, dignity, self-worth, and their right to enjoy fundamental freedoms. Cities, with their impersonality and isolation from extended kin net works, are the breeding grounds for domestic violence. On the other hand, it is argued that creating of opportunities for women through access to credit, awareness raising ,and skill development training for income generating activities have enhanced the self-esteem and status of women at the household level in Bangladesh and reduced the domestic violence against them. Empirical studies reveal that women's participation in income generating activities has had varied effects in relation to vulnerability to violence at the household level. For example, Hadi (2005) shows that women who participate in income generation are less likely to be victims of domestic violence than non-participants women. Contrarily, Ahmed et al. (2001) and Schuler et al. (1996) suggest that women's participation in income generating activities sometimes creates tension between the husbands and wives along with the other in-laws which may lead to domestic violence against women. If it is the fact for the normal situation of women, then what can be happen to the sick women who are not able to perform the household activities along with other responsibilities? This paper is an attempt to examine to what extent the arsenic affected women are being victims of domestic violence in connection with desertion, separation and divorce, along with the physical and psychological torture and as a result of being victims of trafficking.

CONCEPTUAL ISSUES

Arsenic is one of the most common and important trace elements with toxic medical properties (Tarafdar, 1998). The low amount of arsenic is not harmful but the high amount (more than 0.05 milligram per liter of drinking water) may demonstrate adverse effects on health (WHO, 1984). Accordingly, in Bangladesh the maximum permissible level of arsenic in drinking water has been fixed at 0.05 milligram per liter water (GOB, 1997).The concept of arsenicosis is associated with the diseases due to consumption of high amount of arsenic in drinking water and other food items (Sarker, 1999: 217).More specifically, any kind of sickness or illness or morbidity related to arsenic is defined as arsenicosis. Chronic arsenic exposure may result in manifold symptoms affecting the vital organs of the body, viz. skin, nervous system, liver, cardiovascular system, kidney and respiratory tract (Landrigan,1992). But the severity depends upon the duration of exposure, amount of arsenic accumulated in the body, immunity level of individual, consciousness level and the nutritional status of the victims (ibid).

The term domestic violence refers to many types of harmful behavior directed to the married women by their husbands due to their subordinate status in the patriarchal society. Violence is an attempt to regain, through use of emotional and physical force, something that has been lost (Denjin,1984: 488). According to Article 1 of the declaration of United Nations, violence against women includes: any act of gender-based violence that result in, or is likely to result in, physical, sexual or psychological harm or suffering to women, including threats of such acts, coercion or arbitrary deprivations of liberty, whether occurring in public or private life (United Nations, 1993). Gelles and Straus (1979), for instance, defined violence as "act carried out with the intention, or perceived intention, of physically injuring another person. The injury can range from slight pain, as with slap, to murder". The violence against women and children are two distinct concepts (Haugaard, 1999). Many acts many be considered domestic violence and child abuse. The domestic violence against women is defined here as the abuses that are committed by the husbands in terms of physical, psychological and economic torture, along with the dissolution of marital tie in relation to desertion, separation, divorce and practice of polygyny and thus affects the abuse and neglect of children are involved.

RESEARCH METHODOLOGY

This paper is based on data taken from the study "Arsenicosis and its Impact on Reproductive Health of Women and Children in two Districts of Bangladesh". The research was conducted in 2003-2004. The author was the principal researcher of the project. The project was funded by Grameen Trust, Dhaka. The sample of this study was 185 pregnant women who were the victims of arsenicosis. The complete enumeration was conducted using the methods and techniques of survey and observation. Use of key informants method was applied to supplement the survey data. Case study method has also been used in order to get more in-depth information. Although the main objective of this study was to examine the reproductive health of the arsenicosis affected mothers and their children, a few questions were added in the questionnaire to know how the arsenicosis victim women and their children are the subject of domestic violence.

THE ARSENIC VICTIMS

The main symptoms of arsenicosis are melanosis and keratosis. Due to melanosis, the complexion of the victims gradually changes. The limbs and chest are affected first, then the rest of the body may show gradual complexion change including appearance of black or brown pigmentation. Sometimes the skin is marked by black and white spots side- by- side, and that is called the leucomelanosis. In keratosis, the palms of the hands and foot-soles become symmetrically hardened. It is not painful or itchy at the beginning stage but later on it may start rotting and develop into dangerous ulcer. This is said to be pre-cancerous stage, which may develop into skin cancer. Wart-like seeds may be seen growing on palms and soles, which is known as hyperkeratosis. The table below presents the data collected in this study about the various symptoms of arsenicosis in the different stages of life cycle of the victims.

It is evident from the Table-1 that about 47.1 percent victims are suffering from melanosis compared to 12.5 percent are keratosis. Similarly, 33.7 percent victims are suffering from leucomelanosis compared to 4.2 percent hyperkeratosis. Only

2.5 percent are affected by keratosis ulcer. The percentage of female victims is higher than males. It seems to be females are malnourished more than males in a patriarchal social system of Bangladesh. On the other hand, the percentage of victims among the children and youth is significantly high compared to adults and elderly because high consumption of arsenic contaminated water from childhood.

NATURE OF DOMESTIC VIOLENCE

The culture of Bangladesh allows men to have substantial control over the behavior of women which represents a consistent list of events known as domestic violence. These include; not obeying the husband, talking back, not having

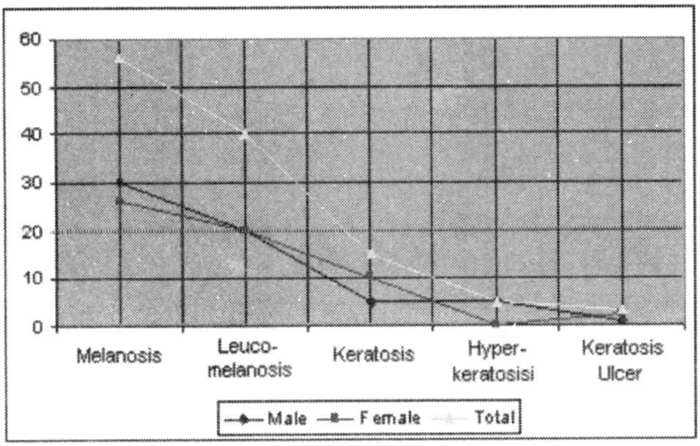

Keratosis

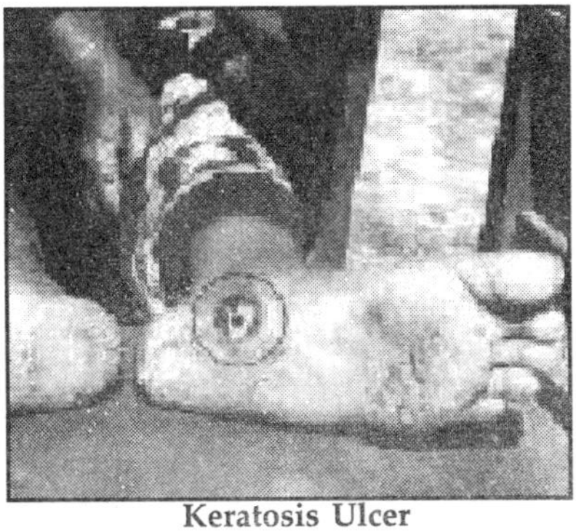
Keratosis Ulcer

Table 1
Arsenicosis in the Stages of Life Cycle of the Victims in Gender Perspective

	Male					*Female*					
ofArsenics	*Children (o-14 yrs.)*	*Youth (15-29 yrs.)*	*Adult (30-57 yrs.)*	*Elderly (57 yrs +)*	*Total*	*Children (o-14 yrs.)*	*Youth (15-29 yrs.)*	*Adult (30-57 yrs.)*	*Elderly (57 yrs +)*	*Total*	*Grand Total*
Melanosis	9	12	2	3	26	15	7	6	2	30	56
	(7.6)	(10.1)	(1.7)	(2.5)	(21.9)	(12.6)	(5.9)	(5.0)	(1.7)	(25.2)	(47.1)
Leuco- melanosis	j	16	4	j	20	3	7	6	4	20	40
		(13.5)	(3.4)		(16.3)	(2.5)	(5.9)	(5.0)	(3.4)	(16.8)	(33.7)
Keratosis	j	8	2	j	10	j	3	1	1	5	15
		(6.7)	(1.7)		(8.4)		(2.5)	(0.8)	(0.8)	(4.1)	(12.5)
Hyper- keratosis	j	j	j	j	j	j	2	3	j	5	5
							(1.7)	(2.5)		(4.2)	(4.2)
KeratosisUlcer	j	j	2	j	2	j	j	1	j	1	3
			(1.7)		(1.7)			(0.8)		(0.8)	(2.5)
Total	9	36	10	3	58	18	19	16	7	61	119
	(7.6)	(30.3)	(8.5)	(2.5)	(48.9)	(15.1)	(16.0)	(15.1)	(5.9)	(51.1)	(100.0)

Note: Figures within the parentheses indicate percentages

food on time, failing to take care of the children adequately, questioning about money or girl friends, going somewhere without permission, refusing sex, and not observing seclusion and suspicious infidelity (Bradley, 1985; Gonjaley, 1998; Hassan, 1995; Schuler, *et al.*, 1996; Viseria, 1999). In addition, the women patients of arsenicosis were being abused by the husbands when they could not fulfill the desired demands of their husbands. On the other hand, Aziz and Maloney (1985: 26-27) pointed out about a ideal wife; if she remains satisfied with little food and clothing she is praised in her husband's household as a *bhalo-bou* (good wife) and she is said to have been born in a *bhalo-bongso* (good lineage). But the nature of violence may vary from one person to another in the different segments of the same society which depends upon the social status, needs of the people and cultural milieu in which they live. The information against domestic violence of 12 women is given in the following table .

Table 2
Domesic Violence Against Women Who are Victims of Arsenicosis

Symdoms of Arsenicosis	*Physical Torture*	*Dese-rtion*	*Sepa-ration*	*Divorce*	*Dowry*	*Polygyny*	*Total*
Melanosis	1 (8.3)	–	–	–	1 (8.3)	–	2 (16.7)
Leucomelanosis	–	–	2 (16.7)	1 (8.3)	1 (8.3)	1 (8.3)	5 (41.7)
Keratosis	–	–	–	–	1 (8.3)	–	1 (8.3)
Hyperkeratosis	–	–	–	1 (8.3)	2 (16.7)	–	3 (25.0)
Keratosis Ulcer	–	1 (8.3)	–	–	–	–	1 (8.3)
Total	1 (8.3)	1 (8.3)	2 (16.7)	2 (16.7)	5 (41.7)	1 (8.3)	12 (100.0)

Note: Figures within the parentheses indicate percentages.

The Table-2 reveals that 8.3 percent women are the victims of physical torture by their husbands. The same percent of women are the victims of desertion and polygyny. Desertion means a husband fled away from his wife without any information and responsibility. Polygyny is that the husband may have more than one wife at the same time. On the other hand, about 41.7 percent women are the victims of dowry. Dowry is a certain amount cash along with kinds are given to the groom by the parents of the bride at the time of marriage. About 16.7 percent are living separately and the same percent of women are divorced by their husbands due to their arsenicosis. In case of separation, the husband forces his wife to go to her natal residence. It is evident from the table-2 that the women who are suffering from leucomelanosis and hyperkeratosis are the main victims of domestic violence.This likely to be because these manifestations of arsenicosis change the complexion of the victims to a great extent and gradually they become disfigured and physically inactive which instinct the husbands to discard their marital tie. Under the circumstances, directly or indirectly the children are affected by domestic violence of their parents in different perspectives. For example, a child who observes violence between parents would not be considered 'involved,' although it is acknowledged that witnessing violence is often very traumatic for children.

MODEL OF DOMESTIC VIOLENCE

The culture of violence is a learned and transmitted behavior which is reinforced by norms and value system that equate masculinity with aggression (Prigoff, 1994). In the concept of Muzumder (1992), domestic violence is the destructive use of aggression, verbal or physical against women. Societal and individual values sometimes instinct the husbands to be violent on their wives especially in patriarchal society like Bangladesh when the wives could not fulfill the demand of the husbands. This model is developed on the basis of the findings of the research that how the domestic violence takes place at the individual, family, community, and societal levels.

The reality of the findings of this research work is that women who are victims of arsenicosis face aggression from their husbands and in-laws aimed to physical and psychological torture and lastly are debarred from family

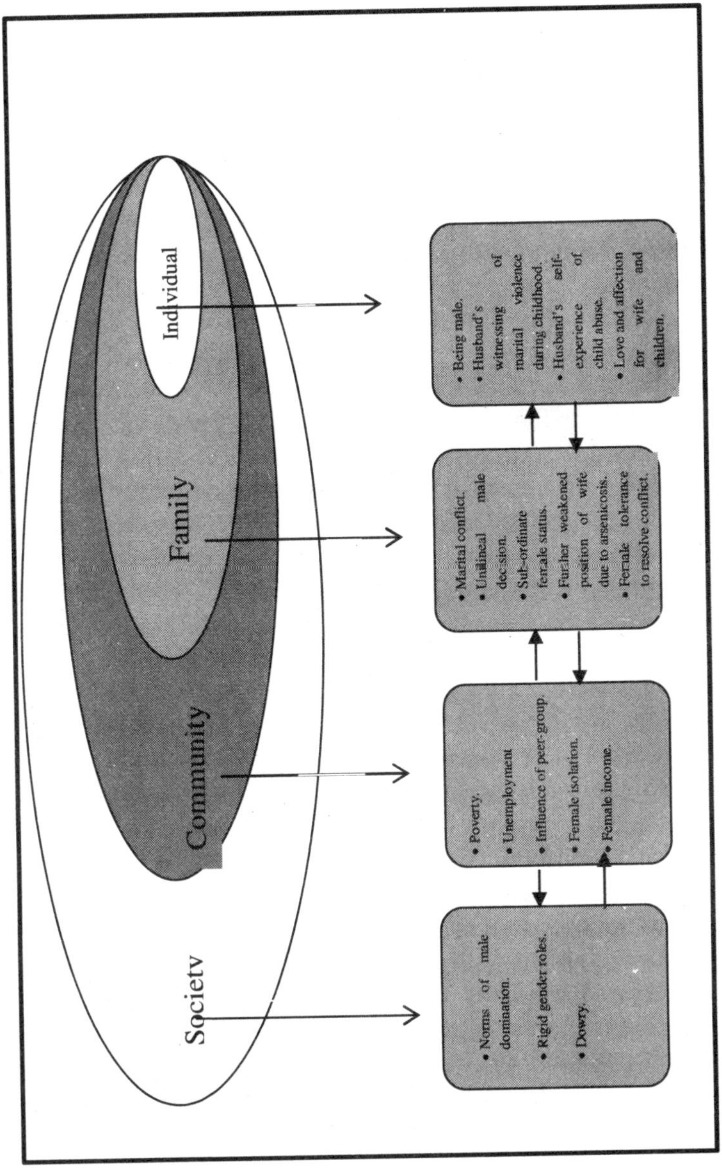

Model of Domestic Violence against the Arsenic Affected Women and their Children

either in desertion or separation or divorce. No single factor is found responsible for domestic violence against women; rather a multiple factors are combined to instinct a particular man in a particular setting to act violently towards a particular woman. It should be noted that in this study the dominant factor is arsenicosis i.e., women health and inactiveness but other factors are also associated with the dominant factor. A model of domestic violence against women is cited here which is associated with social, economic, cultural and psychosocial factors in the ecological framework of a patriarchal social system.

The model reveals how the domestic violence takes place against the arsenic victims in the social framework of Bangladesh. The model is visualized into four circles. The inner circle represents the gender identity of an individual as a man since his childhood and during socialization in the kinship network system. The ecological structure of social norms and values assert men's inherent superiority over women – combined with individual factors such as whether man was abused himself in his childhood or witnessed of marital conflict of his parents which reflects in his adulthood and thus may affect the domestic violence and as a result the arsenic affected women are the victims of domestic violence.

The second circle indicates the male control of wealth and property and he is responsible to take unilateral decisions as a husband about any affair of the family which may generate family conflict and thus affect violence against women (Hoffman *et al.*, 1994). The bargaining power of the wife in the family is usually weak due to their sub-ordinate status and culture of feminization of poverty in a patriarchal society like Bangladesh. Arsenicosis may make this bargaining power weakened and result is domestic violence which is directed to the wife for physical, psychological and economic tortures along with desertion, separation and divorce .

In the third circle, poverty, unemployment or under-employment, and influence of peer-group along with the inactiveness of his wife due to arsenicosis are the contributing factors for violence against women. This circle refers the behavior of the husband that actually inflicts physical harms of the wife which generates stress and frustration. Under the circumstances, if the wife is the victim of arsenicosis that also affect negatively and may lead her to live with husband in burning situations and that ultimately instinct to marital dissolution in terms of separation and divorce.

The fourth circle is societal issues along with the problem of arsenicosis that leads to violence against women. The societal issues are norms and values which are associated with male domination, rigid gender role, and failure of commitment of dowry, and the culture of tolerance of women that helps to adjust in any adverse situation. It has been reported that under this male dominated environment, if the women is inactive and disfigured due to arsenicosis automatically she is the subject of violence. Verbal aggression and emotional abuse can be just as harmful; however, these forms of maltreatment generate physical violence and marital disagreement.

IMPACT OF ARSENICOSIS

This section deals with the impact of arsenicosis on domestic violence against women and their children. Violence against women such as physical torture, desertion, separation, divorce and polygyny system of marriage is linked with other problems such as trafficking that disturb the normal physical as well as social functioning of the victims. Not surprisingly, physical violence is a major cause of injury to women ranging from relatively major cuts and bruises to permanent disability and death. In developed countries like Canada, about 43 percent of women injured by their partners had to receive medical care and about 50 percent injured had to take time from work (Rodgers, 1994: 5).It has been reported that abused women also have reduced physical functioning than non-abused women (Golding, 1996; Laserman *et al.*, 1996). Physical violence may lead to many kinds of physical ailments including irritable bowel syndrome, gastrointestinal disorder and various chronic pain syndromes. Many of the women are found to be suffering from these complications in the arsenic vulnerable areas due to the violence against them. But, many women do not volunteer information, and many of them are reluctant to disclose violence unless they are asked directly about violence after establishing rapport. Still, it is difficult to provide accurate numerical data on the impact of physical abuse associated with physical ailments. The information has given in this paper is based on case study.

Many women consider the psychological consequences of violence to be even more serious than its physical effects. The experience of abuse often erodes women's self esteem and puts them in greater risk of a variety of mental health problems including depression, post-traumatic stress disorder and suicide. These are also associated with desertion, separation, divorce and polygyny. In Bangladesh, the majority women are dependent on their husbands but in case of separation or divorce they become destitutes if they do not get support from their natal families. Under the circumstances, many divorced women become the victims of trafficking with the false of employment and remarriage by the traffickers otherwise they have to depend on begging to survive. Paul and Hasnath (2000) in their study stated that New Delhi and Karachi are the major South Asian centers for the international buying and selling of trafficked women from Bangladesh as slaves, maids or prostitutes.

The violence against women not only creates problems for them but also it affects the care and protection of their children (Halim,1995: 41). Children who witness marital violence of their parents face increased risk for such emotional and behavioral problems as anxiety, depression, poor school performance, low self esteem, disobedience and physical health complaints (Jouriles *et al.*, 1989: 454; McCloskey *et al.*, 1995). It seems to be many children of arsenicosis-affected women and trafficked victim fled away from their houses and became street and working children due to unhappy family life of their parents and also for marital dissolution. It has been reported that the divorced mothers are in great anxiety about the fate of their daughters, how they can arrange money for dowry for the marriage of their daughters when they will be grownup. Under the circumstances, many of the children become the victims of child trafficking. It has been found that many of the girls become floating child prostitutes in urban settings. Floating prostitution is the most vulnerable form of prostitution in which the girls are exposed to a variety of exploitation (Khan and Arefeen,1990: 35). Moreover, child labor is also outcome of domestic violence against women. It has been observed that many children could not adjust with their second families and ultimately they join with the street children.

The probability of consequences of trafficking are the divorced women and their young daughters may be the victims of deception with the false hope of employment and marriage and ultimately many of them may be involved in sex trade, many trafficked children may be compelled to camel jockeying, many children of the divorced mothers may be the subject of bondage labor, and many trafficked victims are to be sold by the trafficker for organ harvesting (Sarker and Panday, 2006:7). Many sex workers in Bangladesh are trafficked victims who are involved in sex trade either in prostitutions or hotels or hired houses. The traditional culture does not permit to reintegrate of the women at the family and community levels once they were victims of trafficking because their loss of chastity which is highly praised in Bangladesh (Sarker,2006:52). Under the circumstances, there is a possibility of expansion of HIV/AIDS due to unsafe sex. In Bangladesh, prostitution is illegal; therefore the sex workers are not officially managed and their health is not monitored and as a result there is a probability of infection with HIVAIDS of sex workers.

CONCLUSION

Arsenic contamination in ground water of Bangladesh is a well established fact that has put millions of lives at risk while hundreds have been already died of its poisoning. The women and children are worst sufferers not only involving health but also in psycho-social problems. The donor agencies like UNICEF, WHO, World Bank, UNDP, SDC and so on are working in close cooperation with the government of Organizations (GOs) and the Non-Government Organizations

(NGOs) to mitigate the problems of arsenic contamination in groundwater and the resultant arsenic poisoning. But, these donor organizations, GOs and NGOs did not extend their cooperation and help towards the women patients of arsenicosis and their children who are suffering from physical, economic and psycho-social problems that already polluted the social environment in the arsenic vulnerable areas of Bangladesh. In the circumstances, to get rid of these problems the following policies may be adopted for the wellbeing of the women and children.

- Awareness campaigns should be initiated at the individual, family and community levels to motivate the people that arsenicosis is neither a contagious nor an inherited disease. This campaign should motivate the husbands not to discard marital tie by desertion, separation and divorce.
- Female empowerment is one of the important preventive measures to get rid of violence against women. Empowering women is not only a worthy goal in their own right but also a key strategy in eliminating gender-based violence. Women will never escape violence as long as they are financially dependent on men and derive their social values exclusively from their role as wife and mother.
- Sensitize the law enforcement personnel is an essential measure in reducing violence against women in Bangladesh. The procedural barriers, gaps and biases undermine the law's ability to deter violence as well as trafficking of women and children to get social justice..
- Compensation for the divorcees along with their children from their husbands should be maintained strictly in order to maintain minimal standard of living so that they can live like other members of the society.
- The Government of Bangladesh should introduce shelter house program in close cooperation with NGOs specially for the women and the children who are

victims of violence and trafficking. In the shelter house, there will be skill development training and employment opportunities for the victims so that they can stand on their own feet

REFERENCES

Ahmed,SM., Chowdhury, M. and Bhuiya, A.(2001), "Microcredit and Emotional Well-Being: Experience of Poor Rural Women from Matlab, Bangladesh,"*World Development*, 29 (11),pp.1957-66.

Alder, C. (1992), "Violence, Genger and Social Change". *International Social Science Journal*, 132 (2) pp.267-76.

Ammerman, Robert T. and Hersen, Michel (1999), "Current Issues in the Assessment of Family Violence: An Update." In Ammerman, R.T. and Hersen, M(eds.) Assessment of Family Violence: A Clinical and Legal Source Book. New York, John Wiley & Sons, Inc.

Aziz, A.K.M. and Maloney, C. (1985), *Life Stages, Gender and Fertility in Bangladesh*. Dhaka., ICDDR,B..

Bachman, R. and Saltzman,LE (1995), Violence Against Women: Estimates from the Redesigned Survey, National Crime Victimization Survey, Bureau of Justice Statistics, Washington DC..

Bradley, C.S. (1985), "Attitudes and Practices Relating to Marital Violence among Tolai of East New Britain". In: Toft, S. (ed.), *Domestic Violence in Papua New Guinea*. Boroko, PNG Law Reform Commission.

Cain, M. , khanam, SR and Nahar, S. (1979), "Class, Patriarch and Women's Work in Bangladesh". *Population Development Review*, (5), pp.405-38

Denjin, Norman K. (1984), "Towards a Phenomenology of Domestic, Family Violence. *AmericanJournal of Sociology*, 90(3). pp. 483-513.

Fletcher, Ronald (1981), Sociology: The Study of Social System. New York, Charles Scribner's Sons.

Gelles, R,J., and Straus, M.A. (1979), Determinants of Violence in the Family: Towards a Theoretical Integration. In W.R. Burr, R. Hill,F.I.. Nye, and I.L.Reiss (eds), Contemporary Theories about the Family. New York, Free Press.

Golding, J.M. (1996), "Sexual Assault History and Limitations in Physical Functioning of Two General Population Samples". *Research in Nursing and Health*, 19 (1). pp. 33-44.

Gonjalez, Montes S. (1998), "Domestic Violence in Cuetzalan, Mexico: Some Research Questions and Results." In: *Proceedings of The Third Annual Meeting of the International Research Network on Violence against Women.* Mexico, Center for Health and Gender Equity.

Government of Bangladesh (GOB) (1997), *The Environment Conservation Rules, 1997.* SRO 117-Law/17, 27 August.

Hadi, A.(2005), "Prevalence and Correlates of the Risk of Marital Sexual Violence in Bangladesh" ,*Journal of Interpersonal Violence*.15 (8) pp..181-89

Halim, M.A. (1995), *Women's Crisis within Family in Bangladesh.* Dhaka, The Bangladesh Society for the Enforcement of Human Rights.

Hartmann, B.and Boyce, J.(1983), *A Quiet Violence:View from a Bangladesh Village*, London, Zed Books..

Hassan, Y. (1995), *The Haven Become Hell: A Study of Domestic Violence in Pakistan.* Pakistan, Cantt. L.

Haugarrd, Jefferey J.(1999), Epidemiology of Family Violence Involving Children. In Ammerman,R.T.and Hersen, M. (eds.) Assessment of Family Violence: A Clinical and Legal Source Book. New York, John Wiley & Sons, Inc.

Hoffman, L.K., Demo, D.N. and Edward, J.N. (1994), "Physical Wife Abuse in a Non-Western Society: An Integrated Theoretical Approach". *Journal of Marriage and Family*, (56). pp. 131-146.

Jouriles, E.N., Murphy, C.M. and O'Leary, K.D. (1989), "Inter-Spousal Aggression, Marital Discord and Child Problems." *Journal of Consulting and Clinical Psychology*, 57 (3). pp. 453-455.

Kabeer,N. (1989), Monitoring Poverty as if Gender Mattered : A Methodology for Rural Bangladesh, IDS Discussion Paper255, Briton, Institute of Development Studies

Kantor, P.(1996), ViolenceagainstWomen:AglobalIssue. http://metab.unc.edu/ucis/pubs/Carolina_Papers/Abuse/figure1.html.

Khan, Z.R. and Arefeen, H.K. (1990), *The Situation of Child Prostitutes in Bangladesh.* Dhaka, Center for Social Studies.

Koenig,MA., Ahmed, S.,Hossain, MB. and Mozumder, ABMKA. (2003), "Women Status and Domestic Violence in Rural

Bangladesh: Individual and Community Level Effects". *Demgraphy*, (40), pp.269-88.

Kottak, Philip (2005), Miror for Humanity. Mcgraw Hill, New Work.

Landrigan, Philip J. (1992), Arsenic. In: William, N.R. (ed.). *Environmental and Occupational Medicine*. Boston, Little Brown & Company.

Leserman, J., Drassman, D.A.U.Z., Toomey, T.C., Nachman, G. and Glogan, L. (1996), "Sexual and Physical Abuse History in Gastroenterology Practice: How Types of Abuse Impact Health Status." *Psychosomatic Medicine*, 58(1). pp. 4-15.

McCloskey, L.A., Figueredo, A. J. and Koss, M.P. (1995), "The Effects of Systematic Family Violence on Children's Mental Health." *Child Development*, 66(5). pp.1239-1269.

Muzumder, Kalindi. (1992), Women and Violence. An Unpublished Research Paper. Bombay, Nirmola Niketon.

Paul, Bimal K. and Hasnath, S.A. (2000), Trafficking of Women and Girls , *Geographical Review*.90 (2), pp,45-56.

Prigoff, Arline (1994), "Research on Gender: Implications for Social Work and Social Development." *Social Development Issues*., 16(1). pp. 3-17.

Rahman, Habibur M. (1984), "Changing Status of Women in Bangladesh." *Current Sociological Perspective*, 3(1). pp. 30-38.

Rodgers, K. (1994), "Wife Assault: The Findings of a National Survey." *Canadian Center for Justice Statistics*, 14(9). pp. 1-22.

Sarker, Profulla C. (1997), Social Structure and Fertility Behavior. Dhaka, Center for Social Services.

Sarker, Profulla C.(1999), "Beliefs and Arsenicosis and their Impact on Social Disintegration in Bangladesh." In: *Proceedings of Joint Conference of AASW, IFSW, APASWE and AASWE*. Brisbane, Australia.

Sarker, Profulla C.(1999), "Gender Dichotomization, Use of Contraceptive Devices and Their Impact of Social Development in Bangladesh." *Indian Social Science Review*, 1(1). pp. 203-211.

Sarker, Profulla C. (2006), "Gender Inequality and Its Impact on Trafficking, Sex Trade and Probability of HIV/AIDS in Bangladesh: Challenges to Social Work Intervention. Journal of Societal & Social Policy, 5(3) pp49-61.

Sarker, Profulla C. and Panday, Pranab K. (2006), Trafficking in Women and Children in Bangladesh. Asian Journal of Social Policy 2(2) pp.1-13.

Schuler, S.R., Hashemi, S.M., Riley, A.R. and Akhter, S. (1996), "Credit Programs, Patriarchy and Men's Violence against Women in Rural Bangladesh." *Social Science and Medicine*, 43(12). pp. 1729-1742.

Tarafdar, S.A. (1998), Arsenic Contamination in Ground Water of Bangladesh: Analytical Aspects. Dhaka, An Unpublished paper of Bangladesh Atomic Energy Commission.

United Nations General Assembly (UNGA) (1993), Declaration on the Elimination of Violence against Women. In: *Proceedings of the 85th Plenary Meeting*. Geneva.

Unicef (2000), Domestic Violence against Women and Girls. Innocenti Research Center, Folrence, Italy.

Viseria, L. (1999), "Violence against Women in India: Evidence from Rural Gujarat,." *Domestic Violence in India*, (1). pp. 9-37.

World Health Organization (1984), *Guidelines for Drinking-water Quality*. Geneva.

9

PROBLEMS OF MARRIED WORKING WOMEN IN INDIA AND THEIR NATURE OF ADJUSTMENT

Bhaswati Roy
Soumyajit Patra
Samita Manna

INTRODUCTION

The women, facing such problems and conflicts, accept it as a challenge and continuously try to cope with the stressful situations. If adjustment means 'to enter into a harmonious relationship', the married working women have to facilitate a two way adjustment with their family members and with their colleagues and authority in their work place, which is more difficult and more problematic.

Universally, women's natural place is in home, whether they are employed or not. From time immemorial, the caring for and rearing children are their most important role. Karl (1995) states,

Women are almost universally responsible for caring for children and other members of the household and for all the domestic work

that their caring roles entail. They often have primary responsibility for their families' health and for the provision of food, water and fuel, and their work is not only unpaid, but largely unrecognized as well. Their major responsibilities for the household's well being do not always mean decision making power within the family.

In respect to men, their identity and status are always derived from the roles of mothers, daughters and wives. Domestication or housewification of women is purely an attempt to show them as dependent and subordinate to men because a housewife is a woman who does her household work and performs her role as a family role. According to Hunt(1968),

A housewife is "the person, other than a domestic servant who is responsible for most of the household duties (or for supervising a domestic servant who carries out these duties)".

Patriarchy or patriarchal family is one, which has perpetuated 'oppression of women'. Male–female relation in such a system is hierarchical (Rani: 1988). The hierarchical gender relations in patriarchy retain the oppression of women in society. They are subjugated in all spheres. Patriarchy does not grant equal status and power in the family. The work roles of men and women are not identical. Women's status is considered as inferior even if they equally share men's activities under patriarchal system. Their property right is also circumscribed sometimes.

Patriarchy actually means male power over the female. Power is personal, physical and institutional. The male dominance sustains through systems of ideas and beliefs and views as 'normal' and 'right'. The subordination of women by men and male coercion is perpetuated through social arrangements, cultural traditions and political management. As Coppock et al (1995) opine,

Although the degree of subjugation within and between any of these relations may differ, all women throughout the world experience the institutionalized and interpersonal dominance of men

The inequalities in a patriarchal system exercise violence towards women. All kinds of women violence are actually generated from the peculiar idea of women as property and as objects of exchange. As Maynard (1993) envisages,

> *... it was the extension of a system of practices and laws which sanctioned men's rights to regard women as their property and therefore to keep them under their control.*

Indian society is always hierarchical and patriarchal. In the Indian social structure the status of woman is always secondary. The concept of equality between men and women is alien to the Indian society. In the man dominated family structure, women are subordinate to their fathers, husbands or sons. Their job is to manage and perform the household chores and rear the children. Traditionally, they had no freedom and had to manage the house whatever with money the husband put in her hand. Indian tradition has always encouraged the subordination and subservience of women, praised their self-sacrifice and promoted their subjugation. The Indian women are also treated as an appendage of men. They were regarded as degraded and just like slaves (Devi : 1982).

Indian value system plays an important role for making the poor status of women. Devotion to the husband is regarded as very important in Hindu religion. It is originated from the Hindu concept of *patibrata* (loyal to huṣband) that denotes a wife who has gladly accepted the devoted service to her husband as her ultimate goal of life. In Hindu tradition, the women always live under the male control. The ideal women never try to break the bond of such control. Their happiness depends on the virtue and chastity as daughters, wives and widows.

Within the family (mainly in traditional and rural), which was joint and patriarchal in nature, women were treated as male's property just like men's own land and. the sons were only eligible to inherit the family property. Women could not sacrifice to the gods, because their presence was often considered as polluting (Liddle and Joshi : 1986).

But it was not the position of Indian women from the beginning of the society. Even in the early Vedic period (2500Be to 1500BC) women enjoyed freedom in their family, marriage and religions life. But gradually during the ages of Upanishads

(500BC to 500AD) the position of Indian women was going to be worsened. Slowly and gradually the arrival of the Arabs and Turks in 11th and 12th centuries and the Mughals in the 16th century made the condition of the women more critical and problematic.

Thus polygyny, child marriage, *purdah* (seclusion) system, *sati* custom, illiteracy, permanent widowhood and women subordination to men were the main characteristics of the Hindu society. The society demanded faithfulness and sincerity from a wife but she could not expect these from her husband. In this way women's freedom was snatched gradually and they were assigned to a status of unpaid domestic servants. (Chakraborty : 1978).

After the advent of the British rule and expansion of new western education, many wide opportunities had been opened to the women and as a result, a new horizon appeared leading towards the modernization of Indian society. Western education tried to bring a sense of nationality and liberty among the Indians. Actually expansion of education along with industrialization and urbanization increased women's skills and qualities. Indian joint families, which were the origin of different rigid social norms, gradually became weak under the impact of urbanization. People left their villages and began to live in different towns and cities. The new environment of these towns and cities were quiet free from the rigid traditional norms of the society. New opportunity of education and liberal social attitude of these urban areas facilitated the advancement of women's status. Industrialisation generated many job–opportunities due to increasing demand of productivity which did not require laborious physical work but the technical skills, intelligence and patience. Women entered in economic activities as they had acquired of such qualities and achieved the skills through training and higher education.

The age-old hindrances came to be faded in facing the economic crisis of the present age. The middle class women, who were engaged in different gainful employment, were regarded as precious property of the family (Mehta: 1975). Women began to join in outside job more and more. This helped to raise their status both in the families and society. That the actual reason behind all kinds of oppression is economic dependence on the male members of the family was realized by the women. In this connection Karl's(1995) opinion is remarkable.

Women's unpaid household work is usually not valued or considered a contribution to the economy. Lack of income, or lower income, also reduces women's decision-making power in the household and their ability to participate in social and political activities.

II

THE WORKING WOMEN

Women who are employed outside their homes and who work for fixed hours and who are paid regular wages or salary by their employers, can be termed as working woman. As Kapur (1970) opines,

Those women who are gainfully employed and not for those who are engaged in social work or are doing honorary job.

Similarly, according to Anjana (1993)

A 'working women' today refers to a woman who works outside her home for a wage or salary.

A large number of women have participated in Indian work force but it remains meagre in number in relation to their male counterpart. Female work participation rates were 23.31, 27.93, 14.22 and 20.85 percents in the census of 1951, 1961, 1971 and 1981 respectively. Under the new definition of work in 1971 census the rate was 12.06 percent and 13.99 percents in 1981 census showing a slight improvement (Swarnalatha: 1993). According to the 1991 census the total number of working women is 278.35 million, which represents a growth rate of 26.12%. One third of the labour force of India consists of women (Anjana: 1993). It has been recognised in the 48th session of the International Labour Conference (1963) that women play a vital role in the economic and social life. In the world as a whole, 27 out of every 100 women are economically active and about a third of the world's labour force is made up of women (Chakroborty: 1978).

Even the women who have gained the working status, always are considered as inferior or subordinate in relation to the men. In all patriarchal societies the position of women in the family are clearly defined by men (Hareven: 1977). McDowell and Pringle (1992) also write,

Women are constantly defined in relation to men. Whether they are similar to men, different from or complementary to them, men, masculinity and male behaviour are always the reference points.

Female tasks are primarily serving her husband, looking after her children and doing all household duties whether they are employed or not. The load of these household activities is no less important and vast but always accord low status) (Agarwal: 1988).

A married-working woman confronts a triple burden of children, home and work. This idea is deeply rooted in our social condition and men feel that it is below the dignity to help in the household chores. Some times it is also thought that men are incapable to do domestic activities. As Lewis (1992) opines,

Men and women in many cultures and subcultures subscribe to the view that men are inept or incapable of domestic work and this serves to excuse men's non-participation in family work....

Thus, the woman overstrains herself to manage both the domestic and the work spheres effectively. She has to perform the multiple roles of as wife, mother and worker and spent all her energy for this. Motherhood to such women creates difficulties. A working mother often suffers from a guilty complex. She feels guilty of neglecting her children and the family because she gets less time to spend with them. The women continue to strive harder and try to prove that no one will suffer from their dual life. In counting their workload Rowbotham (1992) shows,

Women received less than one tenth of the world income, but do two-thirds of the world's work. Although earning less than men, they longer hours 2 to 5 hours more in developed countries, 5 to 6 hours more in Latin America and the Caribbean and as much as 12 to 13 hours more in Africa and Asia. When housework and child-care are taken into account, women on average have a 60 to 70 hours week.

Maladjustment denotes disorder in adjustment condition. Proper adjustment is achieved by a balance between the expected role and performed role which brings conformity with the role demands (Mathur: 1992). Adjustment denotes a process by which an individual enters into a harmonious or healthy relationship with his/her environment by fulfilling all kinds of needs. Joshi (1999) points out that,

... term used to refer the process whereby an individual or a social unit enters into a healthy relationship with his environment, physical or social.

In this connection, Reber's (1985) definition is worth mentioning. He defines the word adjustment as,

A state of complete equilibrium between an organism and its environment, a state wherein in all needs are satisfied and all organismic functions are being carried out smoothly.

It is an on going process in which a person develops his/her potential in reacting to and in turn changing the environment in healthy effective manner. To describe the etmological meaning of the word adjustment, Joshi (1999) says,

The word adjustment has been taken from the Dutch word 'Aanpassen' which means associating one self with someone or adjusting one self to certain circumstances, to a new environment.

Thus, it can be said that the process of adjustment takes place when any person tries to modify his/her action process or behaviour or thinking process to adapt with a complex and stressful or new situation. In any stressful situation, men or women continuously try to alter the environment in a healthy manner using their own intelligence and potentiality. This is known as adjustment process. As Sutherland (1989) mentions,

Modifications in behaviour or thought process that capable the organism to deal adaptively with changes in its environment or in its own capacities.

Different coping strategies from the stressful condition or maladjustment state are adopted by the working women as multiple roles. The intensity of distress can be minimized through three important processes namely, *rationalization, compartmentalization* and *adjudication*. *Rationalization* gives a redefinition of unpleasant situations and thereby makes those socially and personally acceptable. Through the technique of compartmentalization a carrier woman keeps apart the opposing role. *Adjudication* is a formal procedure to reducing individual guilt feeling by turning over the burden to the third party (Mathur: 1992).

III

SOCIO-ECONOMIC PROFILE OF THE WORKING WOMEN

The survey was conducted on 385 married working women at Kalyani Township[1] under Nadia district[2] (Table 1). Table 2 describes different socio–economic profiles[3] of working women. Various problems of adjustment of working women have been observed as the working women have to perform the dual role: House wives and office employees. Many important areas of adjustment are located in this work and finally the coping strategies of them are also noticed for survival óf their better future.

Radical feminists often suggest a complete reallocation of power even at the cost of family ties, abolishing every form of gender division of labour in order to establish a gender-just society. Definitely their emphasis is on establishing multidimensional economic bonds between the women and the wider society, apart from the services to which they are assigned traditionally.

The waves of modernisation, and now globalisation, not only inculcate new values pointing to qualitative changes in the relation between two sexes, but also create a need for recognition not as a subject but as a citizen. We can say that western notion of equality is severely hunting the 'culture of hierarchy' which emphasises on 'self denial' '*sublimating* the ego' (Chitnis 1988). These new values can not act in a 'vacuum and need new institutions for their sustenance and expression' (Beteille 2000).

The adjustment problems of the women in general and working women in particular, should be analysed from this perspective. The need for recognition, in popular metaphor identity, is for obvious reasons, more acute among the working group. They are not only economically self sufficient, not to say economically empowered, but also exposed to global views regarding the status of women and new gender relations which are continuously being advocated by the western feminists. And this is what led Beteille (ibid. 2000) to conclude that women's movement, in our country, is 'confined largely to urban, westernized middle–and upper-middle-class women'.

May be this is a transitional period in which the women have been caught between the two worlds. Though there is a growing consensus among the sociologists that participation of the women in 'collective organising actions' outside the family is a prerequisite to gender equality, till now the shackles of tradition confine them (Helen 1994). Our observation also justifies it.

All the family members of the married working women think of themselves progressive as they allow their 'home manager' to go to the work place. We particularly emphasise on this aspect of Indian mind. Sharma (2000) analysed the importance of 'cultural psychy' in reinforcing the mechanism of 'cultural hierarchy'. Through a rigorous gender socialization this psyche is developed which assigns the women to their primary and essential responsibilities related to domestic affairs. Thus, as Chowdhury (1999) thinks, the adjustment problems of the working women, particularly those who are married, arise from the discrepancy between 'individual right of women on the one hand' and the right of cultural and the religious practices on the other'. But these people think that official responsibilities are primary for the men as the women are mere 'social appendix' to their husbands

IV

But there is a fundamental difference between the attitude of Indian and western women towards patriarchy or, simply towards male domination. Indian feminism is some how compromising, 'the anger in western feminism' is absent here (Chitnis: 1988).

The dialectic between the gradually emerging value system which emphasises on individualism, particularism and identity consciousness and peculiar attitude of Indian women towards patriarchy has given rise to the notion of adjustment.

The influence of social surroundings plays a vital role on developing the adjustment capacity of any working woman. In a patriarchal society, a woman always learns to adjust with the male domination in every sphere of her life. On the other hand, in a matriarchal society she learns to behave differently. So whether she will give importance to male domination or female hegemony is also determined by the socialisation process. Perhaps the glorious heritage of Indian family system has been maintained generation after generation by the Indian women–thanks to their extreme adjustment capability.

The women are socialised to be an ideal wife and good mother and learn the virtue of adjustment and patience from their very childhood. Sengupta (2000) in her study on *Socio-Cultural Dimension Influencing Status of Rural Women*, gives the view that women from very childhood, learn to carry out all the responsibilities as wives and this also helps them to accept the subordinate status in a system of hierarchical relation within the family. Generally, the traditional Indian wives must consider their husbands as their god and must obey their instructions without any question.

With motherhood, such women face much more difficulties. Working mothers often suffer from various guilty complexes because they think that they are unable to spend sufficient time for their children. Dual responsibilities in office and home create a situation of maladjustment for the working women. The roles of mother, wife, daughter-in-law and official roles of working women are often conflicting and confusing. Women who are working frequently suffer from the problems of adjustment. Such problems of adjustment are more prominent when a working woman's children, husband and other family members do not cooperate with her. But the working women always try to win over conflicting situations by formulating their own coping strategies. Such coping strategies are not capable of removing all such problems fully but to some extent give relief to the working women to maintain their dual life smoothly.

Major problems of the married working women are, in many of the cases, created by their in-laws. They demand more and more time and service from them. In the present study out of 385 respondents, 153 (39.74%) respondents have opined that their in-laws constantly pressurised them to resign from their service. A highly educated respondent in Block B described her experience during the time of field work:

I got the appointment letter a few months after my marriage. My husband was liberal and he encouraged me to join. I imagined a shackle free life. But the first objection came from my mother-in-law. She was uncompromising. I was too. And I joined. The conflict became serious. From the very beginning of my joining my mother-in-law and gradually my father-in-law stopped conversation with me. I convinced my husband and made a separation from my in-laws. Now we are happy.

Out of 385, 220 (57.14%) respondents have said that their in-laws allow them to continue their services. But at the same time most of them have also opined that their in-laws do not generally co-operate with them in domestic activities.

However, in general, all respondents of the present study have unanimously agreed that they have to take extra care to manage or satisfy their in-laws. But in most of the cases it is found that the non-cooperation and ill behaviour of the in-laws lead to separation. The married working women strategically adopt four measures to make a balance. These are :

1. they take extra responsibilities in domestic activities and work more for the family members so that the in-laws could not have anything to say. The measure are taken by the 14.03% respondents;

2. they try to appease the family members in all possible ways. The study shows that 14.55% married working women take this measure;
3. they spend more money for the family members. Some respondents think that the in-laws become more non-cooperative when they think that they have no claim on respondents' income. This are adopted by 10.65% respondents;
4. in extreme cases they have to become separated from the in-laws and establish a new household with their husbands. The present study shows that in more than 60.78% cases the respondents could not continue with their in-laws (Table 3).

To measure the adjustment capacity of the respondents two inventories have been used. First is the *Indian Adaptation of Bell's Adjustment Inventory*[4] and second is the *Marital Adjustment Questionnaire*[5]. The Bell's Adjustment Inventory is prepared by Dr. L. Sharma who suggests different scores for measuring four areas of Adjustment-*Home, health, social* and *emotional,* separately. In this context Sharma wrote

Home adjustment refers in terms of healthy relationship with family members possessed healthy and balanced home life, adjustment of health, in terms of physical as well as mental illness, social adjustment in terms of social behaviour extroversion-introversion, submissiveness, shyness etc, and emotional adjustment refers to nervousness depression and other factors of emotional aspect of life.

Marital Adjustment Questionnaire is developed by Dr. P. Kumar and Dr. K. Rohatgi (1987) to measure marital adjustment capacity. Married couple must learn to live together to share, accommodate, compromise, adjust and plan together. When the couple fails to develop a relationship characterised by mutual acceptance there arise the problems in marital relationship.

The working women have opined that in their parental family the dominance of the father is much more than their mother (57.14%) as per the rule of patriarchal society. Such influence of patriarchal dominance no doubt put a great impact on the respondents in their own married life by which they easily adjust with the dominance of their husbands in different family matters.

The difference in *family adjustments* scores has been studied through t-test between different categories of the respondents (Table 4). For this purpose Bell's Adjustment Inventory has been used. The married working women of Kalyani have been categorized in eight distinctive groups[6] considering their education pattern of family and nature of job.

Again these eight distinctive groups have been arranged into four sets of groups[7] for making comparison in each set of groups by which *familial adjustment* pattern of different groups of working women can be assessed.

Bell's Adjustment Inventory for measuring *family adjustment* is consisting of 21 items. Possible score range is 0 – 21. The objective midpoint is 10.50. High score indicates low family adjustment and low score indicates high *family adjustment*. All the mean scores of different groups lie on the positive side of the midpoint. So it can be said that the respondents definitely have family adjustment problems among different groups but as the scores are not too high the *family adjustment* problems are not so serious among them(Table 4).

No statistically significant difference has been found when the respondents are categorised on the basis of their education. But the difference is statistically significant between the respondents living in nuclear family and those living in extended family (t value is 3.29, significant as 5% level of significance). For obvious reasons the married working women living in extended family have more adjustment capacity. The difference of the family adjustment scores between married working women with teaching profession or without teaching profession is not statistically significant. At the same time the difference of the family adjustment scores between Group-D staffs and officers among the married non-teaching working women in Kalyani is also not significant statistically.

Out of 385 respondents, only 111(28.83%) respondents have opined that their husbands are cooperative and no conflict arises between them regarding their employment. But most of the respondents have denied this.

If they do not return home in time or go to office earlier than usual their husbands express dissatisfaction. As a consequence the family environment is spoiled. In 88.32% cases the consequence turns towards no conversation between the husbands and wives when conflict becomes acute. One respondent has also opined that her husband beat her if she argues with him. It is important that respondents having higher educational qualification also have to face these undesirable situation. Devendra (1996) in his work on *Changing Status of Women in India* has shown that the ambivalent attitude of a husband towards a working wife imposes much strain on her and leads to a greater physical and even emotional stress. Sengupta (2000) thinks that the husbands of married working women seem to suffer from psychological insecurity because of the working status of their wives as they fear that their position in the family may be dismissed. A greater need to control the working wives are seen among them.

The problems, in case of the working women are often created by the in laws, relatives and sometimes by their own children who think that they are deprived due to her service. The consequences of such conflict turn into different forms of torture. In majority of the cases the husbands unnecessarily stop conversation with them. This is one form of mental torture which the wives face occasionally. Majority of the respondents have opined that they just tolerate such type of torture (96.36%). But they are not ready to give up their job. At the same time, it has been noticed that generally they do not protest against such torture. Only 3 respondents (1.09%) want to give up their job. They want to resign from their jobs in order to get relief from the torture and misbehaviour of their husbands. 7 respondents (2.55%) who face serious conflict in their daily life want to live separately from their husbands.

But husband–wife relation is so idealised that mere conflict can not break it. Ramu (1988) beautifully illustrates :

This is because domestic relation are not commodity relations with clear notions of gains and losses ... Despite the hierarchical nature of marital roles with the structural potential for conflict, coercion and oppression, they are constructed on mutual understanding, affection, sensuality and attachment which permit couples to realise the fundamental objectives of marriage and family.

The same thing has been reflected in this study. 83.78% respondents' evaluation of their conjugal relationship is positive and satisfactory. Out of 385 respondents only 4(0.64%) have expressed an opposite view. This figure is negligible. As a whole it can be said that despite occasional conflicts the husband-wife relationship in case of the present respondents, is good. It is also true, at the same time, that this has much been possible due to the adjustment capacity of the women, which is consciously built among them through a peculiar gender specific socialisation. Though some emphasis on the role of males in women empowerment is placed recently in the name of gender equality or gender empowerment, the researcher personally thinks that women always have to develop some conflict management strategies to continue husband–wife relationship and family life. Generally the husbands take very little responsibilities in their daily life than their wives.

In the present study the *marital adjustment* of different categories of respondents has been statistically measured (Table 5). For this purpose Marital Adjustment Questionnaire has been used[8]. The married working women of Kalyani have been categorised into five distinctive groups[8] considering their education and nature of job.

Again these five distinctive groups have been arranged in to three sets of groups[9] for making comparison in each set of groups by which marital adjustment pattern of different groups of working women can be assessed.

Marital Adjustment Questionnaire is consisting of 25 items. Possible score range is 0 to 25. The objective mid point is 12.50. All the mean scores lie on the positive side of the mid point. The calculated scores are high enough. High score indicates high *marital adjustment* and low score indicates low *marital adjustment* between husband and wife. Table 5 shows that the difference in *marital adjustment* scores between the respondents who are educated in below graduation level and those who are educated in above graduation level is statistically significant at 5% level (t = 3.26). But no statistically significant difference has been found when the respondents are categoriesed officers and teachers. In the same way there is also no statistically significant difference between Group-D staffs and officers.

The relationship between various attributes of wife, and husbands-wife relationship has been studied through c^2 test. For the present purpose four attributes of the respondents have been selected. These are respondents' education, income, employment and age. Table 6 shows that education, income and age of the wife have no statistically significant impact on husband-wife relation. But there is statistically significant difference between various categories of employment and husband-wife relations (value of c^2 is 35.58 which is significant at 5% level).

The major source of conflict between husbands and their working wives is related to child care. The children of the working mothers often do not get the company of their parents, and as a consequence many problems arise. In the present study 161(43.28%) respondents have said that the problem of their children is mainly mental (Table 7). Out of 372 respondents who have children, 22(5.91%) respondents also have opined that their absence hampers the study of their children. Mostly, the working mothers have to take more initiative to solve this problem than their working fathers. 40(10.75%) respondents also think that they will resign from their services for their children and family if necessary (Table 7). Majority of them have higher educational qualification.. But more than 72.00% respondents prefer to take leave when necessary. They have also opined that when their children suffer from any problem, physical or others they are used to take leave. But their husbands rarely stay in home for their children.

Thus the married working women always have to adjust with their family members on the one hand and with their office colleagues on the other. They loss their energy, they sacrifice their career and accept the role of housewife as primary. Though the impact of women liberation movement is found among them, they always try to adjust emotionally with these situations. So they often think that this is somehow a normal situation. In order to inquire whether or not there is any significant difference in the *emotional adjustment,* Bell's Adjustment Inventory has been used. The married working women of Kalyani have been categorised in eight distinctive groups and four heads of group are framed from it (vide note 6 and 7).

Bell's Adjustment Inventory measuring *emotional adjustment* is consisting of 18 items. Possible score range is 0 to 18. The objective midpoint is 9.00. High score means low emotional adjustment and low score indicates high *emotional adjustment.* It has been observed that all the scores lie on the positive side of the midpoint so it is clear that the *emotional adjustment* problems exist among the married working women. The difference in emotional adjustment scores between the different categories of the respondents is not statistically significant (Table 8).

For quite obvious reasons the working women interact more with the people of different categories than the housewives. So they also have to adjust with the wider society in various ways and for various reasons. In order to examine the difference in the *social adjustment* scores between different categories of married working women, Bell's Adjustment Inventory has been used.(vide note 6 and 7)

Table 9 shows the test of significance of the difference between *social adjustment* scores of different categories of married working women. Bell's Adjustment Inventory for measuring *social adjustment* is consisting of 21 items. Possible score range is 0 to 21. The objective mid point is 10.50. High score indicates low social adjustment and low score indicates high social adjustment. All the mean scores lie on the positive side of the mid point. So it can be said that definitely some *social adjustment* problems exist among them. No statistically significant difference in the social adjustment scores is found between the respondents when they are categorised on the basis of their education. The differences in social adjustment scores between the respondents living in nuclear family and extended family are statistically significant at 5% level (calculated value of is 3.07). No statistically significant difference in the *social adjustment* scores is found between the respondents when they are categorised on the basis of their occupation.

Health adjustment is crucial for all individuals. Good adjustment in social, family and emotional state also influences the health adjustment of anyone. Adjustment problems in other three spheres bring problems in health adjustment as a result most of them are affected by physical and mental illness. Table 10 shows the test of significance of the difference between *health adjustment* score of different categories of married working women. For this purpose Bell's Adjustment Inventory has been used.(vide note 6 and 7) .

Bell's Adjustment Inventory to measure *health adjustment* is consisting of 20 items. The objective midpoint is 10.00. All the mean scores lie on the negative side of the midpoint. As high score indicates low *health adjustment* and low score denotes high health adjustment. Here it can be said that as the mean scores lie on the negative side of the objective mid point the respondents have good *health adjustment*. No statistically significant difference in *health adjustment* is found between the respondents of different categories.

Actually high occupation status and nuclear family give the respondents more freedom in social interaction. But the respondents have opined that whether they occupy high occupational position or not, restrictions are always imposed on their social interaction. They are not allowed to contact with their male colleagues or friends outside the office. In this regard, the working women, as a whole, have to depend on their husbands or their family members. Even in some cases restrictions are imposed on them in maintaining occupational relations. In these cases again the married working women have to find out a conflict management tactic. Thus employment in case of the married working women brings numerous problems in various ways which often break the normal rhythm of their life.

V

The conflict is between the growing need for self identity and the shackles of traditional values. But as Ramu (1988) points out that the 'domestic relations are not perceived by the most couples as commodity relations' the married working women start what is called 'Aanpassen' i.e. they try to adjust with the situation. If adjustment means entering into a harmonious relationship with others, the problem of adjustment of the married working women starts from the dilemma mentioned above.

A higher age of marriage of most of the educated urban woman makes the problem of adjustment difficult. In modern urban families the unmarried educated working women enjoy much freedom in their own families and in course of time they develop their own self image. Till now marriage is a *traditionally defined* obligations, which were developed on the basis of values like pativrata (obedient to husband), *snehashila* (affectionate) and *kartabyaparayana* (responsible). Beteille (2000) has rightly argued in favour no new institutions to accommodate the new values, new culturally prescribed goals.

Here we should mention that the married working women often have to bear the burden of double way adjustment – in their family and in their office. Sometimes they have to complete their official tasks in their home after managing all domestic responsibilities, overstraining themselves. More than 50 per cent of the respondents face this problem – they often complete their official duties in their home and thus adjust with the official responsibilities bestowed on them.

This leads us to two serious questions, Firstly, does economic self-sufficiency of the women automatically brings total empowerment for them ? No doubt economic self-sufficiency is a prerequisite for their participation in social arenas other than the demands of family. It also gives self confidence which is essential for developing their self image. But till now the occupation of the wife is not considered as an important 'resource' to determine the husband-wife relationships and the balance of power inherent in it. Here is an example. In our study, at least 12.50 per cent women, who financially help their parents, have opined that their husbands dislike it that means they do not have sufficient control over their own income. It is also more interesting that all women of this study take permission of their husbands before any expenditure from their own income. The same is not always true for their husbands. The wives often (or is most of the cases) are not consulted when their husbands spend money.

We are not denying that economic self sufficiency of the women has no alternative, but at the same time it is also true that Indian social system itself is a hindrance towards economic empowerment of the economically self sufficient women. And from this discrepancy again a conflict arises with which the women have to adjust again. This is the story of the *subjugation of an otherwise expanded ego*. Therefore, the women, here, not only adjust with their husbands or other family members, but also adjust with their self and perpetuate the marital bonds.

At present the Work Participation Rate (WPR) of the women in our country is closer to 25 per cent, we can expect it will increase in future (The Times of India 8-9-2004). Our second crucial question is if role conflict is inherent in women's employment, how long they will be able to bear the strain of adjustment?

The problem for the women is that they are forced to reinforce both the roles-in one sphere for legal compulsions and in other for traditional obligations. And if the number of working women increases what will be the future of family system? Working women's economic self sufficiency, self esteem, need for identity and globalised world view demand total empowerment. If we accept the zero sum concept of power we should admit that the empowerment of women at the same time disempowers their male counterparts. This may have a bearing on family ties. But it should not be the argument that the women should sacrifice generation after generation to maintain the fundamental solidarity of the family.

Here comes the question of conscientisation of the men to solve the problem. Sharma (2000) has rightly pointed out the 'exclusionary bias' in this regard. Once we argued (Manna and Patra 2001), following Beteille's (2000) stance, that it is not possible to remove authority as such from any social institutions.. What we want is a democratic environment and sympathetic co-operation to reduce the burden of women and at the same time to remove 'all obstacles to individual freedom' (Manna and Patra, 2001).

NOTES

This is the text of the UGC sponsored project sanctioned in the year 1999 and financed by the University Grants Commission. I express my deep sense of gratitude to the Secretary, UGC New Delhi for providing necessary financial support for this project.

1. Kalyani town is divided into three Blocks-Block A, Block B, Block C. Block B is purely residential and industrial and Block C is comprised of housing complex. The University of Kalyani is also situated in Block C. Some residential areas like Majherchar, Simanta colony, Natunpally Kanthaltala etc. are situated within the jurisdiction of Kalyani Municipality which have been referred to as Other Residental Areas, in the present study.
2. Nadia is one of the districts of West Bengal. It was acknowledged as a separate district in the year 1987. Nadia was within Jessore Division. Later on, Nadia Division was formed and Krishnagar was its head quarter. In 1860, the quarter of this Division was shifted by the then British Govt. to Alipore. It was composed of four districts and Nadia district was one of them. But the present Nadia was formed in 1948 after the partition of Bengal.

   From the time of Lord Chaitanya i.e. fifteenth century, AD, the district Nadia has distinct cultural and spiritual environment. Its cultural ethos and ideological structure was strongly influenced by Vaishnabism. It is a district of glorious educational and cultural heritage and has a long and deep-rooted tradition of learning.

3. All the respondents are working in different Govt. and semi Govt. organizations and majority of them are teachers in different Schools, Colleges and Universities.
4. The inventory consists of 80 questions of which, 21 questions measure adjustment in home, 20 questions measure health adjustment, 21 items measure social adjustment and 18 items are used to measure emotional adjustment of the respondents. In this inventory, for each question either one or zero score is given. The questions are either positive or negative. High scores on the inventory indicate low adjustment whereas low scores indicate high adjustment in different areas of adjustment.
5. The marital Adjustment Questionnaire consists of 25 questions with various aspects of marital. The question is put before both the husband and wife and it is recommended that a score of 1 should be given if both partners (husband and wife) answer an item as 'yes' showing their agreement except for items 4, 10 and 19 in which cases the reverse is to be applied. The higher the total score the better would be the marital adjustment of the couple.
6. *Eight groups are as follows:*
   1. married working women having education in below graduation level;
   2. married working women of Kalyani having education above graduation level;
   3. married working women of Kalyani living in nuclear family;
   4. married working women of Kalyani living in extended family;
   5. married working women of Kalyani with teaching profession;
   6. married working women of Kalyani without teaching profession;
   7. married working women who are officers among the non-teaching working women;

8. married working women who are Group-D staffs among the non-teaching married working women.

7. *Four sets of groups are as follows:*
   1. married working women of Kalyani having education in below graduation and above graduation level;
   2. married working women of Kalyani living in nuclear family and in extended family;
   3. married working women of Kalyani with teaching profession or without teaching profession;
   4. officers and Group-D staffs among the non-teaching married working women.

8. *Five groups are as follows:*
   1. married working women having education in below graduation level;
   2. married working women of Kalyani having education above graduation level;
   3. married working women who are officers;
   4. married working women of Kalyani who are teachers;
   5. married working women who are Group-D staffs.

9. *Three sets of groups are as follows:*
   1. married working women of Kalyani having education in below graduation and above graduation level;
   2. married working women who are officers and teachers;
   3. married working women who are Group-D staffs and officers.

REFERENCES

Anjana, M.S. (1993), *Women in a Changing Society*, Ashis Publishing House, New Delhi.

Agarwal, K. (1988), 'Status and Role of Middle Class Educated Earning Women in the Indian Family', in *Women and Work in Indian society* by T.M. Dak (ed.), Discovery Publishing House, Delhi.

Beteille, A. (2000), *Antinomies of Society: Essays on Ideologies and Institutions*. New Delhi: Oxford University Press.

Chitnis, S. (1988), 'Feminism: Indian Ethos and Indian Convictions', in R. Ghadially (ed) *Women in Indian Society*, New Delhi, Sage Publications.

Chakroborty, K. (1978), *The Conflicting Worlds of Working Mothers*, Progressive Publishers, Calcutta.

Choudhury, M. (1999), 'Gender in the Making of the Indian Nation-State', *Sociological Bulletin*, 48 (1 & 2).

Coppock, V., Hayden, D. & Richer, I. (1995), *The Illusions of Post Feminism: New women Old Myths*, Taylor & Francis Ltd, London.

Devendra, K. (1996), *Changing Status of Women in India. Vikash Publishing House: New Delhi.*

Devi, U. L. (1982), *Status and Employment of Women in India*, B. R. Publishing Corporation, Delhi.

Hareven, T. K. (1977), 'The Family and Gender Roles in Historical Perspective' in *Women and Men; Changing Roles, Relationships and Perceptions Workshop on Men and Women* by L. A. Cater, A. F. Scott, W. Martyna (eds), Praeger Publications, New York.

Hunt, A. (1968), *A Survey of Women's Employment*, Vol. 1 HMSO, London.

Helen, O. (1994), *Women and the Family*. London: Zed Book Ltd.

Joshi, S. C. (1999), *Sociology of Migration and Kinship*, Anmol Publications Pvt. Ltd., New Delhi.

Karl, M. (1995), *Women and Empowerment: Participation and Decision-making*, Zed Books, London.

Kapur, P. (1970), *Marriage and the Working Women in Indian*, Vikas Publications, Delhi.

Lewis, S. (1992), 'Introduction: Dual-Earner Families in Context' in *Dual-Earner Families: International Perspectives* by S. Lewis, D. N. Izraeli, H. Hootsmans (eds), Sage Publication, London.

Liddle, J. and Joshi, R. (1986), *Daughter of Independence Gender, Caste and Class in India*. Zed Books, London.

Mathur, D. (1992), *Women, Family and Work*, Rawat Publications, Jaipur.

Maynard, M. (1993), 'Violence Towards Women' in *Introducing Women's Studies* by D. Richardson and V. Robinson (eds), Macmillan, Houndmills.

McDowell, L. T and Pringle, R. (1992), 'Defining Work' in *Defining Women. Social Institutions and Gender Division* by L. McDowell and R. Pringle (eds), Polity Press, U. K.

Mead, M. (1964),*Male and Female,* Penguin Books, Middlesex.

Mehta, R. (1975), *Divorce Hindu Women,* Vikas Publishing House Pvt. Ltd., Delhi

Manna, S. and Patra, S. (2001), 'Women Empowerment, Civil Society and Institutional Well being', *Journal of the Department of Anthropology, 7 (1 & 2).*

Mcdowell, L. T. and (1992), 'Defining Work', in L. T. Mcdowell and

Pringle, R.R. Pringle (eds) *Defining Women,* Social Institution and Gender Division, UK : Polity Press.

Ramu, G. N. (1988), 'Wife's Economic Status and Marital Power: A Case of Single and Dual–Earner Couples', *Sociological Bulletin* 37 (1 & 2).

Rani, K. (1976), *Role Conflict in Working Women,* Chetana Publications, New Delhi.

Reber, A. S. (1985), *The Penguine Dictionary of Psychology,* Penguin, Great Britain.

Rowbotham, S. (1992), *Women in Movement Feminism and Social Action,* Routledge, New York.

Sengupta, N. (2000), *Women on the Move: Socio-culture Dimensions Influencing Status of Rural Women. Minerva Associates: Calcutta*

Sharama, S. L. (2000), 'Empowerment without Antagonism: A Case for Reformulation of Women's Empowerment Approach', *Sociological Bulletin,* 49(1).

Swarnalatha, E. V. (1993), *Women's Education and Occupational Aspirations,* Discovery Publishing House, New Delhi.

10

WOMENıš BID FOR EQUALITY IN THE UNITED STATES: TWO STEPS FORWARD AND ONE STEP BACK

Katherine Van Wormer

Women in the US have made great strides in achieving equality and human rights as a result of activism and the political climate of the late 1960s. This paper will recall that progress but then show that a counter-reaction has set in, a reaction that is being paid by women ;at the lower economic levels and among poor members of minority groups even as students who attend professional schools such as law and medicine and professional women are thriving in American society.

THE FEMINIST PERSPECTIVE

Worldwide, in every society, women as a category are subordinate to men. Girls and boys are socialized into distinct social roles. There is variation in the level of women's equality across the globe and also within societies depending on many elements—the state of the economy, the election of conservative or liberal governments, the passage of human rights laws, the need for women's labor, and the power of fundamentalist religious leaders (Epstein, 2007).

Feminism which sprang out of the women's movement offers a woman-centered approach to understanding human behavior across the lifespan from the treatment of infants and little girls to the challenges facing elderly women. The women's movement is often described in terms of three waves, *the first wave* during the struggle for women's suffrage which ended with the passage of the 19th amendment in 1920 giving women the right to vote. From the late 1960s onwards, *the second wave* was concerned with equality of opportunity, an end to blatant sex discrimination, and an acknowledgement of the physical victimization of women whether on the street, in the workplace, or in the home. An interesting fact about the women's movement was the extent to which it made (white, middle, and upper class) women aware of their own powerlessness apart from their connection to a powerful man which so many had never had, would never have. It made women aware for the first time that the word *man* and pronoun *he* were not universal after all but mostly referred to just the male of the human race. For years "women's lib" was mocked in the media and by the general public as a joke. But the biggest joke was on the opponents of the women's movement in an action designed to defeat the movement for civil rights legislation. This action had in fact happened several years earlier when a southern Senator who was a segregationist added sex to the 1964 civil rights act. This was his way of making a mockery of the act and ensuring its defeat. Curiously, the fact that women actually could claim discrimination was given no legal notice until about a decade later.

Stemming from the same historical period as the mass people's rights movements and peace activism of the 1960s and 1970s–feminist perspectives challenging the taken-for-granted patriarchal social structure filtered through the landscape. The feminist perspectives are basically reactions to the vestiges of sex discrimination in society. *Feminism* is defined by Van den Bergh and Cooper (1995) as "a conceptual framework and mode of analysis that has analyzed the status of women (and other disempowered groups) cross-culturally and historically to explain dynamics and conditions undergirding disparities in socio-cultural status and power between majority and minority populations" (p.xii). The central definition of feminism entails the conscious, explicit awareness that women are denied equal rights, opportunities, and access to goods and services (van Wormer, Besthorn, & Keefe, 2007). Feminism is associated with social action in that it derives from political movements. However, it also represents a mode of analysis that has attracted extensive scholarship. Feminist scholarship offers an enormous source of information and link the political to the personal more effectively than any other theory. As theories about discrimination in the society; they relate to micro as well as macro dynamics in showing the impact of discriminatory attitudes and practices. These theories say a lot about human behavior and the tendency of some people privileged by their gender to fight to maintain that privilege. These theories also show how societies tend to maintain their institutionalized patterns of oppression through various means and how such patterns affect the behavior of the persons regarded as other, persons whose needs are not met. Feminist theorists are primarily concerned with issues pertaining to women although even here, different analyses exist with respect to the fundamental source of oppression in society (Mullaly, 2002).

Dominelli (2002b) and Payne (2005) have filtered out from the feminist literature the following four types of feminism or feminisms:

- *Liberal feminism* seeks equality between men and women mainly through legislation and socializing children to enjoy more flexible roles.
- *Radical feminism* focuses concern on patriarchy, celebrates the differences between men and women, and promotes women's own separate structures.
- *Socialist or Marxist feminism* emphasizes women's oppression as part of structural inequality within a class-based social system. All oppressions are seen as interconnected and stemming from the same source. Power and violence in relations between men and women are not emphasized.

- *Black feminism* starts with racism and draws parallels between racism and sexism. Black women's experience of oppression is heightened compared to that of white women.

To this list we can add ecofeminism. *Ecofeminism* is an environmental philosophy that starts with a view of the oppression of women and the oppression of nature as inextricably linked. There is much focus here on Mother Nature and on nurturance of human and non-human life. The involvement of women in environmental policies bolstered this movement. Ecofeminism asserts that the dichotomy between human beings and nature is a false one, and that famine and overpopulation are rooted in oppressive power structures (van Wormer et al., 2007).

Related contemporary developments in feminism is the inclusion of the rights of women who choose to make their contribution in the home, a global consciousness of the repression of women in other cultures, a recognition of biological differences between the sexes that affect brain development, and a reinterpretation of feminism by the younger generation.

Third Wave Feminism consists of the daughters (and in some instances, sons) of the Second Wave. Their contribution to women's history builds on the foundation of the Second Wave. The somewhat negative view of the foremothers' contributions or activist style is typical of the younger generation, of both those who reject the movement and those who understandably wish to carve out their own definition of feminism without giving up the fight for equal rights.

In *Feminism Is for Everyone* bell hooks (2000) applies her critical analysis to misconceptions about earlier feminism, the belief by many people that the movement was only about equality and that feminism was anti-male. "Their misunderstanding of feminist politics, she states, "reflects the reality that most folks learn about feminism from the patriarchal mass media" (p.1). She goes on to further explain, however, that there was indeed a great deal of anti-male sentiment among some early feminist activists who were responding to male dominance with anger: "It was that anger at injustice that was the impetus for creating a women's liberation movement" (p.2).

Today, according the Seyler (2007), American women are shying away calling themselves feminists. She cites a 2001 Gallup opinion poll that showed only that only one in four women were willing to call themselves feminists. This was a decline since the 1980s when a majority of women identified with the term feminist. Now, like then, however, the majority state that they support the women's movement and women's equality in the workplace.

A popular book written for Third Wave feminists is *Manifesta* by Baumgardner and Richards (2000). Written for young people, these writers differentiate the various waves of feminism without deriding any of them. They define the new feminism as an expanding feminism that is reclaiming the word *girl* but with a difference. Girlies, she tells us, are girls in their 20s and 30s who are into manicures, hair styles and the color pink. They are "reacting to anti-feminine, anti-joy emphasis that they perceived as the legacy of Second Wave seriousness" (p.80). Baumgardner and Richards believe that young feminists should build on the legacy rather than rebuild it. All feminisms, they suggest, share a struggle for justice and equality, rather than paternalism or protection (or domination and violence). They see a common ground as the young women pursue their course, "pushing voter registration, organizing against date rape, becoming women in rock, blowing the whistle in sexual harassment...and fighting for women's reproductive rights" (p.79).

Feminism in all its forms focuses on the empowerment of women. Empowerment is a basic theme, in fact, of all the macro theories discussed in this chapter except for structural functionalism in any of its iterations. Empowerment is a core concept of all social work practice, almost to the point of becoming a cliché term.

U.S. MEDIA ATTACKS ON FEMINISM

Because feminism is yesterday's story, and there's always the incentive to come up with something new or to put a new spin on things, challenges to feminist thought are given prime coverage and their proponents elevated to star status on the talk shows. Popular literature echoes the contemporary sentiment, and, in reflecting on it, reinforces it. Sadly but predictably, the myth of the "new female criminal" has resurfaced in recent years to coincide with and justify woman's harsh treatment by the courts, civil (child custody) and criminal. Books such as *When She Was Bad: How and Why Women Get Away with Murder* by Pearson (1998). For another example of this kind of misrepresentation of the facts, consider this article published in the last-month-of-the-century issue in *Psychology Today.* Tellingly entitled "Bad Girls" the article written by Yeoman (1999) begins: "Violence by women has skyrocked in the latter part of this century. Have they taken 'women's liberation' one step too far—or are they just showing their natural killer instinct?" In fact, the claim is more political than factual. (See Pollock, 1998 and van Wormer & Bartollas, 2007 as well as the Bureau of Justice Statistics for a review of the official statistics on women's crime.)

The focus of the media hype has shifted from the girl gang member to the "violent girl" to the "mean girl" (Chesney-Lind, 2006). *Odd Girl Out: The Hidden Culture if Aggression in Girls* is a best-selling book by Rachel Simmons, (2003).Now the focus is on "bad girls" again (See for example, the Newsweek article, "Girls Gone Bad?" Deveny, 2007). Such media hype, as Chesney-Lind suggests, has created a "self-fulfilling prophecy" that has had dramatic effects on girls' arrests, detentions, and referrals to juvenile courts. Racial discrimination is certainly a factor here as African American females are disproportionately oppressed under harsh enforcement of the law.

The shift in direction evidenced in criminal law and sentencing is paralleled in a turnabout in domestic violence research with a new focus on the victimization of males by female perpetrators. See, for example, Cook (1997), *Abused Men: The Hidden Side of Domestic Violence* (1997) and Buttell and Carney, (2005) *Women Who Perpetrate Violence.*

In an appropriately critical article, entitled "Husband Abuse: Equality with a Vengeance," Canadian criminologists

Minaker and Snider (2006) draw on the facts to disprove the false claim that men and women are equally prone to violence. They demonstrate how the very successes of feminism, combined with neo-conservative governance, the burgeoning power of men's movements and new communications media, have given rise to a frightening turnabout in national ideologies and practices.

The mass media both reflect and shape the climate of opinion. Driven by market imperatives (crime sells) and unprecedented competition from multiple news sources, especially related television and newspaper news editors are under pressure to produce fear-generated, sensationalized stories. The mass media, therefore, are playing a role, unwittingly or not in putting down the feminist movement.

The War Against Boys: How Misguided Feminism is Harming Our Young Men (Sommers, 2001); *The Surrendered Wife*, (Doyle, 2001); *Women Who Make the World Worse and How Their Feminist Assault is Ruining Our Schools, Families, Military, and Sports* (O'Beirne, 2005).

Such writers define themselves as feminists, but their dismissive attitudes toward feminist issues—from sexual harassment to domestic violence to rape to pay equity to child care to welfare rights—are actually an attack on women' equality and on the women who have fought for it.

THE FEMINIZATION OF POVERTY WORLDWIDE

How are women doing worldwide? According to a report from the World Health Organization (WHO) (2000), 70 percent of the world's people living in poverty are female. The United Nations (2003) in a recent report entitled "The World's Women 2000" provides the following statistics:

- In many countries of the developed regions, more than half of mothers with children under age three are employed.
- Women now comprise an increasing share of the world's labor force - - - at least one third in all regions except northern Africa and western Asia.

- Self-employment and part-time and home-based work have expanded opportunities for women's participation in the labor force but are characterized by lack of security, lack of benefits, and low income.
- The informal sector is a larger source of employment for women than for men.
- More women than before are in the labor force throughout their reproductive years though obstacles to combining family responsibilities with employment persist.
- Women, especially younger women, experience more unemployment than men for a longer period of time than men.
- Women remain at the lower end of a segregated labor market and continue to be concentrated in a few occupations, to hold positions of little or no authority and receive less pay than men. (www.unstats.un.org)

For women, the impact of globalization has generated opportunities for some, especially persons with higher levels of education and access to capital. But, for many poor women, globalization has intensified existing inequalities and even loss of livelihoods and labor rights (UNI Fem, 2000). In India, for example, Dalit women continue to experience discrimination in all areas, including access to education and health care, and lack of control over their bodies and sexuality (Ross-Sheriff, 2007). The women who benefit from changes stemming from the global economy are not ordinary women or poor women who are members of deprived minority groups.

In their book, *Global Woman: Nannies, Maids, and Sex Workers in the New Economy*, Ehrenreich and Hochschild (2003) put a human face on the extreme vulnerability of women who migrate, often thousands of miles, to work in the new global economy. The theme linking many of the stories in this collection is the impossible choice many of these impoverished women face: stay in your own country and fight for survival or leave your children behind and provide for their support through work in a prosperous nation. Some of these women will nurture children of women in wealthy nations who themselves are working too many hours to provide that care. We also read in *Global Women* of rural girls sold into sexual slavery in Thailand and destined to get AIDS. And we learn of the exploitation of foreign domestic workers in the United States who are not legally allowed to change employers. In such situations of vulnerability and dependence, women have nowhere to go and they are invariably subjected to physical violence.

The often touted success stories of women who get to work for the transnational corporations is refuted by international human rights organizations. As the executive director of MADRE, a women's human rights organization, Stromberg (2001) states in response to such claims:

In our experience with recently opened markets, women are virtual prisoners inmany factories, subject to physical violence including sexual assault, strip searches, attacks on union organizers, and forced consumption of amphetamines to increase output. Women work longer hours than their male counterparts, are paid half the wages, and suffer from serious work-related health problems, including lung damage, memory loss and numbness from exposure to toxic materials. And they are forced to live in overcrowded slums that lack basic municipal services and are rife with contaminated water, rats, insects, and industrial pollutants. (p. 2 of 3)

For an international comparison of all nations, we can consult the Gender Empowerment Measure which is contained in the UN Human Development Report (2006). This report ranks all nations on the basis of the following categories: life expectancy, literacy rates, power over economic resources, representation of women in government, and earned income levels. The purpose of this ranking is to determine how well nations are doing compared to others in terms of economic and political equality. The Scandinavian countries are at the top with the U.S. ranked number 8 and China no. 81. Hong Kong at rank 22 is ahead of many Eastern European countries. Within China, urban/rural differences are pronounced. For a breakdown by provinces, see the UN Human Development Programme's (2005) comprehensive China Human Development Report.

Since the research was done several years ago, it is likely that advances have been made since that time, especially in China given today's increasing economic and educational opportunities. This index is not complete because health care access is not considered as a standard; the U.S. would receive a lower ranking and China a higher ranking were these criteria included.

Freedom for women in China goes back to the Chinese revolution. Chairman Mao outlawed foot binding in 1950 and passed equal marriage laws. Well before women's liberation in the U.S., Americans were struck by the unisexual dress styles of Chinese women and their protection from sexual harassment. It is only in recent times in the U.S. that wearing pants on formal occasions is acceptable for women. (Dress styles are significant as a sign of gender equality, because historically, as women have moved toward greater equality, women and men are permitted to wear similar clothing {Epstein, 2007}). As Liu (2006) indicates, however, the Cultural Revolution (1966-1976) was a tremendous setback for Chinese women given the Cultural Revolution's emphasis on class conflict. 1978 marked the starting point of the contemporary women's movement as the All China Women's Federation was restored at this time; tens of thousands of women visited the Federation's offices about various problems. In the 1990s, the Chinese government passed a law to implement the Convention on the Elimination of All Forms of Discrimination Against Women. Since 2005, women in China have made progress in holding ministerial positions and pledges have been made by the government to fill at least 22% of legislative seats with women. This rate is comparable to that of the U.S. but well below that in Scandinavian countries.

Unlike the history of women's bid for equality in the U.S., movements in India and China were significantly influenced by the agenda adopted by the United Nations Fourth World Conference on Women. China, in fact, hosted the conference, their aim being to highlight China's national development, however, not women's rights, as Liu (2006) indicates. Nevertheless, the Chinese and Indian movements drew on the international agenda to pursue similar national policy goals. This agenda for gender equality was an agenda for women's empowerment; the platform contained plans to tackle gender disparities in employment and education and domestic violence against women. According to Lui, the means of achieving similar goals was different in India and China; in India progress was made through grass root activism; in China progress came through cooperation with the government. Marxist ideology became the official justification for asserting women's equality; this ideology was consistent with economic reforms. The skewed sex ratio improved in India, but the literacy rate of girls did not improve, and malnutrition has continued as a problem. The opposite was the case in China as government funding was provided to promote literacy of girls.

ECONOMIC PROGRESS OF WOMEN IN THE U.S.

In the United States, the divorce rate is high, and there is a high rate of babies born to single mothers. Of families headed by single women, 37.1 percent are below the poverty line. (This is the line below which people cannot afford adequate food, housing, and so on.) The term *feminization of poverty* applies to the disproportionate numbers of women compared to men who live below the poverty line. When the ratio of women's full-time income reached 80 percent of men's income in 2004, it was an all-time high (U.S. Bureau of Labor Statistics, 2005). The inequality for white women is that they earn 80% of what white men do; African American women do better at 89%, and Hispanics at 87%. Although Asian Americans earn the most of all ethnic groups, Asian American women earn only 76% of what their men folk do. Before the women's movement, women earned only little more than 60% of what men did. This narrowing of the gender earnings gap, especially in recent years, do not reflect a rise in women's income as much as a decline in men's income in the trades and manufacturing during this period.

The rising jobless rate is harder on women than on men in many ways. Women's unemployment reached nine percent in 2003. It is significantly harder for women to maintain steady employment, given their low wage and part-time, often interrupted work (Curphey, 2003). Keep in mind that women are more likely than men to leave their jobs due to family illness, also there may be problems pertaining to sexual harassment or domestic violence.

The causes of female poverty are complex. The high divorce rate coupled with the infrequency of mothers receiving child support from the fathers forces many women to find jobs immediately or go on welfare. Low-paying service jobs – such as waiting tables in fast-food restaurants and motel housekeeping work - - drive many women to welfare dependency as a means to escape from such daily drudgery, lack of essential work benefits, and childcare concerns. Programs designed to compensate for the absence of a male breadwinner in the family are means-tested and highly punitive. When men are absent, women's prescribed role as family caretaker is ignored and devalued by the system – a fact which reinforces women's marginality in society and ensures women and their children's high representation among the destitute. Until the importance of nurturing and shaping young lives through domestic caretaking is regarded as primary work, the feminization of poverty will continue. The federal and state program reductions in job training, education, and childcare implemented by the Reagan, Bush, Clinton, and George W. Bush administrations have had a major impact on already poor women and children.

In the best-selling book, *Nickel and Dimed,* Ehrenreich (2001) set out to see for herself what life at the margins of low-wage jobs is like. She discovered that for women even without children affordable housing was hard to get. Her co-workers often lived in their cars or shared crowded apartments with relatives.

Women who are mothers of small children can qualify for welfare benefits for short periods of time only, and they must be involved in employment training to qualify for a job. This pressure to work has come about through laws that were passed in the Clinton administration, the 1996 Personal Responsibility and Work Opportunity Reconciliation Act. Collectively, this accumulation of cutbacks has served to legitimize the negative attitudes held by many Americans toward the poor. Also as long as working and middle class mothers with children are joining the labor market (to help ends meet), the sentiment is that other women should not have another option.

At the end of the life span, women pay again for their abbreviated, low-paid work careers. Qualifying far less frequently than men for adequate pension plans, most elderly women must rely on Social Security as their sole source of income. Accordingly, 14 percent of elderly females compared to 8.4 percent of elderly males are in poverty (Kijakazi and Primus, 2000).

DOMESTIC VIOLENCE

Violence against women is both a consequence and a cause of gender equality. According to a World Health Report based on 48 surveys from around the world, between 10 and 69 % of women report having been physically assaulted by a partner. In the United States, 22 % report domestic violence (Lite, 2002).

In traditional societies, wife beating is largely regarded as a consequence of a man's right to inflict physical punishment on his wife—something indicated by studies from Bangladesh, Cambodia, India, Mexico, Nigeria, Pakistan, Papua New Guinea, and Zimbabwe (WHO, 2002). Research from industrialized and non-industrialized nations alike shows that partner violence is justified by the perpetrator on the following grounds: the woman's arguing back, refusing sex, not having the meal ready, suspected infidelity, and disobedience. Studies reviewed by the WHO suggest that women stay in abusive situations because of fear of retribution, lack of means of economic support, concern for the children, and the stigma attached to being unmarried. Research also showed that leaving such a relationship was not a one-time thing, that most women leave and return several times before making the final break (LaFraniere, 2005).

In a comparative study of 16 societies, Counts, Browns and Campbell (1992) found that societies with community sanctions against partner violence and support for abused women had the lowest levels of partner violence. Because maintaining shelters is expensive, many poor nations have set up an informal network of "safe houses" to deal with the emergency of domestic abuse. Nongovernmental organizations often offer specialized services for victims of abuse in countries in which they are active (WHO, 2002).

Sexual abuse is a common co-occurring component of partner violence. In most countries, in fact, marital rape is considered an oxymoron. Pregnancy is a high risk for physical abuse and loss of the developing fetus as well. Estimates of abuse during pregnancy range from 3 to15 % in population-based studies in Canada, Egypt, Nicaragua, Chile, and the United States (WHO).

BACKLASH AGAINST WOMEN IN THE SOCIETY

The anti-intellectual thrust is decidedly anti-feminist. Susan Faludi, noted this development as early as 1991 which marked the publication of her national bestselling *Backlash: The Undeclared War against American Women.* Backlash is a phenomenon borne out of success; one party makes claims, advances and another party feels left out, resentful threatened. "This counterassault," writes Faludi (1991, p. xviii), "stands the truth boldly on its head and proclaims that the very steps that have elevated women's position have actually led to their downfall." Liberation now, as Faludi further suggests, has became the true American scourge. Just when women's quest for equal rights had started to gain ground with extensive affirmative action programs in place; just when women had joined the ranks of virtually all the male dominated and prestigious and even macho professions; just when laws protecting rape victims and battered women from being belittled and attacked in court, almost predictably an antifeminist resistance set in. Two steps forward and one step back.

First, the two steps forward. Although women are still a long way from achieving full equality, the changes that have taken place—notably in the areas of control of reproduction, fairness in employment, and legal protection from harassment and other victimization—were resented by many men, especially those facing employment insecurity. Despite male resentment, the clock cannot be turned back on women's bid for equality in those countries where women have entered the power structure. Women continue to enter the professions such as law and medicine in record numbers and legislation tightened up to protect female victims of domestic assault while a new awareness of date rape and its connection with substance abuse has led to prevention measures such as on the college campus. Globally, women are beginning to organize to bring media attention to the needs of girls and women sold into sexual slavery and ravaged by genital mutilation.

The step back relates to the punishment of women, both biologically and legally. I am referring here, first, to the preoccupation with control of women's bodies under the guise of protecting the unborn child. The restriction in federal funding for abortions, as always brought a disproportionate effect to bear on poor and minority women. Internationally, the American Right to Life movement has been successful in preventing ratification of human rights conventions because of the refusal of international bodies to protect the rights of children "born and unborn" as well as in jeopardizing the funding of family planning programs worldwide.

A related issue, because it also relates to the female body, and again reveals the interplay of race, class, and gender in the areas of pregnancy and motherhood, is the criminalization of high risk pregnancy. The prosecution of drug-addicted mothers is a part of an alarming trend toward greater state intervention into the lives of pregnant women under the guise of protecting the fetus from harm (van Wormer and Davis, 2008). Still, this post-pregnancy prosecution does little to protect the child. Because of their closer contact with government agencies and their unlikelihood of having a private physician, poor black women bear the brunt of the prosecutors' punitive approach. These issues, moreover, are all of the "equality with a vengeance" or the "you can't have it both ways" variety of getting back at women. Thus in the name of equality, single mothers on welfare are forced to look for work. Ironically, a program instituted to enable mothers to stay home with small children has now been turned on its head.

Faludi (1999) goes further than other writers to explain the origins of the backlash. She does this remarkably well in *Stiffed: The Betrayal of the American Man* which indirectly refers to economic forces that have a bearing on men's social and work roles. In reading the personal narratives of very average and often sexist men, we get a sense of a lot of anger and of where there anger is coming from—from pressures from work, pressures that are related to forces in the global economy—downsizing, privatization, outsourcing, reduction in benefits. From the devastation of feeling they are losers in their breadwinning roles, men express a sense of emasculation and a longing for the security of the past. The visibility of women taking men's work roles has caused many men, as Faludi suggests, to feel oppressed by the image culture. Places of work that represented a particular vintage of masculinity such as the shipyard are no longer male bastions of pride. "If they were the losers, women had to be the winners" (p. 420). Such putative accomplishments by women would be bound to be resented. The blame they placed not on the workplace or politics or the economy but on another nationality, another race, and another sex. Sometimes they join right wing male bonding groups such as the Promise Keepers or Fathers' Rights groups. Sometimes they resort to violence, displacing their aggression onto weaker family members. Faludi cites James Gilligan, an expert on male violence, who contended that the emotion of shame is a primary factor all male violence. To the extent that this is true, one can detect a sense of shame, in the personal narratives of the working class males that Faludi interviewed for her book, men who had been laid off from shipyards, mines, logging, and so on, men whose hopes of fulfilling the American dream were jeopardized.

BACKLASH AGAINST WOMEN IN THE U.S. CRIMINAL JUSTICE SYSTEM

Resistance to feminism and to women's bid for equality is played out worldwide not only in religious fundamentalism but also in a backlash that accuses feminism of promoting anti-family ideologies that threaten the well-being of children and communities.

The treatment of female victims of male crime by the courts, we can view as a microcosm of the wider society. Women's experiences and participation here tell us a lot about the cultural norms as these pertain to gender expectations. Issues that the wider society is wrestling with—should men and women be judged according to the same criteria (such as physical fitness standards) or should gender differences be taken into consideration—also come into play with regard to the law and its enforcement. This issue is as relevant for victims of rape and partner battering as it is for individuals in trouble with the law.

Welfare women, pregnant out-of-wedlock women, mothers with drug problems, female offenders, and even, to some extent, battered women (whose plausibility is being undermined): all are singled out for the new medicine. The message was loud and clear: the day of entitlements for many welfare services is over; women are now equal and most work (regardless of child care responsibilities) was echoed in the halls of justice where the message was, "You as the equal of a man will be punished like a man."

The execution of Karla Faye Tucker in 1998 in Texas, a young woman who was guilty of horrible crimes involving axe-murders but who turned her life around in prison is a case in point, a woman who paid with her life for the new equality standards as she had to bear the penalty of death like a man. As of 2007, ten other women have followed her to the execution chambers; there are 51 women on death row. Feminists do not raise their voices on behalf of such women because to do so would imply that women were weak and therefore unequal. The paradox is that women without education or opportunity to advance—those most likely to be arrested for criminal behavior—held to the very standards of equality which have opened the doors professionally for another class of women altogether. Few female offenders are feminist and fewer still have benefited in any tangible way from the various affirmative action programs which have helped women advance up the ladder of the prestigious and academic professions.

As compassion takes a back seat in a punitive society, women connected to crime through family ties—mothers who protect their drug dealing children, wives and girlfriends of drug using men, for example—are now subjected to punishment under the "firm arm of the law." Chesney-Lind and Pollack (1994) deemed this trend, "equality with a vengeance." More recently, Chesney-Lind (2006) uses the term "vengeful equity" to refer to the gender blind treatment of women by the major institutions of society.

Among some striking examples of punitive policies pertaining that are especially relevant to poor and minority women in the U.S. are the following:

- the social construction of the "new female criminal," the typical variety of which is a drug-dependent mother who lives in the inner-city and got swooped up in an anti-drug operation;
- conspiracy drug laws that are used to incarcerate large numbers of the female partners of drug dealers;
- the passage and enforcement of fetal abuse statutes which criminalize maternal drug use
- increase in the incarceration rates of drug using women that is significantly greater than the increase for men;
- new adoption laws that remove all custody rights from mothers in prison who are serving lengthy sentences;
- use of dual arrest laws to arrest both partners in domestic violence situations;
- laws that persons convicted of drug offenses cannot receive welfare aid.

While gender-neutral policies have dumped single mothers off the welfare rolls, gender-neutral mandatory sentencing for drug law violation has brought unprecedented numbers of women and especially black women into prison. Equality for these women subjects them to discipline according to the male model without allowance for their motherhood roles or their history of personal victimization. A flawed notion lurks beneath the current policies: the assumption that women have achieved full equality and that men are suffering the consequences. The backlash is felt most by the women least able to take advantage of the new professional opportunities and the least feminist identified. The media demonization of the new violent female, especially young girls in trouble with the law, further aggravates the female offender's plight.

This vengeful equity phenomenon comes into play most concretely in the correctional arena. This fact is seen in connection with the masculinization of correctional services and standardization of treatment philosophies The bulk of the funding here has gone to high-tech security systems and to surveillance rather than to educational and counseling services. Consistent with the new mythology, the rate of construction of women's prisons now exceeds the male rate. And in accordance with the new thinking on female criminality, these structures are designed according to the male model of high-security fortresses; such facilities now are often male-run and male-administered with predictable results. The fact that the majority of women in confinement have been convicted of nonviolent, mostly drug-related offenses tends to be overlooked. For the female offender, chivalry is out; "equality" is in, and how can feminists argue for special treatment for women involved in crime while demanding equality for themselves? In any case, with public sentiment now turning against them, offenders with a history of personal victimization, chided for using the "abuse excuse" are apt to be further victimized by the legal process when charged with crime.

The Impact of the Backlash on Domestic Violence Services Buttell and Carney (2005), in their edited anthology, *Women*

Who Perpetuate Relationship Violence, state as their purpose the desire "to strip away political correctness and take a frank look at the issues surrounding female violence in intimate relationship" (p. xvi). The first paper by Canadian social scientists Dutton, Nicholls, and Spidel (2005) cites study after study from the social science literature to show that women initiate violence as much as men. Had the authors consulted the Bureau of Justice Statistics (Rennison, 2003), they would discover that men kill women about three times as often as women kill men. Had they consulted the National Victimization Survey, these researchers would have learned that women make up 85% of all intimate assault victims (Rennison). The authors made the same mistake as the North American media in basing their conclusion that women are more violent than men from survey data gathered in the 1980s that relied on an instrument, the Conflict Tactics Scale that asked the number of times they had slapped, kicked or otherwise hit a partner. This instrument is problematic because its exclusive focus is on acts performed rather than on the context in which the slapping, kicking, etc. occurred.

From an economic perspective, the impact of market-driven measures of capitalism is causing the reduction of female-oriented social services through cut-backs, privatization of services, and the de-professionalization of workers. At the same time, global market forces pave the way for social service agency consolidation and corporate management techniques with the result that men displace women managers (Dominelli, 2002). In the current backlash climate, the opportunity is being seized by right wing constituents to reduce funding for feminist-based social services. The loss of welfare benefits and services by the state, in conjunction with de-institutionalization of mental patients, in turn, has increased the numbers of homeless young people roaming the streets; this fact has intensified the vulnerability of girls and women to sexual victimization, sexual exploitation, and drug use. A parallel reduction in funding for victim assistance services and women's shelters has been pronounced.

THE LEGACY OF THE IRAQ WAR

Unique to the military is the training of men (and women) to kill. In warfare, combat conditions the soldier to kill almost as a reflex in a situation of danger. Military socialization "to make a man out of the boy" not only attempts to obliterate all that is feminine but also breeds misogynous heterosexuality in the soldier as well (Farr, 2005). The degradation of traits such as weakness in battle, squeamishness, and compassion of traits associated with femininity, helps create or preserve masculine detachment and aggression desirable for battle. Such conditioning can be devastating for later family functioning.

On the homefront, a condition such as post-traumatic stress disorder (PTSD) or a state of intoxication (even being suddenly aroused from sleep) can trigger violence. Depression related to PTSD can lead to suicide. Anderson (2005) studied the seven homicides and three suicides that have taken place in western Washington State by returning soldiers from the war on Iraq. Five wives, one girlfriend, and a child have all been killed. Two of the suicides were committed after murder. These cases and others like them reported across the United State seem to suggest that as an anti-war slogan popular in the sixties said, "War is not good for people or other living things."

Female soldiers returning from the wars in Iraq and Afghanistan are often suffering from PTSD of a gender-specific sort—rape victimization, not at the hands of the enemy but by fellow soldiers. This fact was highlighted in a cover story in the *New York Times* Magazine by Corbett (2007). The rates of sexual harassment and assault are known to rise during wartime, as stated in the article.

CONCLUSION

There are two kinds of backlash we have discussed in this paper—institutionalized and personal. *Institutionalized backlash* operates at the societal level, typically as laws that are written or enacted as a reaction against progress by a minority group. *Personal backlash* may have its origins in social or work stress and is manifest as displaced aggression onto another person such as a family member. Sometimes this backlash takes the form of violence. That much of family violence is associated with the stress on men in a competitive, global economy is a major argument of this paper. Both forms of backlash, whether at the macro or micro level, are cultural in origin and derive from basic prejudice against girls and women, but especially against girls and women who are seen as competitive with men and therefore threatening. Resentment against the progress of affirmative action in western countries is matched by resistance to these democratic ideals in totalitarian nations. In the Western part of the world, new laws that move old protections have been introduced in combination with budget cuts of feminist-based services, while in the Middle East, old laws restricting women's freedom have been reintroduced. Women's bid for equality has been used against girls and women in the United States, and poor and minority women in trouble with the law have paid for the male resentment against their more liberated sisters. Much of the backlash that we considered took the form of attempts to reverse feminist-inspired policies and activities.

Meanwhile, women from another part of the world have seemingly been punished for the advances made by women far away. Cultural clash often leads to violence as a means of holding girls and women down. Backlash, at its most basic level, is about power and control and fear of loss of that power and control. Backlash is also a response to anger and resentment by individual males whose place in society is undergoing rapid change, often faster than they can psychologically handle.

The current backlash mentality is pervasive worldwide. Today we are living in a globalized economy characterized by rapid change and strenuous competition among nations, corporations, and workers. The stress on families and communities is severe; men whose "sense of their own manhood flowed out of their utility in a society" as Faludi (1999, p. 607) terms it, are often seen to be "fighting a world transformed by the women's movement" (p. 413). Every social movement breeds a counter reaction, and as some individuals are losing their place in the world, even from forces that have nothing to do with the women's increasing equality, some men are lashing out at the most vulnerable people in their lives—women. Psychologists call this *displaced aggression*. In the western world, two decades of the corporate media's demonizing of girls and women has become as Chesney-Lind (2006) contends, a self-fulfilling prophecy as reflected in a masculinization of the treatment of women in the criminal justice system. Such attacks on girls and women are under the guise of equality. Another form of displaced aggression is seen in the privacy of the home in domestic violence. In some non-western nations, the form that the displaced aggression takes is a virtual war on women's self-expression and their rights.

Advocacy for gender specific rather than gender neutral treatment of women, in the courts as in correctional institutions and family life is a must. It is a must because equality laws and arguments are being used against girls and women, for example, in defining domestic violence situations as fights and in arresting both parties, in according men equality in child custody hearings, in overlooking battered woman defenses in drug cases in which the partner is prosecuted along with the offender.

In this era of political backlash, above all, feminist analysis is essential to criminological research, research to counter the myths of female violence being perpetrated in books, and media hype based on the "revelations" about girls and women in such books. Feminist criminologists can help spread the word on what the research data show by writing letters to the editor and contacting reporters on a regular basis to clear up such fallacies that are being spread. Awareness of conditions and strategies that lead to equality-with-a-vengeance traps is essential so that women's advocates can avoid falling into one of these traps. Activism through lobbying legislators on behalf of increased funding of domestic violence and victim assistance services is paramount. As educators, feminist criminologists would do well do adopt a global, human rights perspective on violence against women worldwide and on the remedies provided through non-governmental organizations such as Human Rights Watch and Amnesty International.

Human rights are women's rights. This saying refers to women's rights globally and has become a motto of the international movement for human rights. Attention is increasingly drawn to the 1948 United Nations International Declaration of Human Rights which included women as an at-risk population and which as in the U.S. Constitution states that no one shall be subjected to cruel; inhuman or degrading treatment or punishment (United Nations, 1948: Article 5). In 1995, Amnesty International took up the call

Such a global, human rights perspective provides for justification for demands of social justice by drawing on principles from a higher authority. Just as the demands of social justice are new, so we must think anew. And such new thinking is enhanced through the globalization of information through the new communications technologies. The U.S.'s failure to ratify many important human rights documents underminesit leadership andcredibility as a global leader.Learning to believe in oneself as a woman is a lifelong process in a patriarchalsociety. Learning the functions that violence and the threat of violence serve for theabuser in suppressing all criticism and dialogue is a part of that process.

REFERENCES

Anderson, R. (2005), September 6). Home front Casualties. Seattle Weekly. Retrieved June 2006 from *www.seattleweekly.com.*

Baumgardner, J. & Richards, A. (2000), *Manifesta: Young Women, Feminism, and the Future.* New York: Farrar, Straus & Giroux.

Buttell, F. & Carney, M. (2005), *Women Who Perpetrate Relationship Violence: Moving Beyond Political Correctness.* Binghamton, NY: Haworth Press.

Chesney-Lind, M. and Pollock, J. (1994), Women's Prisons: Equality with a Vengeance.

In A. Merlo and J. Pollock (Eds.), *Women, Law and Social Control* (pp. 155-177).

Boston: Allyn and Bacon.

Chesney-Lind, M. (2006), Patriarchy, Crime and Justice: Feminist Criminology in a Era of Backlash. *Feminist Criminology 1* (1), 6-26.

Cook, P.W. (1997), *Abused Men: The Hidden Side of Domestic Violence.* Westport; Conn.: Praeger.

Corbett, S. (2007), March 18, New York Times Magazine. Retrieved June 2007 from *http://www.nytimes.com/2007/03/18magizine/18cover.*

Counts, D., Brown, J., & Campbell, H. (1992), *Sanctions and Sanctuary: Cultural Perspectives on the Beating of Wives.* Boulder, CO: Westview Press.

Curphey, S. (2003), May 9, Safety Net is Weaker for Unemployed Women. Women's e News. Retrieved from *http://www.womensenews.org.*

Deveny, K. (2007, February 12). Girls Gone Bad? *Newsweek*, pp. 41-47.

Dominelli, L. (2002a), Anti-oppressive Social Work Theory and Practice. Hampshire, UK: Palgrave MacMillan.

Dominelli, L. (2002b), *Feminist Social Work Theory and Practice.* New York: Palgrave.

Doyle, L. (2001), *The Surrendered Wife.* New York: Simon & Schuster.

Dutton, D.G., Nicholls, T., & Spidel, A. (2005), Female Perpetrators of Intimate Violence. In F. Buttell and M. Carney (eds.) Special Issue, *Journal of Offender Rehabilitation*, *41* (4), 1-32.

Ehrenreich, B. (2001), *Nickel and Dimed: On Not Getting by in America.* New York: Metropolitan Books.

Ehrenreich, B. and Hochschild, A. (2003), *Global Woman: Nannies, Maids, and Sex Workers in the New Economy.* New York: Metropolitan.

Epstein, C.F. (2007), Great Divides: The Cultural, Cognitive, and Social Bases of the Global Subordination of Women. *American Sociological Review*, *72*, 1-22.

Faludi, S. (1991), *Backlash: The Undeclared War Against American Women.* New York, Doubleday.

Faludi, S. (1995), March/April). "I'm Not a Feminist but I Play One on TV." *MS*, 31-39.

Faludi, S. (1999), *Stiffed: The Betrayal Against the American Man.* New York: William Morrow & Co.

Farr, K. (2005), *Sex Trafficking: The Global Market in Women and Children.* New York: Worth.

Kijakazi, K. and Primus, W. (2000), Options for Reducing Poverty Among Elderly Women by Improving SSI. Center on Budget and Policy Priorities. Retrieved from www.cbpp.org

LaFraniere, S. (2005), August 11, Entrenched Epidemic: Wife-beatings in Africa. *New York Times*, A1.

Lite, J. (2002), October 3, Report Indicates Gender-Related Violence is Global. *Women's E News*. Retrieved from *www. womensenews.org*.

Liu, D. (2006), When Do National Movements Adopt or Reject International Agendas? A Comparative Analysis of the Chinese and Indian Women's Movements. *American Sociological Review, 71*, 921-942.

Mason, R. (1995), June 1-4, An Agenda for Women's Empowerment. *Quaker United Nations Office Briefing Paper*, p.1.

Minaker, J. & Snider, L. (2006), Husband Abuse: Equality with a Vengeance. *Canadian Journal of Criminology and Criminal Justice, 48* (5), 753-780.

Mullaly, B. (2002), *Challenging Oppression: A Critical Social Work Approach*. Don Mills, Ontario: Oxford University Press.

O'Beirne, K. (2005), *Women Who Make the World Worse: And How their Radical Feminist Assault is Ruining our Schools, Families, Military, and Sports*. New York: Sentinel HC.

Payne, M. (2005), *Modern Social Work Theory* (3rd ed.) Chicago: Lyceum.

Pearson, P. (1998), *When She Was Bad: How and Why Women Get Away with Murder*. New York: Penguin.

Pollock, J.M. (1998), *Counseling Women in Prison*. Thousand Oaks, CA: Sage.

Rennison, C.C. (2003), *Intimate Partner Violence 1993-2001*. Bureau of Justice Statistics (BJS), Washington, D.C.: U.S. Department of Justice.

Ross-Sheriff, F. (2007), Globalization as a Women's Issue Revisited. *Affilia*, 22, 133-137.

Seyler, M. (2007), April 25, Feminism: It's What Women Don't Want. American Observer. Retrieved August 2007 from *http://www. americanobserver.net/2007/04/25/feminist*.

Simmons, R. (2005), *Odd Girl Out: The Hidden Culture of Aggression in Girls*. Darby, PA: Diane Publishing Co.

Sommers, C.H. (2001), *The War Against Boys: How Misguided Feminism is Harming Our Young Men.* New York: Simon & Schuster.

Stromberg, V. (2001), May 11, Letter to the Editor. *Madre.* Retrieved from www.madre.org http://hdr.undp.org/statistics/data/pdf/hdr05_table_25.pdf.

UNI Fem (2000), *Progress of the World's Women 2000.* New York: United Nations.

United Nations (1948), *Universal Declaration of Human Rights.* Resolution 217A (III). New York: United Nations.

United Nations (2003), *The World's Women 2000: Trends and Statistics.* New York: United Nations.

United Nations Development Programme (2005), *China Human Development Report.* Retrieved August 2007 from http://hdr.undp.org/docs/reports/national/CPR_China/China_2005_en.pdf

United Nations Development Report (2006), *Beyond Scarcity: Power, Poverty and the Global Water Crisis. Gender Empowerment Measures.* United Nations. Retrieved August 2007 from http://hdr.undp.org/hdr2006/statistics/indicators/230.html

U.S. Department of Labor Statistics (2005), September, Highlights of Women's Earnings in 2004. U.S. Department of Labor. Retrieved August 2007 from *http://www.bls.gov/cps/cpswom2004.pdf.*

Van Den Bergh, N., & Cooper, L.B. (1995), Introduction to Feminist Visions for Social Work. In J.E. Tropman, J.L., Erlich & J.Rothman (Eds), *Tactics and Techniques of Community Intervention* (3rd ed.) (pp. 74-93). Itasca, IL: F.E. Peacock.

Van Wormer, K., Besthorn, F.H. & Keefe, T. (2007), *Human Behavior and the Social Environment, Macro Level: Groups, Organizations, and Communities.* New York: Oxford University Press.

Van Wormer, K. & Davis, D.R. (2008), *Addiction Treatment: A Strengths Perspective.* Belmont, CA: Thomson.

World Health Organization (WHO) (2000), Gender, Health, and Poverty (fact sheet #251). Geneva: World Health Organization.

World Health Organization (WHO) (2002), *World Report on Violence and Health.* Geneva: WHO. Zamichow, N. and Perry, T. (2003, June 25). Home is where the hurt is. *The Los Angeles Times,* A1.

Yeoman, B. (1999), November/December). Bad Girls. *Psychology Today,* 54-57, 71.

11

WOMEN AND PATRIARCHY IN RURAL CHINA

Maria Cheung
Meng Liu
Toula Henonen

"While the policy of equality has been advocated in China for half a century, patriarchal ideology is still sustained in many aspects of social and family life. Men play the dominant public roles, while women are taught to be virtuous wives and good mothers" (Liu, 2001, 87-88)

INTRODUCTION

China was under Communist rule since 1949 with a centralized and planned economy. Land was collectivized. Despite a number of land reforms during the 1950s, the establishment of commune system in 1958, and radical production policies during the Great Leap Forward, China was unable to increase its economic productivity. In 1978, leader Deng Xiao Ping decided to change course and embarked on economic reform by introducing market mechanisms, privatizing state owned enterprises and dissolving rural collectives. Since implementation of the reforms, China's economy grew over three fold (National Bureau of Statistics of China, 2001). From 2006 to 2007, its average economic growth was over 10% (National Bureau of Statistics of China, 2006, 2007). In the era of economic growth, have rural women enjoyed benefits similar to other groups in society? Has China achieved more gender equality in rural areas? In this chapter, we employ a gender lens to analyze inequality between women and men in China and examine institutional barriers, such as the household responsibility, household registration (*hukou*) and political systems and traditional cultural values. The complex interplay of economic, political, social, and cultural forces will be addressed in analyzing the marginalization of rural women in China.

The majority (approximately 60%) of the Chinese population remain rural (United Nations, 2005). Some authors (Gupta, Lee, Uberoi, Wang, Wang, & Zhang, 2000; Coady, Dai & Wang, 2001) have argued that the economic reforms have brought about substantial benefits to China's rural areas. On one hand, the standard of living of rural women has been raised. On the other hand, the reforms have deeply divided the urban and rural sectors of China, creating a greater dichotomy between the rural and urban, and coastal and inner regions. Attane (2002) explains, "there are in fact at least two Chinas, one urban and one rural" (p.150). Rural women occupy the lowest social and economic status in society (Xu, 2004). Between urban men and women and rural men and women,, rural women remain at the bottom of the social strata. During the commune period from the late 1950s to 1960s, men earned more than women despite their similar participation in economic production. After economic reform, rural women's marginality was further intensified by the economic discrepancy between urban and rural areas. Despite the significant contributions of rural women in the rural economy, they are still seen as a pool of reserve labour and a dispensable group in the economy.

Since the mid-1980s, women have become the main productive force in agriculture. With the rapid economic growth in cities, rural men serve as a steady supply of cheap labour to perform work that city residents refuse to take up, such as construction and garbage collection. With rural to urban migration, agricultural work once performed primarily by men is now carried out by women, especially middle-aged women. Furthermore, the process of women's marginalization is aggravated by the regional discrepancy between coastal and inland provinces. Many rural women in the poorer Western regions are locked in the cycle of poverty as a result of the feminization of agriculture (Jacka, 1997; Rempel, 2002). In some of these provinces such as Guangxi, Yunnan, Guizhou, Sichuan and Inner Mongolia, women make up 80% of agricultural work force (Song, 1999). In these poorer and more remote regions, women are confronted with poor arable lands, limited infrastructure, and a lack of access to loans, technology, knowledge and training.

Many programs providing social security and public provision aimed at fostering women's rights were reversed after economic reform. Universal health care and other elements of the social safety net have been dissolved. The Communist Party came into power mainly through the support of the peasantry during the civil war in China. However, once the Party consolidated its power, the government shifted its attention from reducing rural poverty to alleviating urban poverty (Tian, Wang, & Ke, 2003). The government has perceived that urban poverty poses a political risk to the ruling Chinese Communist Party. Many benefits, such as Minimum Living Allowance and Old Age Security have been established in cities but not in rural areas. After economic reform, the reversal of welfare policies in rural areas greatly increased gender inequality in rural China. Under the current market economy, Chinese rural women's marginality continues to be reinforced by perpetuation of the patriarchal social structure in rural areas and revival of patriarchal values after the economic reforms. The household responsibility system, household registration system, and the monolithic political system pose fundamental structural barriers for rural women's advancement..

PATRIARCHAL SOCIAL STRUCTURE AND VALUES

Gender relationships and family structures in rural China have been shaped by Confucian values which embody a rigidly patrilineal kinship system that has existed for the past three thousand years. It emphasized the subordination of women to men where patrilineality was characterized by the passing of social-economic membership through the male line. Records of lineage were only documented along the male line. Access to key economic and social assets depended on men's position in the lineage. Families without sons were seen as dying out. Only men constituted and reproduced the social order (Gupta et. al., 2000). Daughters and wives were regarded as dependents and sometimes even property of the family (Liu, 2002). Traditional Chinese cultural values did not regard a married daughter as part of the household. Rather, she was considered as belonging to her husband's family.

Patriarchal values emphasize male superiority versus female inferiority. The patriarchal Chinese culture sees the family as a hierarchy and expects women to subordinate to man (Murphy, 2004). The three cultural principles for the role of a woman are: (1) obedience to the father before marriage, (2) obedience to the husband after marriage and (3) obedience to the son when widowed. It has also been observed that in villages, there is a strong prohibition discouraging women's expression when it could be construed as competing with male prerogatives. Women who are active in the village avoid placing themselves in competition with men.

Gender relationships between men and women have been primarily traditional in rural areas and this has not changed significantly even after the introduction of Communist rule (Friedman, Pickowicz, Sheldon & Johnson, 1991). Women have never enjoyed equal rights with men especially in rural areas. Despite the Communist revolution and subsequent social and land reforms and pronouncements about women holding up half the sky, rural Chinese society remains a patriarchal and patrilineal social network. Despite the state's attempt to eliminate feudalistic cultural values during the collectivization of land, Chinese rural communities maintained traditional values rather than embracing the ideology of the state (Friedman et. al., 1991; Chang 2000). It is reported that even during the collectivist era, discrimination against women's labour existed. The work points assigned by work units to men were always higher than those accorded to women (Judd, 1994, Jacka, 1997).

As gender policies benefiting women receded after economic reform, traditional Chinese gender values have re-emerged as a dominant force in Chinese village life. Growing inequality especially in access to resources and opportunities reinforces women's traditionally lower social status (World Bank, 2002). The re-emergence of traditional culture marginalize rural women significantly and deepen gender inequality. After decollectivization, agricultural production shifts back to rely on the family as the main production unit and the work points system no longer exists. The labour of women became less visible.

The recent migration of men working in urban centres has led to a new pattern of gender relations in rural China. The gender division of labour reflects a change in the cultural dichotomy in men's and women's work. In Chinese patrilineal society, men were responsible for the 'outside realm' of the family and the women the 'inside realm'. It is a common expression in Chinese that "men rule outside and women rule inside" (*nan zhu wai, nv zhu nei*). Although the content of women's work and men's work is changing, the division remains, as does the secondary value placed on women's work relative to men's. The traditional proverb, "men plough and women weave" has now been replaced by "men work and women plow" (Judd, 2002, p. 34). The feminization of agriculture has redefined agricultural production as 'inside work' (Jacka, 1997), meaning that such work that is carried out in the household domain. When more village men go to work in urban centres for a prolonged period, they leave their spouses to manage the household. A wife has more control over daily household decision making as well as how to use the income remitted home by the husband (Mathews & Nee, 2000). However, Jacka (1997) found that important decisions are still made by men in the household. Women's low status and lack of power in the patriarchal social arrangement in rural China is sustained by three major institutional barriers in society, namely: (1) land right issues of the household responsibility system, (2) household registration (hukou) system, and (3) lack of women's participation in the political process.

HOUSEHOLD RESPONSIBILITY SYSTEM

Tinker and Summerfield (1999) underscored that "until women possess a safe shelter for themselves and their families, they will continue to be the poorest in the world" (p.6). Constitutional rights granted in the 1950s on equality of rights between women and men in terms of land and inheriting and possessing property, have not been enforced in rural areas. The Communist government started rural land collectivization in 1952 and established the rural commune system across the country side in 1958. After twenty years of operation, it was acknowledged in the late 1970s that the commune system was a failure. It neither helped to increase agricultural productivity nor improved the living standard of peasants. In 1978, the Chinese government started to dismantle the commune system and replaced it with the Household Responsibility System (HRS).

Under the HRS, plots of land were contracted to rural household for an extended period. The allocated size of the land to households was based on the number of members and labourers in the household. The household entered into an agreement with the government which typically required the household to meet mandatory procurement criteria by selling a fixed amount of food grains or cash crops at below-market prices and paying tax to the government. After fulfilling the above, the household was entitled to the rest of the income earned from what they produced on their land. Anything produced above the government quotas could be sold at higher prices to other buyers. The agreement may have further restricted the household in the ways it could use the land. The right to reallocate land is typically vested in the village (Brandt,

Rozelle & Turner, 2002). In 2002, the Rural Land Contracting Law was adopted to reinforce this change. Peasants did not have property rights over the land but had land use rights instead (Li, 2003). Land use rights are not allocated to the individual but to the household. There is no provision to clarify the land use rights of the individuals within the household. Very often the head of a household, either as a father or a husband, signed the contract. He was therefore considered as the person who held the land use rights.

Even till today, while theoretically women enjoy the same legal rights with men in land contracting, the patrilineal values and social arrangement dominate land contracting at the village level. Women in such social environments only have the rights of maintenance as daughters in their natal home, as wives in their husbands' home, but no rights to lay claim to key productive assets such as land. Rural women as daughters or wives are not regarded as persons who share the land use rights (Jacka, 1997; Li, 2003). This tends to marginalize rural women.

Another issue that put rural women in disadvantage is that villagers are fast to take away the land rights of a newly-wed bride and slow to re-adjust land rights for divorced women and widows (Li, 2003; Liu & Chan, 1999). It is common that rural women married to men outside her village. If the maiden village of a woman married to another village carries out land adjustment, it is very likely that her land rights within her father's household will be taken away. On the other hand, if the village where she married into does not carry out any land rights adjustments, she will not have any entitlement of land use rights in the husband's village. The same problem exists when a woman is divorced or widowed and returns to her native village. Her land use rights under her ex-husband or late husband's household may be taken away and re-allocate to other households while her maiden village have already taken away her land use rights after she was married to another village. A substantial number of rural women lost their land rights as a result of marriage, divorce or widowhood (Li, 2003).

Many rural women felt trapped in a destructive marriage or when domestic violence and abuse occur. The incidence of domestic violence against women is higher in rural and remote areas than in urban and more developed regions (Liu, 2003). Due to the lack of land use rights, the rural women felt dependent financially on the husband's family. In rural China, typical domestic violence includes husband inducing harm to the wife, and in-law abuses especially between mother-in-law and daughter-in-law. It is still common for young couples to live with the husband's parents in rural areas. In such circumstances, the daughter-in-law is expected to be subservient to the mother-in-law and to take over most of the burden of domestic chores. According to Liu's study (2002), the sources of conflict centred around family issues such as disagreements over limited household resources, and competition for love and attention from the husband/son.

Rural women in China have a high rate of suicide, three times greater than that of their urban counterparts (Phillips, Li, & Zhang, 2002). China has one of the highest female suicide rates in the world and is among the few countries where there is a higher suicide rate for women than men (World Health Organization, 2004). According to Philips, Li and Zhang's study (2002), China has a particularly alarming suicide rate among young rural women who are between 25 to 34 years of age; it is the leading cause of death for this age cohort. There is also a surge in completed suicides among elderly rural women. After the age of 65, the suicide rate of rural women (and men) increases dramatically. Family conflict is a more prominent factor, rather than depression, which accounts for suicide of rural women in China. In a detailed case analysis of suicide triggered by family conflict, Liu (2002) explained how a daughter-in-law's suicide is an act of ultimate revenge against the husband's extended family when a woman perceived that her in-laws mistreated her and her husband failed to protect her.

HOUSEHOLD REGISTRATION (*HUKOU*) SYSTEM

While urban-rural disparity is a common phenomenon in many developing countries, seldom is it caused by deliberate policies that maintain and reinforce such disparities. In China, differential wealth between urban and rural areas is sustained by the Household Registration (*hukou*) System in China. This is because the migration of rural people to cities does not involve a simple transfer of household registration to the city area and concomitant access to the social welfare resources located there. Poor people from rural areas tend to become poor migrant workers when they relocate to cities.

Various governments of different dynasties throughout Chinese history adopted some sort of household registration system mainly for taxation purposes and to keep track of changes in local population numbers. There was no law to restrict the mobility of people between urban and rural areas. Shortly after 1949 when the Communist Party took power, the government introduced a *hukou* system as an administrative device to control rural to urban migration. The influx of millions of peasants who worked in the burgeoning state industrial enterprises in urban areas was perceived as undermining the nation's political and social stability. The *hukou* system was then established to; (1) prevent rural migration to urban areas, and (2) increase political control of the Party at the grassroots level (Cheng & Selden, 1994).

The *hukou* system classified the population into two categories: "agricultural" (rural) and "non-agricultural" (urban). At the beginning of its implementation, the *hukou* system is akin to a serf system in which the peasants were tied to the land (Judd, 1994). Between 1961 and 1963, about 18 million migrant workers in cities were deported back to their villages of origin (Wu & Treiman, 2004). Peasants were confined to reside in their own villages and were prohibited to move to or reside in the cities. The *hukou* system also resembles a caste system where household status is inherited. Children inherit their household registration classification from their mother (Judd, 1994; Chan & Li, 1998). In its early years of implementation, the household registration derived its power through the rationing system. The ration of staple food and various essential items was provided to registered households. People who resided outside their original residence could not receive any rations.

This classification system defines the socio-economic and political eligibility and the status of rural dwellers. It also gives rise to profound urban-rural inequalities in many areas, such as incomes, job opportunities, education, social services, health care and physical infrastructure. Gender inequality in rural China is in part reinforced by a structural barrier maintained by the government's policy of *hukou*. This quasi-caste system also marginalizes marriageable rural women because men with urban registration are very reluctant to marry women with rural registration as their children will automatically inherit rural residence status. When rural men move to work in the cities, they would likely leave their families behind as they are not entitled to basic social services such as health care, social insurance and education.

It has been difficult to change rural registration status to an urban one. The most common ways for a rural dweller to change his or her registration classification are through admission to a university, joining the army or becoming a government cadre. Only a small number of rural residents succeed in acquiring urban resident status. Under restrictive quotas, some rural households have been able to obtain forms of temporary urban residential permits either by buying expensive housing units or investing in major urban centres (Wong & Huen, 1998).

Since the introduction of economic reforms, the *hukou* system has been relaxed. The local authorities could no longer hold back rural people on the land through provision of rations as the better opportunities in urban centres appealed to poor rural dwellers. Migration has been considered legal since 1984 (Poncet & Zhu, 2005). However, the *hukou* system has not changed. Urban workers from rural areas can only obtain a work permit. It is therefore very difficult to have the whole family reside in the city as they are not entitled to the social service benefits and privileges enjoyed by their urban counterparts. Migrant workers tend to work at jobs that no urban dwellers want to take. The change in rural migration only aggravates the urban-rural disparity. This further marginalizes rural women because married and older women (and elderly men) and children are left in villages without the agricultural labour previously contributed by the migrant. In interior and Western provinces the feminization of agriculture has become a common phenomenon. The young rural women, who are the second largest population migrating to work in urban centres, are exposed to risks of abuse and harassment once there (Gaetano & Jacka, 2004). Even though young rural women face similar segregation in urban employment as most rural men do, they are usually required to return to marry in the village and remain there while their male counterparts still go back to work in the city after they got married. In order to improve the conditions of rural women, the *hukou* system needs to be reformed to eliminate the inherent inequalities imposed on rural women, and the rural population as a whole.

Although the *hukou* system makes it almost impossible for rural people to migrate to cities in family groups, there are families who do so. These families tend to live in extremely poor conditions. They are not entitled to any of the benefits to which urban residents are entitled. They have to pay extra tuition for their children to attend sub-standard schools. They are second-class citizens who constantly face discrimination in the work environment and in the neighbourhood. Women face yet a greater burden because of gender inequality in the work place and at home (Fan, 2003).

LIMITED PARTICIPATION OF WOMEN IN THE POLITICAL PROCESS

Apart from socio-economic and cultural factors, women's limited political participation is another significant factor which can lead to the subjugation of rural women in a patriarchal society. This is because women leaders can better ensure that women's voices and interests remain on the political agenda. Under the present system, there are few appropriate channels for women to express their needs. Very few women's organizations advocate for rural women's interests in China. While the Women's Federation is active in providing a range of services to rural women, there is a need for enhanced awareness of grassroots women's interests and needs rather than a focus only on the implementation of Party policies. Establishment of more women's NGOs could be helpful in providing specialized services that are geared to the diverse needs of rural women. A social and political environment of openness to welcome the ideas of women at the grassroots level is needed.

In 1989, the Chinese government initiated a system of village management committees whose members are, in principle, elected by all villagers. The function of the village management committee is to deal with issues and matters that affect the village. However, open nomination has not been widely adopted (Zhong, 2004). In many cases, the nomination of candidates is still controlled by the township government and the village Communist Party branch. The work of the village committees is governed by the village Communist Party branch. The village committee chair is usually the Deputy Party Secretary. All major decisions have to be approved by the Party branch before adoption and implementation by the village committee. Moreover, township governments can veto decisions made by the village committees.

The monolithic political structure of the communist state prioritizes those who are members of the Communist Party to form the local political leadership. Female representation in the local village level political structure has been constrained by the patrilocal post-marital residence which restricts women from becoming Party members, a prerequisite for holding political and administrative office in China. Membership in the Party is usually granted after a considerable period of observation and consideration. It may take several years for a person to become trusted and respected by local leaders. By then, rural women may be too preoccupied with family responsibilities (Judd, 1994). Low educational level also directly affects rural women's level of community and political participation (Alpermann, 2003).

After the economic reforms took effect, women's representation in public office declined significantly (Howell, 2001). A survey conducted in 1999 by the UN Task Force on Gender in Shandong Province indicated a significant drop in female representation among the leadership (World Bank, 2002). At most of the county and township levels of government, 95% of office holders are male. Only one per cent of all village management committee chairs and 20% of all village committee members are women, and these are usually local women leaders of the Women's Federation (Howell, 2001). Without adequate representation in political decision-making processes, rural women have limited influence in the resource distribution and policy-making that affect their daily lives.

IMPACT OF GENDER INEQUALITY ON RURAL WOMEN

The above-mentioned patriarchal structure and institutional barriers created by socio-economic and cultural forces have strong impact on rural women's survival in an often-harsh countryside environment. The marginalization of rural women can be traced through all their life stages (Cheung, Heinonen, & Liu, in press). Prior to birth, a female fetus carried by a rural woman faces more risks from targeted abortion as parents tend to prefer to have a boy rather than a girl. This is due to traditional beliefs and practical needs for survival and maintenance of the family line. The state policy of one child per family (in rural areas two children are mostly allowed), when enforced at the village level, is a causal factor (Li & Lavely, 2003). Shortly after birth, a baby girl may face a risk of infanticide should her parents determine that they cannot accept a girl child (Chang, 2000). A female child's medical care may be prioritized lower than a male child's as nearly all medical services have been privatized in rural areas and seeing a doctor is expensive for poor peasant families (Li, Zhu & Feldman, 2004). While attending elementary school, a girl has a high chance of being kept at home to help with household chores or agricultural tasks (Murphy, 2004). It is mainly due to family poverty or because the family views girl's education as less important than boy's. Her chance of receiving education beyond the compulsory nine years is lower than her male counterpart. In rural areas, only about 40% of females complete high school as contrasted with 60% of rural males who do so (National Bureau of Statistics of China, 2001).

The Chinese government has extracted resources but invested little in rural areas (Fan, 2003), at least until recent years. Economic diversification, providing greater employment opportunities in the industrial and service sectors, draws workers away from rural areas to the cities and rural towns of China. Because of the higher income generated through off-farm work by males, men are the first to leave rural villages to seek better work opportunities (Judd, 1994). Due to expansion of the service sector and light industries in towns and urban centres, young female workers were drawn to work in these areas in unskilled low-wage jobs. They earn less than men because of their lower educational levels. They do not enjoy the same benefits as their urban counterparts due to the disadvantage of rural residence status they carry with them. Further, many return to villages to marry and settle on land that often produces poorly.

The influx of rural men and young women to urban centres means that married and older women (and men) remain in villages to farm the land and raise animals. The low profit margin of agricultural products traps them in a cycle of poverty, especially in the interior regions where land is mostly unproductive, and characterized by harsh climate, and poor infrastructure. As a means to counter the harsh environment, villagers in areas such as Inner Mongolia have initiated planting activities to encourage once-productive land to return to its former state (personal conversation with villagers in Balinyouqi, November 25, 2005).

After China's accession to the World Trade Organization, market information and technological skills have become especially important factors for small farmers so they could compete in the market. Support in terms of credit, information resources, infrastructure development and relevant training are paramount. Due to the lack of education and social status, rural women have less access to these supportive mechanisms than do men (Rempel, 2002). Although women's involvement in agricultural work has increased in interior and remote areas of China, the lack of infrastructure and resources (land, loans, information and training) disadvantages women, perpetuating the feminization of poverty in these areas. The breakdown of the collective welfare system after the economic reforms, together with the feminization of agriculture, often involves a triple burden for younger married women who need to perform agricultural work, care for children and household chores, and at the same time, take care of the needs of aging parents-in-law. Performing all these tasks are both physically and psychologically taxing (Chang, 2003). In recent years, there has been an increase in married women migrating to work in city centres (Pan & Huang, 2005). However, their success is limited by reduced job opportunities. Often they are found in domestic work in wealthier people's homes where they are engaged in domestic work.

As women generally live longer than men, they face hardship if they become ill or frail (Zhu & Xiao, 1991). The concept of retirement is nonexistent in rural China. Elderly rural residents do not enjoy the same old age security as do their urban counterparts. Further, agricultural seasons with long hours of physically demanding work is a feature of rural life. Older people continue farming as long as they are physically able.

With the privatization of medical care after economic reform, the rudimentary social security schemes under the commune system were abolished with no replacement. Although elderly women may become too frail to perform agricultural tasks, they do help take care of grandchildren and perform other household chores. It could be said that they work until they drop (Pang, de Brauw, & Rozelle, 2004). The lack of financial security causes elderly parents to be dependent on their adult children. Confronted with ailing health and without strong religious or cultural taboos against suicide in China, older women may seek an alternative to their hardship. Evidence can be seen in the sharp increase in the suicide rate for women (and men) over sixty-four years of age (Phillips, Li & Zhang, 2002).

CONCLUSION

Rural women constitute 31% of the total population in China (National Bureau of Statistics of China, 2001). The majority of them who reside in the interior and Western provinces find themselves trapped in a cycle of poverty. While the living conditions of some rural women in coastal regions have improved after economic reform, a large proportion in the interior and remote areas have experienced no improvement or deterioration of their situation. In rural China, women still belong to the lowest social strata. Although women's situation may improve with greater economic activity and income, there remain traditional beliefs and institutional barriers that deter women's full participation in society. In patriarchal Chinese society, rural women continue to have less influence than rural men in the family and in the community in which they live, as well as in the wider socio-political sphere.

In rural areas, having land is important in reducing poverty and enhancing food security (Agarwal, 2001). The feminization of agriculture and the fact that most women do not have land use rights perpetuate women's poverty and hence marginalization. In the interior and remote areas, it is not only that women cannot generate sufficient income from increasingly barren land, but also an insufficient infrastructure of roads and transport, training and agricultural extension programs, and credit access to support women's agricultural work (personal communication, village women in Kalaqinqi, Inner Mongolia, November, 2004). Rural women in China face multi-faceted challenges throughout their life cycle, from education, health and social security, and from traditional gender values and social exclusion.

In many rural regions in different parts of the world, patriarchy is interwoven into social, economic, political and cultural forces to construct rural women's marginality. The feminization of poverty is perpetuated by gender inequalities in the distribution of income and resources. Rural women in China, especially those who are married and older women, are systematically excluded from more profitable non-agricultural labour market and political institutions which could improve their economic and social situations. They face more constraints and fewer opportunities than men in access to higher education, quality health care and employment, in effect, to improve their lives. Traditional patriarchal values still run deep in Chinese society, especially in rural areas.

Gender awareness initiatives could help to highlight and promote the contributions of rural women. Such programs could involve educational, artistic or dramatic activities and discussions of gender relations and issues grounded in the cultural experiences of the respective communities. Education is a key factor in empowerment of rural women. More education is needed to understand the way patriarchal attitudes and social values affect gender relations at the village level and shape change. The central government's declared policy to foster education at the village level needs to be realized through transferring adequate resources to rural education, especially in the poorer and remote areas. Employing positive measures to encourage parents to send their daughters to school is important to ensure rural girls receive same level of education as boys.

A greater focus on gender in rural policy-making and programs to cater for the needs of rural women is needed. To alleviate rural women's poverty, there is a need for governments at different levels to eliminate institutional barriers that prevent women from full participation in society; such measures would enhance gender equality. Recently the central government has announced a series of new rural policies such as the cooperative medical insurance scheme, abolition of agricultural taxes and fees for the nine years of basic education. As helpful as these initiatives can be for rural women, attention also needs to be paid to land rights for women, especially in situations of divorce or widowhood. The *hukou* system also poses a barrier for women's empowerment because it can aggravate rural women's disadvantaged position. An examination of the way this policy affects rural women (and men) would provide needed information that could effect change that would benefit rural women and men. The new cooperative medical insurance scheme mainly covers acute medical conditions that would require hospitalization. As important as such coverage is for rural people, the scheme needs to extend the coverage for non-acute illnesses as well.

Addressing the redistributive function of the scheme will be a future important strategy to narrow the gap between urban and rural areas. In order to encourage the voices of rural women and reflect them in policy-making, a more participatory environment is called for, whether at the local community level or at the macro policy decision-making level. Grassroots self-help organizations that help rural women to express their needs could be fostered so that women would have spaces to meet and consider their needs and interest together.

REFERENCE

Agarwal, B. (2001), Participatory Exclusions, Community Forestry, and Gender: An Analysis for South Asia and a Conceptual Framework. *World Development, 29*(10), 1623-1648.

Alpermann, B. (2003), *A Discussion and Recommendation on Rural Administration in China.* Retrieved February 28, 2006, from *http://www.chinarural.org/euchinaprog/report_c_alpermann.pdf* (in Chinese).

Attane, I. (2002), A Half Century of Chinese Socialism: The Changing Fortunes of Peasant Families. *Journal of Family History, 27*(2), 150-171.

Brandt, L., Rozelle, S., & Turner, M. (2002), Local Government Behavior and Property Right Formation in Rural China. Department of Agricultural and Resource Economics, University of California Davis, Working Paper Series.

Chan, K. W. & Li, Z. (1998), The Hukou System and Rural-urban Migration in China: Process and Changes. Department of Geography, University of Washington. Retrieved November, 2004, from *http://csde.washington.edu/pubs/wps/98-13.pdf*

Chang, K. S. (2000), Economic Privatism and New Patterns of Inequality in Post-Mao China. *Development and Society, 29*(2), 23-54.

Chang, K. S. (2003), Market Socialism and Ruralist Welfare Reform in Post-Mao China. *Development and Society, 32*(2), 147-171.

Cheng, T. & Selden, M. (1994), The Origins and Social Consequences of China's Hukou System, China Quarterly, No. 139 pp. 644-668.

Cheung, M., Heinonen, T. & Liu, M. (in press for 2008), Gender Analysis of the Marginalization of Rural Women over the Life

Span after the Initiation of Economic Reforms in China. *Journal of Social Development Issues, 30*(2).

Coady, D., Dai, X. & Wang, L. (2001), Community Programs and Women's Participation: the Chinese Experience. *(World Bank Policy on Social Protection, Research Working Paper Series, Volume 1, No. 2622)*. Retrieved October, 2005, from http://www-wds.worldbank.org/external/default/WDSContentServer/IW3P/IB/2001/07/13/000094946_01062804153178/Rendered/PDF/multi0page.pdf.

Fan, C. C. (2003), Rural-urban Migration and Gender Division of Labor in Transitional China. *International Journal of Urban and Regional Planning, 27*(1), 24-47.

Friedman, E., Pickowicz, P. G., Sheldon, M., & Johnson, K. A. (1991), *Chinese Village, Socialist State*. New Haven: Yale University Press.

Gaetano, A. M., & Jacka, T. (2004), *On the Move: Women in Rural-to-urban Migration in Contemporary China*. New York: Columbia University Press.

Gupta, M. D., Lee, S., Uberoi, P., Wang, D., Wang, L., & Zhang, X. (2000), *State Policies and Women's Autonomy in China, the Republic of Korea, and India 1950-2000: Lessons from Contrasting Experiences* (World Bank Policy Report on Gender and Development, Working Paper Series, No. 16). Washington, DC: World Bank.

Howell, J. (2001), April, *Women's Political Participation in China: Struggling to Hold up Half the Sky*. Paper for the 51st Political Studies Association Conference, Manchester, United Kingdom.

Jacka, T. (1997), *Women's Work in Rural China*. Cambridge: Cambridge University Press.

Judd, E. (1994), *Gender and Power in Rural North China*. Stanford: Stanford University Press.

Judd, E. (2002), *The Chinese Women's Movement: Between State and Market*. Stanford: Stanford University Press.

Li, J., & Lavely, W. (2003), Village Context, Women's Status, and Son Preference Among Rural Chinese Women. *Rural Sociology, 68*(1), 87-106.

Li, P. J. S. (2003), Rural Land Tenure Reforms in China: Issues, Regulations and Prospects for Additional Reform [Special Edition]. *Land Reform, 3*, 59-72.

Li, S., Zhu, C., & Feldman, M. (2004), Gender Differences in Child Survival in Contemporary Rural China: A County Study. *Journal of Biosocial Science, 36*, 83-109.

Liu, M. (2001), Re-victimization: An Analysis of a Hotline Service for Battered Women in China. *Asian Journal of Women's Studies, 7*(2), 12-93.

Liu, M. (2002), Rebellion and Revenge: The Meaning of Suicide of Women in Rural China. *International Journal of Social Welfare, 11*, 300-309.

Liu, M. (2003), *Marital Violence in China*. Beijing: Commerce Press. (in Chinese).

Liu, M., & Chan, C. (1999), Enduring Violence and Staying in Marriage: Stories of Battered Women in Rural China. *Violence Against Women, 5*(12), 1469-1492.

Mathews, R., & Nee, V. (2000), Gender Inequality and Economic Growth in Rural China. *Social Science Research, 29*, 606-632.

Murphy, R. (2004), The Impact of Labour Migration on the Well-being and Agency of Rural Chinese Women: Cultural and Economic Contests and the Life Course. In A. M. Gaetano, & T. Jacka (Eds.), *On the move: Women in rural-to-urban migration in contemporary China* (pp. 243-276). New York: Columbia University Press.

National Bureau of Statistics of China. (2001), *Major Findings of the Second Stage Survey on the Status of Women, Part 2*. Retrieved February 28, 2006, from *http://www.popinfo.gov.cn/popinfo/pop_docrkxx.nsf/v_tjzl/41F1595FE7 62E9F 448256BDC 0010D8B5* (in Chinese).

National Bureau of Statistics of China. (2006-2007), *Statistical data-Quarterly*, retrieved Nov. 5, 2007, from *http://www.stats.gov.cn/english/statisticaldata/QuarterlyData/*.

Pan, Z.F. & Huang, A.X. (2005), A Sociological Analysis of Motivating Factors of Rural Married Women finding Employment out of Home Village: A Case Study of Pancun Village. *Collection of Women's Studies, 64*(2), 20-31.

Pang, L., de Brauw, A., & Rozelle, S. (2004), Working Until you Drop: The Elderly of Rural China. *The China Journal, 52*, 73-94.

Phillips, M., Li, S., & Zhang, Y. (2002), Suicide Rates in China, 1995-99. *Lancet, 359*, 835-840.

Poncet, S., & Zhu, N. (2005), Country People Moving to the Cities: The Migratory Dynamic. *China Perspectives, 62*, 11-22.

Rempel, H. (2002). Rural China Adapting to a World market. *Canadian Journal of Development Studies, XXIII*(3), 543-569.

Song, Y. (1999), Feminization of Maize Agricultural Production in Southwest China. *Biotechnology and Development Monitor, 37*, 6-9.

Tian, W., Wang, X. & Ke, F. (2003), Poverty Module China: The Poverty Alleviation Role of Agriculture in China. Paper presented at The Roles of Agriculture Project International Conference 20-22 October, 2003, Rome Italy, Agricultural and Development Economics Division, Food and Agriculture Organization, United Nations.

Tinker, I. & Summerfield, G. (1999), *Women's Rights to House and Land: China, Laos, Vietnam*. Boulder, CO: Lynne Rienner Publishers.

United Nations (2005), *World Population Prospects: The 2006 Revision and World Urbanization Prospects*. Population Division of the Department of Economic and Social Affairs of the United Nations Secretariat. Retrieved November 28, 2007, from *http://esa.un.org/unpp*.

Wong, L. & Huen, W. (1998), Reforming the Household Registration System: A Preliminary Glimpse of the Blue Chop Household Registration System in Shanghai and Shenzhen. *International Migration Review*, Vol. 32 No.4, Winter, 1998, 974-994.

World Bank (2002), *China Country Gender Review*. East Asia Environment and Social Development Unit. Beijing: World Bank Beijing Office.

World Health Organization (2004), *Mental Health*. Retrieved March 10, 2006, from *http://www.who.int/mental_health/media/en/296.pdf*

Wu, X. & Treiman, D. (2004), The Household Registration System and Social Stratification in China. 1955-1996, 41(2), 363-384.

Xu, X. (2004), *Analysis on Peasant Mobility Opportunities and Related Issues*. Retrieved March 10, 2007, from *http://203.93.24.66/shxw/shld/P020040709401145469270.pdf* (in Chinese).

Zhong, Y. (2004), Political Culture and Participation in the Chinese Countryside: Some Empirical Evidence. *The American Political Science Association*, pp. 445-453. Retrieved November, 2005, from *http://www.apsanet.org/PS/july04/zhong.pdf*.

Zhu, C., & Xiao, G. (1991), An Analysis of the Life Cycle of Chinese Women. *Chinese Journal of Population Sciences*, 3(3), 247-257.

12

SOCIO-CULTURAL PARAMETERS OF GENDER DISPARITY AND OLD AGE INSECURITY OF THE WOMEN IN PATRIARCHAL SOCIETY

Profulla C. Sarker

INTRODUCTION

The life span of human being may be divided into four phase viz. childhood, adolescent, adulthood, and old age. During the first two spans, persons usually remain under the care, love, affection, guidance, and protection of the parents. In the third span, he or she becomes self dependent under the existing socio-economic and cultural system and state laws and provides shelter for the dependents (Aziz and Maloney, 1985). The fourth and the last span of life which is indeed crucial and characterized by a loss in vitality and return to the state of dependency upon the traditional joint family system where he or she wants to get all kinds of support to survive in kinship network relations. On the other hand, with the advancement of medical science, public health care services, and technological development the longevity of the people of Bangladesh is improving and as a result the number of aged person is increasing. In the process of urbanization, industrialization, modernization, pauperization, globalization, and migration, the traditional joint family system is declining with the tendency to form nuclear unit and gradually the next generation become individualistic and self centered. Changes are taking place not only in kinship tie but also in parent-child relationship, which putting them in the different worlds. Under the circumstances, the aged persons especially the women are facing different types of problem to survive in the patriarchal social system. In both the developed and developing worlds, the older women are the victims of gender inequality in inadequate access to wealth, property, and resources (World Bank, 1994).These inequalities are often buttressed by legal and political institutions. Older women also suffer from the effects of basic needs and civic facilities. Although a critical synthesis of gender theory and ageing is emerging, until recently, a few research works have focused on the study of women and gerontology in developing countries. Socio-economic status of the older women is partially rooted in the gender division of labor which assumes that women's primary involvement is in reproductive labor, unpaid household work, care provider and unequal power relations at household level. These activities often restrict women's employment opportunities, mobility, educational attainment, skill development, and interaction with the cross-section of people. The main focus of this paper is to examine to what extent the socio-cultural parameters of gender disparity affects the insecurity in basic needs and civic facilities of the women in their old age.

CONCEPTUAL ISSUES

Ageing has various meanings. First, ageing is a social construct. Societies assign different age expectations according to gender, socio-cultural norms and role assignments. Secondly, ageing is a bio-social process that is presumably determined by genes, anxieties and is influenced by environment. Biological investigation suggests that maximum life span is genetically determined, and therefore, it is fixed for each species (Schiender, 1978).Ageing refers to the regular changes that occur in mature organism have under representative environmental conditions with the advancement in chronological age. It is a process of constant change that is universal in all organisms. Although ageing varies in different reasons, such as life style, health, family status, etc. However, old age is considered here as 60 years and above of an individual in connection with the retirement system and state laws.

Gender refers to socially constituted relations between men and women. Gender considers social roles and values attached to each sex. More specifically, it is a socio-economic and cultural contour to analyze roles, responsibilities, opportunities, constraints, attitudes, and needs of men and women in the context of social system in which they live. Gender disparity is meant providing women with a fewer facilities than she legitimately deserve. Gender disparity is associated with the attitudes, expressions, and actions that determine by the society between men and women. Gender disparity here implies gender discrimination, which refers to inequality between men and women in connection with insecurity of the women in their old age.

A society that expects males to dominant females in every sphere of life cycle of women is termed as patriarchal society. It is a system ruled by men in which women are inferior in status as well as basic human rights (Kottak, 2005:198). In patriarchal society, the authority is roughly vested upon man who takes the responsibility for maintenance family and plays dominant role to take any decision of the family (Sarker,1997). More specifically, in patriarchal society, the power is in the hands of males than to females.

THE AGED WOMEN

The longevity of the women is higher throughout the world compared to their counter part men. An insignificant number of research works have focused on the study of women and gerontology especially in developing countries where the patriarchal social system is predominant like Bangladesh. The total population of Bangladesh is about 152 million. Among them 51.5 percent are males and the rest of the 48.5 percent are females. The existing life expectancy at birth is 62.5 percent for men and 61.5 percent for women. The percentage of older women out of total population is given below from 1911to 2001.

The Table-1 shows that in the period between 1911 and 2001, there has been more than a four fold increase in the number of elderly women. During this period i.e. 90 years, the elderly women who belong to the age group of 60 years and above has gone up from 4.4 to 9.1 percent. The mass application of immunization against infectious diseases, improvement of reproductive health, and maternity services, awareness about nutrition and relatively better quality of life have brought about remarkable changes in the age structure of women population in Bangladesh.

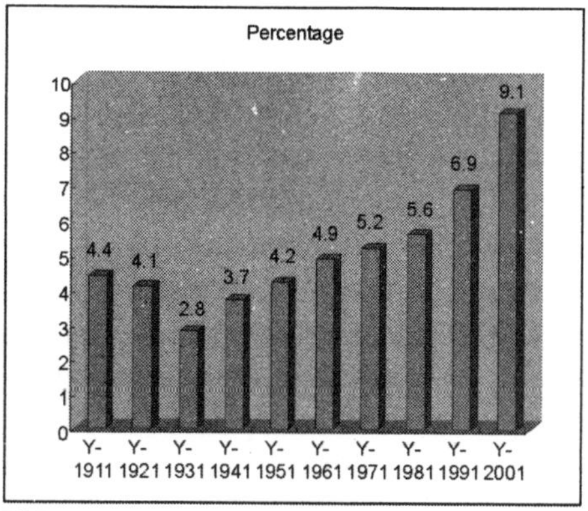

Table 1: Older Women of Bangladesh in the Period of 1911-2001

Source: Sex and Age Composition of the Population. Country Monograph Series No.8, population of Bangladesh, ESCAP, United Nations, Bangkok.

PARAMETERS OF GENDER DISPARITY

In many cultures gender disparity begins before birth. Many parents desperately decide for induced abortion if they found that the fetus is female. Women face inequality every where in the different phases of their life cycle. In many societies, they do not get a chance to even aspire to lead healthy and productive lives. It has found that in many cultures women are devalued as human beings from the day they are born; from early childhood girls are made conscious of the fact that unlike their brothers, who are assets to the family, and they are liabilities. In the process of socialization, girls are made to understand from childhood that once married, they should learn how to adjust to their husbands and other relations either in side of the family or out side (Sarker,1999:205). Girls are taught the two virtues-patience and sacrifice, the deal of *Bangali* motherhood. They girls also learn to accept the essentially inferior status of women in society. As girls grow up they perceived in preferential treatment given to their brothers, fathers and other male members of the family and they also taught that getting less of everything and not complaining about it is the ideal behavior pattern of a good women (ibid). In a milieu of scarcity whatever little is available, be it good food, clothing or opportunities for education and health care facilities, it is first offered to boys. In the culture of patriarchal society, the wives are expected to be modest, submissive, and dutiful to their husbands and other members of the family. In real sense, socially the women have no individual identity; rather, they are addressed by their kinship positions vis-avis others, such as daughter, wife, and mother.

The culture of patriarchal society does not permit equality between men and women. Gender disparity has its genesis in religion. For an example, the women of patriarchal society have to depend upon men in different phases of their life cycle. In childhood and adolescent period they depend on parents as daughter, in adulthood, they depend upon husbands, and in old age they depend on children especially on son or other relatives. It should be mentioned that even employed women are not independent in real sense though they have liberty of movement and social interaction with a cross-section of people. The question is that how many employed women can spend their income without the consent of their husbands? Slaves are purchased with money, but in a patriarchal social system directly or indirectly, especially the illiterate and poorer section of women become slaves by paying their husbands cash and kinds in the form of dowry.

CONTRIBUTION OF OLDER WOMEN

The older women contribute at the family, community, national, and societal levels. In the formal sector, about 25 percent older women were work force, although the nature of their work varies regionally (United Nations, 1995). In

European society, early retirement policies encourage older women to withdraw from workforce permanently. In Middle East, labor force participation of older women is lower than in other developing regions. In Jordan, less than 1 percent of older women work for a wage. On the other hand, in some African countries, labor force participation of women is higher (Rix,1991). In addition, the contribution of older women in informal sector is not recognized in developing societies. Their work is non-remunerative and as a result considered unproductive (Beneria,1979). Many older women work on family farms or participate in family agricultural enterprises. They also contribute to performing household tasks and care giving duties. Many older women remain indispensable but unrecognized asset. In many parts of the world, older women offer their services as unpaid contributors. They contribute as mentors, volunteers, and caregivers for grand children. In many societies the older women perform the household activities such as cleaning, washing, cooking, etc. especially where the son and daughter-in-law are working members of the family. A study of 151 countries unequivocally rejected the idea of older persons as "dependent retirees". It negated the idea as a 'myth' and concluded that many older persons contribute not only for family but also for national economy (Rix,1991). Consequently, the approaching elderly women in many societies are considered as asset rather than liability.

OLD AGE INSECURITY

The old age insecurity of the women is different in socio-economic condition in which they live. The aged women, it has been consistently demonstrated, are disadvantaged in a variety of ways in relation aged men. They are poorer, sick, powerless, and they have to survive with minimum facilities. Most of the older women are widows because the life expectancy of women is higher compared to men. More over, the average age parity is found from the different studies between husband and wife is almost 8 to 9 years. It has been observed that men prefer younger wives in patriarchal societies to get longer time as care giver and sexual partner.

Age inequality is linked with widowhood and poverty. Calleja (1997) pointed out that poverty and ageing has generally proved into the globalization of poverty in late life. Poverty appears in the form of social and economic insecurity, health hazards, loneliness, illiteracy and dependency. It should be noted that poverty among the older women is not accidental rather it is multi-dimensional and their number is increasing rapidly. The socio-economic status of the older women is partially rooted in the gender division of labor which assumes that women's primary involvement is in reproductive labor, unpaid household work, care giving and unequal power relations at the household level. These gender based attitudes often restricted women's employment, mobility, education, skill development training and interaction with the cross-section of people. When they get employment, most of the women are concentrated in low-wage with minimum security (United Nations,1999). In the life cycle women earn less and experienced inequality, at work, family, community and society.

One of the acute problems of the elderly women is poverty since they have lost their energy to work. In Bangladesh, about 80 percent elderly women live in rural areas and almost all of them are unemployed and many of them are widows. It has been found that gender differential in age at marriage is the key factor that has a strong influence in determining how many marriages will end in widowhood. Under the circumstances, they have to depend upon children or relatives. Most of the elderly women do not own any cultivable land. Inheritance laws and practices discriminate against women. For example, under certain legal systems, daughters inherit half as much as their brothers, and mothers less than their children. In rural Bangladesh, land determines who eats and who does not (Hartman andJames,1997). Consequently, many of the women do not get adequate food to survive. They hardly consume meat, fish, egg, fruits, milk, etc. and as a result many of them are malnourished. Malnutrition makes them prone to disease, which leads to increase morbidity and mortality.

Older women experienced higher rates of chronic illness and disability in later life than men. Older women live with numerous chronic conditions, many of which are irreversible but not life threatening. Most of these illnesses are senile dementia. The elderly women are also suffer from diseases like pain, weakness, blood pressure, asthma, diabetes, anemia, cardiac problems, etc. Surprisingly pain and anemia are almost common (Rahman et al.1997).The existing medical facilities especially for the elderly people are inadequate in Bangladesh whish failed to meet the demand for treatment. The health care system in Bangladesh is curative and remedial, rather than preventive and promotional which almost common in other Asian countries(Chow,1996).Many of the elderly women do not get chance for medical treatment and as a result they have to depend on traditional medicine like herbal and folk which accessible and cheaper compared to modern allopathic medicine. The older women suffer from multiple and long term illnesses, as well as greater social isolation in late life. Longevity is a mixed blessing: many women are in a position to enjoy more years of life, yet they experience chronic ailment and often have insufficient assess to resources.

Housing is another problem encountered by the elderly women to get shelter at the end of their life. Two-third of the elderly women in Bangladesh lives with their children especially with the sons and the rest of them live with their spouses or alone. It has been observed that people of many families live in one room in rural areas and slums in urban areas and some of the older people sleep in porch-like area. Many of the elderly women are shelter less (Roy,200).The tendency to form a neo-local residence after marriage among the young generation is increasing. The main reasons to form neo-local residence are individualistic attitude, materialistic benefit, and to avoid conflict between in-laws. The conflict between the mother-in-law and daughter-in-law create mental torture and some times in extreme cases the elderly women commit suicide to get rid of oppression (Sarker,2002 and Moody,1994). It has been observed that the poor elderly women depend on charity through begging other wise they have no alternative.

INITIATIVES OF INTERNATIONAL FORUMS

The United Nations conferences and other intergovernmental meetings have been concerned with the situation of elderly women in global perspective. The first conference on the International Women's Year was held in 1975 in Mexico. The main focus of the conference was the situation and need assessment of the older women across the world. In 1980, the World Conference of the United Nations Decade for Women: Equality, Development and Peace, held in Copenhagen. The situation of the elder women was one of the agenda of this conference. In 1982, in its International Plan of Action on Ageing, the World Assembly on Ageing recommended that particular attention be paid to the situation of older women. In 1985, the Nairobi Forward-looking Strategies, adopted by the World Conference to Review and Appraise the Achievements of the United Nations Decade for Women: Equality, Development and Peace, also addressed the issue of older women and highlighted women's longer life expectancy, their economic situation and special health needs.

In 1986, the Commission on the Status of Women considered a report of the Secretary-General on the status and situation of the older women in their societies. In 1992, the Commission on the Status of Women adopted resolution on the integration of elderly women into development. The Platform for Action, adopted at the Fourth World Conference on Women, held in Beijing in 1995, made recommendations based on a life cycle approach and referred explicitly to women at all stages of life.

In 1998, the Commission on the Status of Women considered a report of Secretary-General, "Older Women Support System: New Challenges". The report included relevant recommendations that resulted from the Expert Group Meeting on Care giving and Older Persons: Gender Dimensions, which was jointly organized by the Division for Advancement of Women and the Division on Social Policy and development of the United Nations Department for Economic and Social Affairs, held in Malta in 1997. On the basis of the report prepared by Commission in 1997, the Assembly called upon States to include a gender dimension in their national programs for the International Year of Older Persons.

INITIATIVE AT THE STATE LEVEL

The Government of Bangladesh and the NGOs have already been taken five approaches for the upliftment of the socio-economic conditions of the women in general that also affects the life of the older women. These approaches are; welfare approach, equity approach, efficiency approach, anti-poverty approach and empowerment approach.

WELFARE APPROACH

The welfare approach was initiated by the Government of Bangladesh in close cooperation of WHO and UNICEF keeping in view for reduction of the maternal and child morbidity and mortality to ensure the economic and social development. The women and the children are most vulnerable groups and their quality of life and well-being are directly related to economic and social development.

EQUITY APPROACH

The Equity approach was initiated emphasizing the participation of women in development process and economic progress by their productive and reproductive roles. The main thrust of this approach is to eliminate gender disparity and ensure the participation of the women in different sectors of nation building department.

EFFICIENCY APPROACH

The efficiency approach was initiated in order to integrate women in the main stream of education and skill development program. About 50 percent of population is women and they deprived from education and other skill development opportunities due to various reasons. The efficiency approach is contributing for the women to involve in employment sectors.

ANTI-POVERTY APPROACH

The anti-poverty approach was initiated to involve the women in development activities for the reduction of absolute poverty as well as feminization of poverty. The women are always victim of feminization of poverty in their different phases of life cycle and as a result they always remain poor in economically, socially, and culturally. So the anti-poverty approach is the poverty reduction process of the women.

EMPOWERMENT APPROACH

The empowerment approach focuses on increasing women's control over the choice in their lives which seeks to increase their self-reliance and self-confidence so that they can stand on their own feet in future. In patriarchal society, power is in the hands of men and they take unilineal decision about any affair of the family. The empowerment approach helps to develop the egalitarian attitude of both the men and the women to take decision in any thing.

SERVICES FOR THE ELDERLY WOMEN

The services are given for the elderly at the traditional joint family system is an old issue in the culture of the people of Asian countries including Bangladesh. A joint family is primarily responsible not only for the dependent of young, but also for the care of the aged members and for any of its member is suffering from illness, accident, or misfortune. It consists of the allocation of a pattern of rights and duties defining that area of life concerned with marital, parental and domestic relationship. The elderly people are very much interested to live with their relatives in kinship network system. They want to share and contribute in love, affection, misfortune, or anything happened of the other members of the family. With the declination of the joint family, the service for the elderly people at the family level is also reducing.

The services are given at the community level are related to charity and alms in neighborhood relation where the family support is not available and the elderly women are destitute. The security like pension, provident fund, group insurance, etc. is given to the employed women after their retirement. There is no public safety net for the poor elderly women. In 1998, the Government of Bangladesh introduced a pension program for the rural elderly poor in the titled of 'Old Age Pension Scheme'. Under this scheme only 10 percent poorest of the elderly poor from each ward get financial support Taka 100 (US$1.40) per month. It should be mentioned that half of the elderly beneficiaries are female. The scheme is executed under the Directorate of Social Services of the Government of Bangladesh. There is a separate committee headed by the Finance Ministry for over all supervision. Though the amount of pension is meager but it is good beginning for the welfare of elderly poor. There are number of other programs of the Government of Bangladesh targeting the poor women. These are the Vulnerable Group Development (VGD), and Vulnerable Group Feeding (VGP). Although these programs are not directly related to elderly women but some of the able bodied aged women are getting benefit from these programs.

The NGOs are involved for the services of the elderly women. For example, Bangladesh Association for the aged and the Institute of Geriatric Medicine (BAAIGM), provide health care, recreation and rehabilitation services for the older persons. Bangladesh Women's Health Coalition (BWHC) involving older women in literacy services for women and children through clinic based using the 'life cycle approach' to health care. Resource Integration Center (RIC) has launched integrated development programs for the older people emphasizing the elderly women. To accomplish these programs RIC primarily focuses on income security, community based medical service, socialization, humanitarian support, and advocacy for change social attitude and inclusion in different programs of older people irrespective of gender. Besides, Service Center for Elderly People (SCEP), Elderly Initiative for Development (EID), Bangladesh Retired Government Employees Welfare Association (BRGEWA), Bangladesh Rural Advancement Committee (BRAC) and so on are working either for elderly men or women or of both in order to provide security in old age so that the elderly people can live with security for the rest of their life.

CONCLUSION AND POLICY IMPLICATIONS

The elderly women are more vulnerable than men due to marital instability in terms of widowhood, separation, desertion, and divorce. The older women are also more likely to be widowed and this life stage has profound economic and physical effects. The economic impacts include reduced income particularly for families in which the male has been the main bread winner. The widows are vulnerable to income in security than are men due to their younger age at marriage, longer period of widowhood, lower rates of remarriage and labor force participation (World Bank,1994). Moreover, the elderly women are not only the victims of absolute poverty rather they are victims of culture of feminization of poverty in connection with socialization, paying dowry for marriage, employment, wage, legal status, health care, education, and participation in decision making process in the different phases of their life cycle which reflects in old age in relation to basic needs and civic facilities.

Women live longer and are less prosperous than men. Despite some improvements in their status, older women continue to be marginalized and erroneously perceived. In order to improve their living conditions, quality of life and well-being the following policies may be adopted.

- The government should amend laws that discriminate against women with regard to property, legal, and inheritance rights.
- Either individually or jointly, the government and NGOs should design and implement policies that would provide minimal income and social safety nets for elderly women in need.
- The government should support family care leaves so that the elderly women can live in kinship net work relations for the rest of their life.
- Both the government and NGOs should create employment opportunities for the able bodied women free of discrimination and ensure adequate benefits.

- The government should open a geriatric unit in the hospital in order to provide better quality of health care service.
- Encourage older women to form self-help groups and network in order to avoid dependency mentality in old age.
- Create an enabling environment for older women to focus on their personal development.
- Free old age home facilities should be provided for the poor and destitute older women.
- Awareness and counseling should be given to the younger generation to take care of their elderly family members because ageing is universal and nobody can avoid it.
- Community based service facilities should be encouraged for the elder women involving the civil society.

REFERENCES

Aziz, K.M.A. and Maloney, C.T. (1985), Life Stages, Gender and Fertility in Bangladesh, ICDDR'B., Dhaka.

Beneria, Lourdes (1997), "Reproduction Production and Sexual Division of Labor," Cambridge Journal of Economics, Vol.3 pp.203-223.

Calleja, James (1997), Eliminating Poverty in Old Age. The United Nations International Institute on Ageing, Malta.

Chow, N.(1996), "Ageing Issues and the National Agenda," Added Years of Life in Asia. United Nations, NewYork.

ESCAP (2001), Sex and Gender Comparison of the Population. Country Monograph Series 8, Population Bangladesh, ESCAP, United Nation, Bangkok.

Hartman,B. and James, K,B.(1997), Needless Hunger: Voice from a Bangladesh Village. Institute of Food and Development Policy, Sanfranssisco.

Kottak, Philip C. (2005), Miror of Humanity. McGrawHill, NewYork

Majumder, S. (1994), "Physical, Mental, and Metaphisical Aspect of

Fitness-ACocept for Aged People". Ageing and Society, Vol.6, Non.11, pp.40-45.

Moody, Harry R.(1994), Ageing Concept and Controversies. Sage Publishing Company, California.

Rahman,M.A., Roy, Sarmistha, Sarker, Profulla C.(1997), "Ageing and Health Problems of Bangladesh: A Situation Analysis of Rajshahi City". South Asian Anthropologist, Vol.18, No.1, pp.9-16.

Rix, Sara (1991), "Older Women and Development: Making a Difference." The Paper Presented to Expert Group Meeting on Integration of Ageing and Elderly Women into Development, Vienna.

Roy, Sarmistha (2000), Instability of Joint Family System and Its Impact on Old Age Insecurity in Rrural Bangladesh. An Unpublished Ph.D.Dissertation, Institute of Bangladesh Studies, University of Rajshahi, Bangladesh.

Sarker, Profulla C. (1996), "Decline of Joint Family System and Old Age Insecurity in Bangladesh." Proceedings of the Joint World Congress of IASSW and IFSW, HongKong

Sarker, Profulla C. (2001), "Kinship Structure and the Care of the Aged People in Bangladesh." South Asian Anthropologist, Vol.21, No.1, pp37-43.

Sarker, Profulla C.(2002), "Ageing and the Problems of Older People in Basngladesh: An Overview. In Antonio Guerci (ed.) Old Age in the World. Erga Edizioni, Italy.

Sarker, Pofulla C.(1999), "Gender Dichotomization, Use of Contraceptive Devices and their Impact on Social Development in Bangladesh." Indian Social Science Review.Vol.1, No.1, pp.213-21.

Sarker Profulla C.(1997), Social Structure and Fertility Behavior. Center for Development Services, Dhaka.

Schniender (1978), The Genetics of Ageing. Plenum, NewYork.

World Bank(1994), Averting the Old Age Crisis: Policies to Protect and PromoteGrowth. Oxford University Press, London.

INDEX